A Taste-Berry™ Teen's Guide to Managing the Stress and Pressures of Life

A Taste-Berry™ Teen's Guide to Managing the Stress and Pressures of Life

With contributions from teens for teens

Bettie B. Youngs, Ph.D., Ed.D.
Jennifer Leigh Youngs

Authors of the national bestseller
Taste Berries™ for Teens

Health Communications, Inc.
Deerfield Beach, Florida

www.hci-online.com

We would like to acknowledge the following publishers and individuals for permission to reprint the following material. (Note: The stories that were penned anonymously, that are public domain or were previously unpublished stories written by Bettie B. Youngs or Jennifer Leigh Youngs are not included in this listing. Also not included in this listing but credited within the text are those stories contributed or based upon comments by teens.)

Making Sure I Don't "Strike Out" with Patrick, by Kimmy Shavers. Reprinted with permission of the author.

The Most Painful Lesson I've Ever Learned, by Mindy Knadler. Reprinted with permission of the author.

Am I Invisible to You?, by Renee Young. Reprinted with permission of the author.

My Life as an Anorexic Teen, by Amanda Wilson. Reprinted with permission of the author.

(Continued on page 307)

Library of Congress Cataloging-in-Publication Data

A taste-berry teen's guide to managing the stress and pressures of life / [compiled by] Bettie B. Youngs, Jennifer Leigh Youngs; with contributions from teens for teens.

    p.   cm.
    ISBN 1-55874-932-2 (trade paper)
    1. Stress in adolescence. 2. Stress management for teenagers. I. Youngs, Bettie B., date. II. Youngs, Jennifer Leigh, date.

BF724.3.S86 T37 2001
155.9'042'0835—dc21   2001024360

©2001 Bettie B. Youngs and Jennifer Leigh Youngs
ISBN 1-55874-932-2 (trade paper)

Publisher: Health Communications, Inc.
        3201 S.W. 15th Street
        Deerfield Beach, Florida 33442-8190

R-08-01

Cover illustration and design by Andrea Perrine Brower
Inside book formatting by Dawn Grove

To: _____

... A taste berry in so many ways!

From: _____

Also by Bettie B. Youngs

More Taste Berries for Teens: A Second Collection of Inspirational Stories and Encouragement on Life, Love, Friendship and Tough Issues (Health Communications, Inc.)

Taste Berries for Teens Journal: My Thoughts on Life, Love and Making a Difference (Health Communications, Inc.)

Taste Berries for Teens: Inspirational Short Stories and Encouragement on Life, Love, Friendship and Tough Issues (Health Communications, Inc.)

Taste-Berry Tales: Stories to Lift the Spirit, Fill the Heart and Feed the Soul (Health Communications, Inc.)

A String of Pearls: Inspirational Stories Celebrating the Resiliency of the Human Spirit (Adams Media Corp.)

Gifts of the Heart: Stories That Celebrate Life's Defining Moments (Health Communications, Inc.)

Values from the Heartland: Stories of an American Farmgirl (Health Communications, Inc.)

You and Self-Esteem: A Book for Young People (Jalmar Press)

Stress & Your Child: Helping Kids Cope with the Strains & Pressures of Life (Random House)

Safeguarding Your Teenager from the Dragons of Life: A Parent's Guide to the Adolescent Years (Health Communications, Inc.)

How to Develop Self-Esteem in Your Child: 6 Vital Ingredients (Macmillan/ Ballantine)

Self-Esteem for Educators: It's Job Criteria #1 (Jalmar Press)

Keeping Our Children Safe: A Guide to Emotional, Physical, Intellectual and Spiritual Wellness (John Knox/Westminster Press)

Developing Self-Esteem in Your Students: A K–12 Curriculum (Jalmar Press)

Getting Back Together: Repairing Love (Adams Media Corp.)

Is Your Net-Working? A Complete Guide to Building Contacts and Career Visibility (John Wiley)

Managing Your Response to Stress: A Guide for Administrators (Jalmar Press)

Stress Management Skills for Educators (Jalmar Press)

Also by Jennifer Leigh Youngs

More Taste Berries for Teens: A Second Collection of Inspirational Stories and Encouragement on Life, Love, Friendship and Tough Issues (Health Communications, Inc.)

Feeling Great, Looking Hot and Loving Yourself: Health, Fitness and Beauty for Teens (Health Communications, Inc.)

Taste Berries for Teens Journal: My Thoughts on Life, Love and Making a Difference (Health Communications, Inc.)

Taste Berries for Teens: Inspirational Short Stories and Encouragement on Life, Love, Friendship and Tough Issues (Health Communications, Inc.)

Getting What You Want Out of Life: Goal-Setting Skills for Young Adults (Learning Tools Press)

Contents

Acknowledgments

We would like to thank some of the "taste berries" in the development of this book.

First, to the many teens who were a part of this new addition to our *Taste Berries for Teens* series. Thank you for sharing what's on your mind and in your hearts, and for thinking deeply about ways to translate your complex feelings into singular applications for fellow teens around the globe.

As always, we extend heartfelt gratitude to our publisher, Peter Vegso, and the talented staff at Health Communications—most especially those with whom we work most closely: Christine Belleris, Lisa Drucker, Susan Tobias, Erica Orloff, Maria Dinoia, Kim Weiss, Randee Feldman, Lori Golden and the others who are intricately woven into transporting our works into the hands and hearts of our readers. As always, it is with big smiles that we thank Andrea Perrine Brower, who designs the gorgeous covers of our books.

A very special thanks to the taste berries in our office who worked closely on this project: Tina Moreno, Carrie Hague and a staff of teens whose valuable input is evident throughout this book.

And to the many important taste berries in our personal lives. This was a stressful year for both of us. We lost our mother and grandmother, and never quite regained equilibrium, though working with so many others in assembling this book in and of itself was a soothing balm. Always the "messenger" arrives when needed, and we never take the work of angels for granted; it is much honored. Thank you, Mom and Grandmother, for being our guardian angel; to Dad and Grandfather, Everett Burres, for being such a wise old sage and a very loving one. To the "guys" in our lives, David Kirk and Dic Youngs, and to our many brothers and sisters everywhere—thank you for sharing the journey and holding our hearts in such a touchingly human way.

As always, we give thanks to God from whom all blessings flow.

Introduction

Welcome to *A Taste-Berry Teen's Guide to Managing the Stress and Pressures of Life.* In this book, teens (ages twelve to twenty) talk openly about the stress and pressures they face in today's times, as well as ways to best manage stress, and, as importantly, use it to their advantage.

Of course, being a teen yourself, no one has to convince you that life is stressful! From coping with the pressures of getting good grades at school, to passing the test for making (and keeping) friends; from finding a part-time job, to having a life once you do; from deciding where you and your friends would like to hang out this weekend, to deciding where you'd like to go to college (or for job training); from finding time to do all the things you have to get done, to having leisure and "down" time for yourself once you do; from meeting the needs and expectations of parents, teachers and activity coaches, to setting and achieving goals of your own, life can be extreme-edge hectic! So much so that teen Geoff Granger labeled it a "balancing act," while Tandy Mann phrased it the "juggle of struggles" and Cindy Morris called it "Zoo-ville in Teenville."

Whatever name you give to keeping up with your life as a teen—regardless of the ups and downs that stress creates—you know you'd better be cool: You've got to cope. Consider this book your taste berry for doing just that. A taste berry? If you haven't yet had a chance to read *Taste Berries for Teens: Inspirational Short Stories and Encouragement on Life, Love, Friendship and Tough Issues,* or the *Taste Berries for Teens Journal* and the latest book in our *Taste Berries* for teens series, *More Taste Berries for Teens: A Second Collection of Inspirational Short Stories and Encouragement on Life, Love, Friendship and Tough Issues,* you're probably asking, "What is a taste berry?" A taste berry is a glorious little fruit that, when eaten, mysteriously convinces the taste buds that all food—even food that is distasteful—is delicious! The bright little berry has been used around the world for countless years to make the sometimes necessary eating of bitter foods, such as roots, tolerable. Have you ever had a day when you felt overwhelmed, down-and-out, or simply "at wits end" or "too out of juice" to effectively cope with the situation at hand? Were you suffering a disappointment, feeling betrayed or nursing a broken heart? Was there a time when you had a million-and-one urgent things to do—and not enough time (or desire) to accomplish them? Or, things didn't turn out as you planned—or you had no plans—and everyone else, it seemed, did? Has life thrown you a curve ball, and you don't know what to do about it, nor whom to turn to? On those days when stress sets in, when anxiety lingers, when the pressures mount, when your cool has turned to ghoul, we could all use a taste berry! This book is yours! *A Taste-Berry Teen's Guide to Managing the Stress and Pressures of Life* will help you:

- understand what stress is (and isn't),
- examine how you respond to stressful times (and determine how effective that is),
- determine how your stress shows itself as physical, emotional and behavioral symptoms,
- check out some terrific (and time-tested) intervention and prevention strategies to minimize stress and stay cool under pressure, and
- learn ways you can use stress to your advantage.

Learning how to cope effectively with stressful situations is more than a good feeling. Handling stressful times in positive ways gives you the confidence to confront other stressful encounters. The more you build a storehouse of positive experiences of seeing yourself as successfully handling difficult times in positive ways, the better able you are to handle other tough times. Having said that, it's important to remind you that, while many teens can handle the day-to-day stress of life, some stresses and pressures are too much for anyone to handle alone. Should you be facing times that are simply overwhelming, rather than suffer alone or resort to doing things that are self-destructive, we urge you to seek help. This is especially true in cases of physical, emotional or sexual abuse, suicidal feelings, eating disorders, depression, pregnancy and/or using drugs or alcohol. If you're uncertain where to go for counseling, turn to an adult (whether a parent, teacher, school guidance counselor or clergyperson) whom you feel you can trust to direct you to the proper place. Also, many schools provide peer crisis counseling, and there are any number of toll-free hotlines that offer teens valuable information and can direct you to other sources of help, as well. (Some are listed in the Suggested Resources section in this book, and may also be listed in the yellow pages of the phone directory.)

This book is divided into seven units, each of which opens with a Message from the Authors, which is our chance to give you a brief overview of the chapter's theme, as well as point out any specific "taste-berry advice" teens have shared with us on the subject of stress collectively, both through their letters and in our workshops. Each chapter opens with a story by a teen, followed by our teaching a specific concept or skill, followed by a worksheet section where you get to work with the skill, applying it to your life.

We want this book to be informative and fun, so as you read through each of these sections, be open to trying each technique and then decide which ones best work for you given the situation at hand. For example, it's unlikely you are going to practice "progressive relaxation" (a skill that requires you to sit calmly so as to relax various muscle groups) should you be running late for meeting up with a good friend or on your way to class. However, later, if needed, it will help you reduce a tension headache and [re]focus so you can get through part of your day. Likewise, applying the "thinking out loud" skill would be a good choice because this particular skill will keep you on target and lead you exactly to where you should be heading! So, welcome aboard. Relax, learn and have fun!

As always, we look forward to hearing from you. We'd like to know which of the stories, comments and skills you liked best—and why. We'd also love to hear about the "taste berries" in your lives—or how you've learned to be better "taste berries" in the lives of others. To that end, we invite your comments as to how you found this book helpful, and welcome your stories as to how you are coping with teen life—the incredibly powerful and positive things you are doing, and the issues that cause you sadness, pain and concern. We are now working on an upcoming third edition of *Taste Berries for Teens*, so if you have a story or poem you'd like to submit, please send it to us at:

Taste Berries for Teens III
c/o Teen Team
3060 Racetrack View Drive, Suite # 101–103
Del Mar, CA 92014

Part 1

Teen Talk: The Stress of Life in "Teenville"

The most difficult years in life are those between ten and seventy.

—Helen Hayes

A Message from the Authors

No one's life is without stress, certainly not yours. Being a teen in today's times is filled with ups and downs—awesome, terrific, thrilling, exciting, tense, embarrassing, "bummer" and downright "Omigosh-I-couldn't-believe-it-happened" experiences. It's a time characterized by hopes and expectations: "Will I be liked, considered cool and asked to be a friend?" "Will there be a special someone out there, someone wanting to be special to me?" "Will I pass this class, get accepted to college, decide what work is best and right for me, find a great job?"

Being a teen is also filled with "first-times": realizing you have "feelings" for someone; going on a first date with a special someone; learning to drive a car, even passing your driver's test, driving a car on your own for the first time; deciding getting good grades are you, and not just something you're doing to be "in good" with your teachers, parents or friends.

It's the strain-filled time of all-important decisions: After high school, should you enter the job market, get into a specialized job training program or head off for college? Should you go steady with that one special person or "date around"? Should you "change" some of your friendships—make some new ones, and leave behind others? Should you get a part-time job or concentrate solely on making good grades?

It's also a time of a feeling that so many of your actions have "do or die" consequences: doing well on those grueling SATs so you can fulfill your dreams of going off to college, finding a job, or finding out who you are and then coming to terms with your identity—and yet, making the grade with your friends so you're one of the crowd.

It's a time of growing up and learning how you can eventually make your way in life. As you learn how to stand on your own two feet, you know the importance of honoring the "rules and rituals" that make your home run smoothly; of living up to your responsibilities within your family—even though you might like to have more time alone to be independent or use it to be with your friends. It's a time when, while meeting the wishes and expectations of your parents, you are discovering—and clarifying—a voice of your own.

Being a teen: What could be more stressful—and more exciting? From pimples and braces to playing truth or dare, stress is "a way of life" for today's teens. So much so, that many of the teens we worked with on this book said being a teen is like living in a "city of one's own, Teenville"—a city that is situated not far from the "land of overwhelm."

In this unit, teens talk candidly about the most current "overwhelm" they're facing—and why it's their "stress du jour." Of course, you could write your own story (and you'll get your chance in chapter 3!), but for now, let's take an up-close and personal look at some of the complex issues teens face.

Stress du Jour: Teens Talk About the Current Big Stress in Their Lives

My Girlfriend's "Ultimatum"

My girlfriend, Stella Anne Harding, has given me an ultimatum: Either I pick her up in a car and take her out on dates—or she finds a new boyfriend! Stella Anne constantly reminds me that she knows plenty of guys—with cars!—who are just dying to take her out. I know it's true. Stella Anne could look at a guy and he'd be drooling. If she decided she wanted to go out with that guy, he'd be there in a heartbeat!

Talk about pressure.

Her having notified me of this ultimatum, my entire quality of life—everything—depends on passing my driver's license test and being able to use the family car. So that's the biggest stress in my life right now.

Passing the driver's test is not as easy as it sounds; my friend Tom Jennings has failed it twice so far! But my stress doesn't end with getting my license. My parents have laid out more rules than the military for even being able to use the car! "If you . . ." or "If you don't . . ." Stuff like that. They've even tied my using the car to getting decent grades. So now I'm not only practicing for my driver's test, I'm also spending all kinds of extra time studying for all my classes so none of my grades fall. Any

slip-up, whether it's grades, being late for class or curfew or accidentally "mouthing" back to my parents, could end up meaning
not having a car even when I've finally gotten my license.

So the pressure to get my license (and get good grades and not
upset my parents) and, of course, Stella Anne's threat hanging
over my head is what's stressing me out right now. When I see
guys who have wheels flirt with Stella Anne, and especially if
she's in one of those moods to put a little pressure on me, well,
that's when I visit the "land of overwhelm."

Zach Shields, 16

Will a Promise Ring Solve My Problem?

The big stress in my life is this: I want to go to the University of Nebraska because they have a great college football team. (They're one of the "Big Eight"!) Of the four universities I've applied to, it's also the one that's shown the most interest in me. The football department has contacted me several times about the possibility of offering me a football scholarship. That would be great, and it sure would help me and my parents afford four years of college. But here's my problem: My girlfriend and I may be going to different colleges—and I'm really stressed out about it.

My girlfriend, Melissa Williams, and I have been high school sweethearts for three years. We really love each other, and I'm positive I want her to be my wife someday. Throughout high school, we talked about going to the same university so that we could be together. Then, after four years of college, right after our senior year, we'd get married. We had it all worked out. But things aren't turning out according to plans. Melissa wants to go to a college in the East where they have a "rated" department in fashion merchandising—which is something she wants to build a career around. She's creative and talented, and this college is the perfect choice for her. But it's not like I can just apply to her university. Unfortunately, her university doesn't even have a college sports program.

I'm so stressed-out about us going to different colleges, but I don't really see a way for us to be together. When I ask her why she doesn't just attend the University of Nebraska with me, she reminds me of her own goals and the reasons that the college she's selected is best for her. She's right, of course, and it really would be best for me to go where I'll have a chance of playing football— and have an opportunity for being considered as a good draft choice by a professional team (which is my ultimate goal).

Seeing my girlfriend only occasionally for the next four years is something I don't even want to contemplate. I'm just so afraid that Melissa and I will grow apart if we are thousands of miles away from each other, with each of us so busy in our studies and focused on our career goals. Plus, Melissa is such a sweet, smart and beautiful girl that any guy would be interested in her. I'm scared that I might lose her if we go off to different colleges; it's very possible that she might find someone new. I can't even imagine what that would be like.

Since I really want to hold on to Melissa, I've considered proposing and offering her an engagement ring—or at least a promise ring. At least we'd have a commitment. But we'd still be without each other. I know I'm going to be really lonely not seeing her every day, even if we both decide not to ever go out with anyone else.

This is one of the biggest dilemmas I've ever faced, and the stress from it overwhelms me. I'm making choices that will affect the rest of my life!

Kevin Walker, 18

Making Sure
I Don't "Strike Out" with Patrick

✳ The biggest stress in my life right now is trying to get a guy I have a crush on—Patrick McCormack—to treat me as nice in front of my friends at school as he does when we're in private. It's not a simple thing. I mean, it's not like he's a jerk or anything. I think he's sort of shy, a little bit at least, so I don't just want to come on strong and tell him "how it's going to be." I have to handle things just right. Time is important here, but the whole situation is trying my patience.

My whole family always goes to everything we kids are involved in. So when my younger brother's baseball season began, of course they attended all the games. As I did. These games were held right after school and sometimes on Saturday mornings. It's a pretty nice gathering, and a really friendly setting—and not at all boring. Even the kids not playing get to be a part of the whole scene. The parents of the players take turns working the concession stand set up to sell food and drinks to raise money for the school sports teams. Often the parents enlist the help of the whole family—with the exception of the players, of course. I'm not really into baseball, but I do help out in the concession stand because it's really fun, and usually my friends are helping out, too, so that makes it even more fun.

On the seventh baseball game, as usual, I went over to the concession stand to see if any of my friends were there. Upon reaching the stand, I saw Patrick, a classmate of mine. The moment I saw him, he looked up and saw me, too. "What are you doing here?" he asked in kind of a mean-spirited sort of way. Patrick is known to be a rather sarcastic sort of person, but he's also very smart and has a quick wit, so he has a lot of friends, too. I don't consider his "cuts" a reason to not like him; in fact, it makes it sort of a challenge. He's really,

really cute, and all the girls think he's "to die for."

Patrick didn't know it, but I secretly had a huge crush on him, and anybody that Patrick "liked" would instantly be considered "in" by the other kids at school. Practically all the girls I knew at school wanted to be his girlfriend, but Patrick always played hard to get. As far as I knew, he'd never claimed anyone in school as his one single girlfriend. Nothing could make me more happy than being his first real girlfriend.

Though Patrick's comment hurt my feelings, I didn't let on. "I'm working," I lied. "Oh, just great!" he groaned in response. Pretending his comment didn't faze me, I looked at the two adults in the concession stand, picked up an apron-belt, tied it on and began to wait on the "customers." I couldn't believe my good luck: I was working within inches of the boy I secretly had a crush on! Things couldn't have been more perfect, and I was thankful for this opportunity to be so close to him. And I was bound and determined to make the most of it. Even if it meant putting up with his remarks and little jabs. It was stressful but in an exciting kind of way!

You could tell by all the noise of claps and cheers on the playing field that it was good game. Everyone is always in a good mood when the games are exciting, so I was happy about that. There was also an interesting "game" going on in the concession stand. For example, most all of the parents in the booth also knew all the players, so when there wasn't more than a couple of persons waiting to be helped, they'd step outside to catch bits and parts of the game. At such times, when it was just Patrick and me in the concession stand, there was a big change in his behavior. He was nice to me! But when the others came back to the booth, Patrick would be sarcastic again, saying things like "Hey *klutz,* toss me another bag of rolls." After two hours in the booth, I mentioned my feet were starting to hurt. (I didn't wear my tennis shoes like I would have if I had known I was going to be working!) With everyone looking on, Patrick reached out and pinched my cheek hard and said, "Ah, poor baby, can't take the work." But then later, when there was no one at the stand requesting food or drinks and the adults had once again stepped out to view the game, in a really nice tone Patrick suggested, "Why don't you sit down so your feet won't hurt?"

This same sort of "two-faced" behavior continued the whole time. When there were others around, Patrick was sarcastic, getting in as many little jabs as possible, but then, when it was just the two of us, he spoke softly and kindly. And, *twice* he "bumped" into me (I know it was intentional). But even with all my frustration at the "ups and downs" of his behavior, I was excited just to have the chance to be so near him. I had never gotten this close to him at school, nor had I ever had a chance to spend so much time near him.

Much to my relief, about the time my brother's game went into the sixth inning, Patrick got even nicer—but still, *only* when no one else was around. As soon as someone else was there, he'd start to tease me again, and act like he thought I was a pain.

Then something very exciting happened, something that has given me a lot of hope that Patrick wants *me* to be his girlfriend. When Felicia Willis, a friend of mine, came to the concession, Patrick was once again putting on his "act," but it didn't fool Felicia one bit. "You two lovebirds should go steady," she teased. "I've been watching you, and you're very cute together." I was very embarrassed that she said that in front of him, but glad, too. And of course, I was all for our going steady!

"On my deathbed!" Patrick shouted at her suggestion. Well, that didn't feel so good, but I'd already had hours of his "on-again, off-again" behavior so I took it in stride. Besides, spending nearly three hours with Patrick was progress! And like I said, in school that could never happen. We don't have any classes together, we don't have any of the same friends, and all our classes are at different ends of the building, so we rarely get a chance to meet up in the halls.

All too soon the game ended, and my parents hurried over to the concession stand and said we had to leave "pronto." Because they wanted to go over and talk to the coach and some of the other parents, they asked me to hurry to come with them. So without saying anything other than, "Good-bye everybody!" nothing more happened between Patrick and me. I'm not sure if he even noticed that I left. On the way home, I learned that my little brother had made a home run, and everyone was pretty happy about it, most especially my brother! He was really in a good mood, but not any better than my own! Although I hadn't made a "home run," I hadn't struck out either! In fact, I'd made it to "first base."

That night in my journal I wrote down everything, including that I just knew he felt as badly about my leaving as I did about having to leave him. Under the heading, "My First Date with Patrick!" I wrote down every single thing that was said and done on that important outing.

The next week in school was really a letdown because I only saw Patrick three times and only from a distance. I made a special point of walking by his locker (which twice made me late to class). Though he glanced at me once, I thought maybe he hadn't recognized me because he didn't say anything, and he didn't even act like he knew me. So, you can only imagine how excited I was for my brother's next ballgame the very next weekend. And, you can be sure I had signed up in advance to work in the concession stand!

Just as I had hoped and prayed, Patrick was there to work the stand, too. This time, though, things were very different! Though Patrick wasn't much nicer to me when others were around than he had been the time before, he was *really* sweet to me when it was just the two of us! In fact, in the bottom half of the fifth inning, Patrick even told me that he "liked me"! I was shocked, and as my friend Lindsey always says when she's really excited about something, "over the moon," too. Then, when the fans went wild in the last inning and when the game was tied, things heated up between me and Patrick even more. Because it was obvious the game was getting really exciting between the two teams, the parents in the booth told us kids in the concession stand to go ahead and go watch the game. With aprons on, Patrick and I dashed out to see what all the commotion was about. As we ran past the bleachers, Patrick pulled me aside and kissed me—on the lips!

The kiss happened so fast, I didn't even have a chance to kiss him back.

So now I know how "over the moon" feels firsthand, and I can tell you it is really, really cool. More like "awesome, wonderful, magnificent." Well, so then I knew for sure I was in love, and Patrick, too.

That was four weeks ago. So here's my big stress: It's only at the ballgames that I have a boyfriend! At school, Patrick still ignores me; I mean, you'd think I had a disease or something. Worse, baseball season is over now, so I won't be spending any more time in the concession stand in order to be near him. And after that kiss, I totally want him to be my full-time boyfriend. I just don't know how to make it happen—which is something I'm totally frustrated about. I mean, it's not like he goes around (like I do) looking for me. So my big stress is trying not to "strike out" with Patrick.

Kimmy Shavers, 14

The Most Painful Lesson
I've Ever Learned

My cousin Bobby and I went to the same high school, and though we were in the same grade, we never had a class together until last semester. Our families weren't all that close (mostly because they didn't really get along), and so there was this sense of distance between Bobby and me, too. But we were getting old enough to realize that just because certain adults in the family were sort of estranged, as they call it, and because it was the reason we really didn't know each other all that well, it didn't mean it had to spill over into our getting to know and like each other as friends and classmates. And this year we did have a class together, so I figured sooner or later Bobby and I would get to know each other better. I was cool with that, and I knew Bobby was, too. We also smiled at each other in a friendly sort of way, and he always looked in my direction and gave me a thumbs-up when, in the homeroom we shared, my name was mentioned as one of the "winning" basketball team members (the principal always announced the names of the players individually).

So I was having more and more of an appreciation for him as not just a relative, but a cool guy with a lot of nice friends. Most everyone at school thought of him as a neat person. Though I really didn't know him all that well, I thought he probably was. So I just knew that this was the semester that he and I would become good friends—even if our families weren't.

Unfortunately, things didn't turn out that way. I don't know if it was just because we were both shy, or because we sat with our separate groups of friends. Maybe it was because we didn't know each other very well to begin with, and didn't know how to begin to connect during that semester-long class, but the semester came and was three weeks from being over and still Bobby and I barely knew each other.

Then, on Saturday morning two weeks before the school year was over, my mother took me aside and, with tears in her eyes, told me that Bobby and three of his friends had been in a car accident the night before. The driver of the car died instantly; Bobby was taken to the hospital in bad shape and was placed in intensive care; the other two passengers were treated and released the same night.

My dad told me that my cousin was in too serious of a condition to have visitors, so I couldn't go see Bobby in the hospital. And then, a couple days later, we got the news that my cousin Bobby had died. I was in shock. It seemed so unreal. I felt sick— both in my heart and in my body.

I am filled with remorse that I never got to tell my cousin good-bye. Something else I regret is that during that semester class together, we both missed out on a perfect opportunity to get to know each other. I am so sorry that I hadn't taken the initiative to be a close friend—and cousin.

It's been four months now, and my heartache is a never-ending one. My feelings—all over the place—are not tiny voices, but rather, crashing waves that flood my mind with anger, sadness and frustration. I daydream that one bright, sunny day, my cousin Bobby, a sensitive young guy who sat not more than ten feet away from me in fifth-hour class, will walk in the classroom and simply tell us all he was out with the flu.

If only I'd taken the time to know him. Death is really hard to get over, especially when it makes a house-call in your life.

Mindy Knadler, 18

They Said It Was "Even Better"—But It's Not

I was fifteen and had lived in West Des Moines, Iowa, all of my life. I loved living there. All of my friends, everything familiar to me—life as I knew it—was there. Then, my father took a new job in Kansas City, Kansas. So, my whole family had to pack up and move. My sister and brother and I were really upset about having to move, but my parents assured us that in Kansas City our lives would be "even better than West Des Moines." To make sure they were, our parents reassured us we'd be renting a house big enough so that each of us kids could have our own room—which sounded great to me because I shared a room with my younger sister, and she's a real pest. She's nosy and is always looking through my things and is always asking a hundred and one questions about my friends. My parents also promised us that we kids could have a phone line "designated" for just us, which also sounded like a great deal since we all have a lot of friends (Mom and Dad do, too), and one phone line for five people is definitely not enough. Our parents told us about other "perks," too. I'm sure they came up with all the angles to get us to look forward to the move. And little by little, we kids were convinced—well, at least resolved—that life could be, as our parents had said, "even better than West Des Moines."

Well, I'm two months into my "even better than West Des Moines" life, and so far, "even better" hasn't happened. Leaving all my friends behind was bad enough, but the new school is so huge that even though I've been in the building for nearly a month, I still worry that I'll take a wrong turn in the seemingly thousands of corridors, and end up being late for class, or worse, lost forever. And, the classes are so much bigger at this school that I sincerely doubt that I'll ever get to know anyone well enough for us to become good friends. To top it all off, the schoolwork is much harder; I'm barely making Cs—and I've never had to work so hard in my entire life!

Going to this school is really stressing me out. But it's not just getting to class and making good grades that's stressful here. Socially, I feel like I don't really fit in. I don't dress quite like the other kids at this school—at least not the "cool" kids. What I wear was very cool at my last school. Now I debate what to wear almost every day. Since we'd already done my school clothes shopping before we moved here, I can't get any new clothes right away. On top of this, my hairstyle isn't the "cutting edge" look it was at my old school. In fact, it's pretty much "on its way out" altogether at this school. I can hardly wait for the style to grow out, so I don't look like such a "wanna-be-cool" failure. Things are just very different all the way around. I'm amazed how different high school is here than in the school I left behind. Like at my old school, I was a star player on the girls' lacrosse team. I was excited to play for my new school, hoping to make some new friends on the team, but wouldn't you know that my new school doesn't even have a girls' lacrosse team.

So I'm stuck here, fighting for my grades, feeling lost half the time and without friends—I'm feeling out of place all the time. I'm stressed to the max! And so far, "even better" hasn't happened. Oh yeah, I'm definitely living in the "land of overwhelm." And all because I left the very cool land of West Des Moines for the nowhere land of Kansas City, Kansas.

Kendra Donovan, 17

Am I Invisible to You?

I see him walking in the halls,
But he acts as though I don't exist.
He's always with his friends—and mine
And yet, he pays no heed, or time.
Why doesn't he see me?
Am I really invisible to him?
It's got me stressing out!

We have two classes together,
And I'm always looking in his direction
So why doesn't he notice me staring at him?
He looks right through me.
Why doesn't he notice, or offer up a little smile?
Am I really invisible to him?
I'm stressed!

I see him every day at lunch,
But he never says a word.
I watch his every move,
But he doesn't seem to care.
Why doesn't he see me?
Am I really invisible to him?
Talk about stressful!

I think of him all the time,
Can't he see? Doesn't he know?
He talks to my friends, but never to me.
Why doesn't he notice me?
Why doesn't he see me?
His acting like I'm invisible
Is really stressing me out.

Renee Young, 17

My Parents' Divorce Became *My* Divorce

My parents are getting a divorce. It may be the best decision for my parents. I mean, when they started not getting along, the whole house was filled with bad vibes. But while it may be a good thing for them, it's a terrible thing for me because now I won't have both of my parents in the same house. I love both of them, and have a really cool relationship with each of them, and it bothers me that our family has broken apart the way we have.

Thinking about living apart from either of my parents makes me feel sad—and lonely.

I'm also disappointed that my life is going to change a lot because of the divorce. As a part of the divorce, my dad moved out a few months ago. I don't have a car of my own and before, I always caught a ride to school with one of my parents—but mostly my dad because he didn't have to be to work as early as does my mother. But now that my father lives nearly fifteen miles away from where my mom lives, I can't see him driving all the way across town in the early morning rush-hour traffic to get me to school. So what will I do on those days when my mother has to be to work early—which sometimes happens once or twice a week? I think it would be embarrassing to have my friends at school ask, "Where's Brian today?" only to be told, "Well, his parents are divorced, so he didn't have a ride to school!"

The divorce is stressful to me in other ways, too. I've played baseball for the last few years, and you have to keep your grades up to stay on the team. It's always been tough for me because schoolwork doesn't come easy to me like it does for a lot of my friends. But now, homework seems so much harder because I just can't concentrate. And I once had two parents in the house when I needed help with my homework, so it was easy to ask

Mom for help on my Spanish assignment. She speaks Spanish, but Dad doesn't. Well, I was staying at Dad's house the other night and I didn't get the help my mom would have given me when it came to my Spanish final—and I got the D to prove it.

And that's just the beginning of my life taking a downward spiral. Now that my parents are divorcing, I have to take turns living at each parent's house. While I'm glad that I still get to see both of my parents, I'm upset that I have to split my life like that. What if I'm at my mom's house and I really need a schoolbook—and I left it at my dad's? Or what if I'm at my dad's for the weekend and the really cool new shirt I want to wear is at my mom's? And how are my friends going to reach me? Do I have to give them a schedule of which house I'm at on which days so they can call me? That could be embarrassing!

And besides, I'm used to having my own room. But now, Dad has this new girlfriend, and she has a twelve-year-old son. They're nice and all, but if she and my dad get married, I'll have to share my room with this new kid I barely know, and I'll have to share my dad with this new woman. My life feels like a complete mess right now, and it's really stressing me out. Somebody should remind parents that when they decide to divorce, everyone in the entire family feels it!

Before all this began, I thought making the cut for my school's football team was the biggest stress in my life—and it was—but it's nothing compared to all the stress I'm facing right now.

Brian Durr, 14

Have You Ever Been to Juvenile Hall— Even to Visit Someone?

When I was twelve, I lived with my mother and my sister, Susan, in Phoenix, Arizona. I liked my school and friends, and I especially liked Sean Andrews. I'd even gone to grade school with him (and started liking him in the sixth grade). Sean didn't know it, of course; I would've died if he found out. I mean, what if the other kids teased him about it, so that he got upset with me? That would ruin everything. And besides, what if he didn't like me back? That would be really embarrassing. So I never told anyone, not even my sister, Susan—and we were really close.

Then, my sister Susan and I had to go live with my father in Florida. I had to leave my mom and all my friends behind. Sean, too. The thing is, I never told Sean "good-bye" before I left. It's not like I didn't want to, I just didn't know what I should say: "Bye. I've liked you for a long time, but now I'm moving and I'll never see you again." That didn't seem cool, so I left without ever telling him I was leaving.

Once in Florida, I didn't think I'd ever see him again. So I tried to just get on with my life. The new school was okay and all, and I made some really nice friends, but I missed Sean *sooo* much. I thought about him all the time, daydreaming about him while sitting in my classes, and especially missing him when I'd be laying in bed thinking about my life in Phoenix—my mom, my room at Mom's house and my friends. Sometimes I'd be so homesick for all of them that I'd just lay in bed and sob.

One night when I was crying, my sister (we shared a room at my dad's place) asked, "Are you crying because you miss Mom and Sean in Phoenix?"

I didn't know she knew I was also missing Sean because I still hadn't told her about him, so I was very surprised. "I just want to go back to Phoenix," I replied, not knowing what she knew about my liking Sean.

"Me, too," she said. "Then we can be with Mom and our real friends again, and you can be with your boyfriend."

I was so surprised she called him my boyfriend. "Sean's not my boyfriend," I told her.

"Yes he is," she said matter-of-factly, and then added really sweetly, "You've liked him for a long time. I know. Goodnight, Vic."

"Goodnight," I replied, feeling relieved that now I could share my hurting heart with someone, especially a good friend like my sister.

With every passing week, I became more homesick. My father must have noticed, because after just that one semester with our father, my parents agreed that my sister and I would return to Arizona to live with our mother again—which, of course, meant we'd be going to school there again. The moment I learned this, my heart felt such a huge relief. I was happy just knowing the days were ticking off, and soon I wouldn't be a zillion miles away from all the things I loved in Phoenix any longer. I just hoped Sean hadn't moved away—and didn't have a girlfriend like so many of the boys in our school had.

Though the semester couldn't end soon enough for me, it did end and I was on my way back to Phoenix.

The second I arrived at my mother's house and settled back into my room, I called around to my friends, casually asking them about Sean. "Was he still around? Did he have a girlfriend (or even *like* anyone)? Had he ever mentioned me?" Stuff like that. I found out that yes, Sean was still around, and no, there was no girlfriend, and no, my name had never come up in his conversations—at least none that anyone knew about or was letting on to.

Excited that there was still a chance he was "available," my dreams were no longer of missing Sean, but of how I could meet up with him—and of how I could let him know I liked him. Of course, all this was in the middle of stressing out about the possibility that he might be mad that I did like him. Some boys are like that, and I really didn't know how Sean was about these things.

The answers to all my "how" questions plopped in my lap one week later, when I was sitting at home watching TV. My sister, who had been visiting her girlfriend (who lived in the neighborhood), came dashing into the TV room. Grabbing my hand and practically pulling me off the couch, she exclaimed, "I was just over at my friend's house, and guess who's there playing basketball? Sean! So get up and go get dressed up!" Out of breath and obviously excited, she added, "I'll take you over there. You can see Sean! Hurry up or you'll miss him."

Instantly my stomach filled with butterflies, and I didn't know what to say. I just ran to my room and began pulling out clothes, wondering what I should wear. I wanted to look really great, but it was the middle of the afternoon, so it's not like I could wear something really dressy, like my church clothes. After trying on just about every piece of clothing in my closet— all in a matter of two minutes—I finally decided on my nice blue dress, which I just love. I put on my platform shoes because they're really cool, and because they'd make me look taller (and older). I brushed my hair, and boy was I ever happy that I had washed it that morning. Then, I ran into Mom's room and sprayed on some perfume—this was an important moment, and what if Sean had grown into liking the smell of a girl's perfume? I hoped my mom wouldn't find out I sprayed some of her perfume on, but wearing perfume might make a difference: I wanted Sean to *really* notice me.

My sister and I practically ran to her friend's house. I was excited, and nervous, too. We got there just as Sean and his friends were taking a break from their game. "Hey, look who's back!" Sean said the moment he saw me. It felt so good to have him start things off like that; it really took the pressure off. Then came his words, "Want to go for a walk?"

"Sure," I said, thinking the best and feeling all giddy inside. So we left our friends and started walking down the sidewalk. And that's when Sean told me something I could hardly believe. "Look" he said, "I've liked you for almost three years, so when you left to go to Florida, I was really upset about it. And I missed you. Don't ever leave again without saying good-bye." My heart jumped into my throat, and for a moment, I was too shocked to speak. All this time he'd liked me, and I never knew! And, all this time, I liked him, and he never knew! And to think I hadn't said "good-bye" to him when I left for Florida!

So that's how our "real" relationship, our "true love" relationship began.

For the next two months, Sean was my boyfriend, and I was his girlfriend. It was a really happy time. My daydreams, and night dreams, too, had all come true.

Then, things took a turn for the worse. I don't know why, but I started doing drugs. Maybe it was because some of my friends were using drugs, so I wanted to be a part of the fun they said they were having. But it didn't turn out to be much fun. In the end, I got in trouble and ended up in a detention center as a result. Now, I'm thirty-five miles away from home because I have to spend the next ten months here in the center. So now I don't see Sean. And it's all my fault—again. Sean knew when I started doing drugs because I asked him if he wanted to try some, too, but he refused. He also told me that I shouldn't use either. He even told me that if I continued to do drugs, he wouldn't be my boyfriend. But even with that warning, I still used.

I can't believe I screwed up my life so bad.

Being in a detention center is just totally awful. Your whole life is "detained." You're cut off from everything that is fun and carefree. Your life isn't even your own; there are meetings, rules and kitchen chores, duties with schedules that are far worse than your parents would ever assign. There are even very strict curfews—and not just for going to bed, but even on the weekends. Plus, you're told what you can wear, when you can eat, when you have reading time, when you can shower, even what time you have to have all the lights in your room off. You can't even listen to music. During the day, you have to get permission to use the bathroom. It's just awful. I miss my mom, my sister, my friends, and worse than when I was in Florida, I'm without Sean again. I miss him *soooo* much. Who knows if I'll ever have a chance to be his girlfriend again; maybe he won't even want to speak to me again.

I'm so stressed-out. I think knowing that I did this all to myself makes it even more stressful. I feel so awful about what I've done to my life—in every way. I'm definitely overwhelmed. Nothing could be worse than my life right now.

Victoria Moore, 15

Senior Stress-Out

I always thought my senior year was going to be a breeze. I guess I felt this way because I have two older sisters, and I can remember them saying, "Work hard now, Sis, so you'll get good grades and a good grade-point average, because it's important for getting into college; work hard because then you'll be smart and have a good score on your SATs—which means you'll have a better choice of getting into college. Work hard . . . work hard . . . work hard." And I did.

So finally I am a senior, a senior with good grades, a high score on the SATs, and a good grade-point average. With my most difficult classes behind me, including having met my foreign-language requirements (two full years of French), I thought my senior year was going to be carefree! Boy, was I mistaken. Nothing could be further from the truth. All those stories my friends told me about the senior year being "a breeze" and the easiest are simply *not* true. Instead of being carefree, my mind is on the pile of college applications I have to finish (some that I still have to start)—all of which require a "personal essay" (I have yet to figure out how to describe "me" in four hundred to five hundred words); the homework that has to be kept up so I don't screw up on my good grade-point average (I'm hoping for a scholarship); and then current things, like the big soccer game tomorrow after school with a rival school we just absolutely have to defeat.

I really don't remember my sisters having as tough and stressful senior years as mine seems to be. Maybe they didn't. Or maybe they did but because I was buried in homework, school activities and in doing things with my friends, or, caught up in the stress of making sure I got those good grades they were always telling me I needed, that I didn't notice how hard they had it. Whatever the reasons, I didn't realize I'd be so stressed still. But here's the thing, I don't see an end in sight. I mean I have a lot of friends who are one year older than me, and now many of them are in college. When they come home to visit, all I hear is how stressful college is. For example, I had one friend who didn't even get all of the classes she signed up for. And another friend's professor informed the class (on the very first day) that the class was overbooked by some twenty students and the test he was handing out would eliminate twenty of those "obviously not quite ready to be in the class." (Of course, this meant that a test was being administered that would fail twenty students in the class—and on the first day of class no less!) Another friend is freaking out because she didn't get to room with the friend she applied to room with, and another friend told me she heard that nearly 30 percent of all freshman college students fail their first year! I mean the stories are just horrendous! And there's another thing, too. As much as my friends who are already in college were looking forward to their "freedom" and getting away from home, many of them are homesick and also miss all their friends. Now that I've thought about it, I'm sure I will, too.

I was hoping that when I was a senior all my school stress would finally be behind me, but lo and behold, all my friends who are in college let me know I'm in for a whole new world of stress once I get there. So now I'm feeling all this *new* stress, wondering if I even want to go to college. If only my senior year could be focused on my life as a senior, instead of my college life next year. Even the teachers are totally wrapped up in our life a year from now. They say, "You need to start thinking about what your major is going to be in college," or "Don't let your study habits slip; you need to keep them up for college next year," or "This is going to be really useful when you're off in the real world at college."

So, while I thought my major school stress was behind me, I can see it's not. Am I overwhelmed? You bet, especially when I hear the word *college.*

Katherine Wellington, 18

Big Expectations

I am absolutely enthralled with Camryn Manheim's character (Ellenor Frutt) on the television drama *The Practice*. I mean, here is a woman lawyer who is tough, yet compassionate; no-nonsense, yet has a good sense of humor; sure of herself, yet open to others; has the mind of a steel trap, yet vulnerable. Oh, and I forgot to tell you, she is, like me, a "big" girl.

The only difference about her being "overweight" and my being overweight is that no one on the television show in which she is a big star (and I'll bet the same is true in real life, too)—not her partners in the law firm, nor the attorneys, judges and clients she deals with on a daily basis—remind her of it. Unlike my daily life, in which I'm reminded of my weight on a daily basis—either in how I'm "sized up" by certain looks or in unkind remarks—which range all the way from the little offhanded ones, like when Dan Pointer, who plays on our school's football team remarked, "You ought to try out for the (football) team; we need a good blocker" or in outright smart-aleck remarks, like just yesterday when Josh Berstein said, "Hey Maria Rosa, I got a new truck and it weighs nearly two tons—just a little less than you!"

I tolerate these unkind gestures and remarks from my friends and classmates as much as I can. I mean, I try to be a good sport about them and try not to make too much of them, but the remarks hurt my feelings. Though others may not see my tears, it doesn't mean they aren't painful to me. Whenever I do show my feelings, then whoever said the remarks tries to pass it off by saying a little insincere remark like, "Oh, can't you take a joke?" Well, it's not a joke to me. These remarks—whether in weird looks or in words—make me feel that I'm not liked as much as other "normal weight" kids or accepted for who I am. I mean, I'm smart and nice to others. So I don't see myself as deserving rudeness from others. I want to be just one of the group, to be accepted for my intellect and sense of self, just like Camryn Manheim is both in real life and on the television show.

I have big expectations of myself and I'd like my classmates to see those in me, too, and not call attention to how much I weigh. I'm a great gal who is working on being a good student, and I've got great goals that I'm working toward achieving. As importantly, I am working on being healthy and fit. With the exception of how much others feel the need to judge me on my weight, I'm actually quite happy with my life. What's my stress? Unfortunately, it's that I have to deal with the opinions, rejection and criticism of others about my weight. I wish others would just get off my case about it, and stop using it as a reason to see me as somehow less worthy than those whose pounds don't add up to what my scale shows.

Maria Rosa Rios, 15

How Do You Know (for Sure) If You're Gay?

When you're different from most other guys, it's really hard to feel good about yourself. And I've always been different from most other guys my age. At least, I've always felt that way. Now, I think maybe I'm gay, but I'm still not sure.

I've been trying to figure it out for awhile now. At first, I just started listening very closely every time the subject of being gay came up on television. As soon as I heard the topic or the word "gay," it was like I had radar—I zoomed right in on the program. It had my complete attention. Then, I began reading about famous men who were known to be gay—hoping to find some kind of clue for how I could figure out if I was gay, too. Next, I started reading everything I could about it—but there aren't many sources written for teens—and I would think that if you are just trying to figure this out for the first time, as opposed to knowing it for years and years, it makes a difference. I looked everywhere I could think to look. It wasn't easy, because I didn't want anyone to see that I was doing it or else they might guess that I really was gay. So, I still didn't know for sure.

One thing I do know: I'm just not interested in girls, like all the other guys I know. But I pretend I am. I even passed notes with Paula Mathews in math class all last semester and told her that I liked her. But I was only doing it because I want to be like everyone else. I wasn't really interested in her at all, or any other girl. What's more, over the past year I sometimes kind of even feel like I might be interested in guys instead. Does that mean I'm gay? Being so different can really be confusing, which is really stressful.

I'm not quite sure how to sort this all out, but I hope that I'll know for certain by next year. I don't want to go through all my high school years so confused, because this confusion is definitely not at all fun. And I feel alone. I've tried to think of who I could go to for help with this, and I'm thinking about talking to Mrs. Wilson, my school counselor. Last semester I went to talk to her about changing my history class, and we ended up talking about other things, too. She was really understanding and easy to be honest with. I'm hoping she can help me know myself better. I don't think I've ever faced anything so stressful in my life. And for me, I don't know when the stress will let up. Much of the stress I feel comes from inside of me. But even though others don't know the turmoil I'm going through (and if they did, that would add even more to my stress), it's a very real strain for me, one that doesn't end when school lets out, or when my homework is finished. Nothing makes my turmoil go away. That's my stress du jour—though it seems more like stress de la millennium.

J.M.P., 15

If I Could Wash Away My Past . . .

Because of my past,
Awful and dreadful I've been cast.
I feel lost, knowing not what to do . . .
Where to go now or whom to turn to.
Totally stressed . . . inside and out.

Because of those days
Stumbling around in a haze,
As my beautiful candle burned out.
Shadows now haunt me . . .
Stressing me . . . inside and out.

I'm clearly not here.
I have lost all that was dear.
I should give up—or perhaps already have.
I feel my life is over, there is no salve,
Only stress . . . inside and out.

I'm embarrassed and hurting,
And so terribly ashamed
Guilt-ridden and sorry for the troubles for others
On whom I've blamed. For them, and me
I cry . . . inside and out.

Through my fingers life has slipped,
My heart feels pummeled, broken, ripped.
Can I throw these dark memories into the sea,
Like cremated ashes, all that old me?
Cleansing . . . inside and out.

My soul craves a new start,
Need to jumpstart my heart.
Could I really start over again?
Am I sincere, a fool, or fooling?
Another pretend . . . inside and out?

I need fresh wax, a new candle mold
A spirited scent for someone to hold.
To light it and wish for sweet inner-peace
To burn at one end, the old life to cease.
No more stressing . . . inside and out.

I pray the lost child hiding in me
Will come take my hand, help me to see
I'm not really alone, just lonely inside.
It's a stressful world where "little me" hides.
Time to evolve . . . inside and out.

My chrysalis is hard, not easy to break,
Endurance I know, but the goal to re-awake
Means to re-love myself—and treasure that wealth.
I've got to commit mind, body and soul . . .
Time to de-stress . . . inside and out.

Leigh Kirk, 18

Is There a "Dream Dad—Not!" in Your Life?

My real father moved to another state after he and my mom got divorced, which was over ten years ago. I've seen him a few times, but it's not like we have a real close relationship anymore. So when my mom first married Al, I was really excited, especially because Al spent a lot of time doing things with me that most fathers do with their kids, like taking them to the batting cages, and to baseball and football games. Things like that. Al took me everywhere. He and I did a lot of guy things together, just the two of us. It was great!

So, of course, when they said they wanted to get married, I was all for it, because I knew Al was going to be the answer to my having a "regular" dad. And he was in the very beginning, but now he's changing, and I don't like it one bit.

It seemed to me that the change was almost immediate. After my mother and Al married, Al and I hardly ever did anything together. In fact, it seems to be that Al doesn't really want me around all that much. And there's another thing, too. I've lost private time with Mom. Now there is no such thing as just Mom and me having dinner or discussion time alone, without Al. I miss that. Even worse, he takes part in the decisions that affect me. I don't think he has any right to be a part; Mom and I can decide things, as usual. Things aren't as I thought. That my "dream dad" is just not so "dreamy" is the most stressful thing in my life.

Ricky Toole, 16

My Life as an Anorexic Teen

Not too long ago, I developed a very serious eating disorder: anorexia. Basically, anorexia is when an already-thin enough person feels she stills weighs too much, therefore she begins to eat very little—obviously not enough to stay healthy. I was also bulimic, which means you eat a lot, but then gag yourself so you throw up after meals (and yes, it is as ugly as it sounds). When you "binge and purge" in this way, it's called bulimia.

My illness began last year on August 4 when, while taking a shower, I looked down at my stomach and noticed that it stuck out a little bit. Right away I thought I was fat and better start losing some weight—even though I only weighed seventy-six pounds as it was. There was next-to-no fat on my body, but you couldn't tell me that. I was convinced that little roll of fat on my belly meant I was obese. Repulsed, I promised to rid myself of it as soon—and as fast—as I could.

My goal was to lose fifteen pounds, which I got right to work on. I literally made a promise to myself that I wouldn't be satisfied until I lost every single one of those pounds. So every day, without fail, I would diligently exercise. I'd do sit-ups, jumping-jacks and push-ups. And, I'd eat very little, sometimes nothing more than an apple for breakfast and some toast for dinner.

I was losing weight fast, and I was very proud about that. It gave me a real sense of accomplishment and self-control. Willpower! Now *that* I had. Or thought I did.

Around the first part of November, I discovered that I couldn't control my mood swings. Probably this was caused by the fact that I wasn't eating enough to feed my body, or my brain. By the end of November I became so depressed that I tried to slit my wrists. Hurting myself physically was a confusing thing, because while I wanted to hurt myself, I was also upset about wanting to hurt myself. It was obvious—even to me—that I didn't understand myself—or my needs—at all.

By Christmastime, my mother noticed how skinny I was getting (as well as the cuts on my wrists) and took me to a doctor. I was admitted to a hospital that helps teens with their emotional problems.

Being admitted to the hospital was a very difficult time for me as well. I love my parents very much and even though they visited me daily, it was a day-by-day struggle for me just to get through the "program" I was on. For starters, I had to eat. Food, real meals, were put in front of me, and then I'd be handed a fork and spoon and told, "You have to eat." It was very hard to get used to eating "normal" food and normal-size portions of food again. Because I had gone so long without eating, my body actually didn't want to eat (because my body was so adjusted to *not* eating). My long spell of not eating had caused other health problems, like my kidneys began to fail. The doctors said if I didn't eat I would die, so I tried very hard to eat, but every time I'd take even one bite, I'd get nauseated.

Still, starving seemed easier than being so nauseous, so I wouldn't. When the staff member who served me my meals saw that I didn't eat, she then stayed to make sure I did. I was a girl who was so sick, I could no longer be counted on to save my own life—so others were assigned to see that I did. Then, when the staff discovered that I didn't eat because I couldn't (without throwing up) they put large tubes into my nose and down into my stomach so I'd get nutrition. It would hurt so badly, and felt so intrusive—like a big snake crawling inside my nose, down my throat and into my stomach.

I thought I must be pretty close to dying, because it wasn't long before a hospital staff member stayed by my side day and night. I was never alone: A staff member would watch me eat, take my prescriptions, take a shower, a nap, and even stay in my room all night long. It was terribly confining, but it worked. Little by little I began to eat, gradually increasing the amount of food my body would tolerate without being sick and wanting to throw it up. Seven weeks after I was admitted, everyone thought I was well enough to continue treatment on an outpatient basis. So, I got to go home.

I guess I wasn't ready to go home. Only one week later, feeling so low and depressed, I took thirty-nine of my depression pills in hopes I'd die. It might have worked except for the fact that the first thing that happened was that I got very dizzy and then so sick I threw up (which relieved my stomach and bloodstream from some of the prescription pills). My parents rushed me to the hospital, where they stuck tubes down my throat and into my stomach so they could pump it out. I also had to drink this charcoal stuff to make me throw up anything that was left of the "overdose" of medication. This horrible experience left my body so numb, I couldn't even go to the bathroom without help. Once again I was admitted to the hospital. This time my stay included a short stay in the intensive care unit, then I was placed back in the eating disorder program at the hospital for more treatment.

Today, one grueling year later, I'm better. I'm still terrified that my eating disorder will return, but I'm working hard at being a healthy, normal-weight teenager. It's a day-by-day process, though, because there's still a lot of pain and suffering going on for me. I'm seeing a counselor, and that's a big help. I am hopeful I'm going to get "all better," as my little cousin says. I know that I am lucky to be alive. Certainly I am grateful I didn't die.

I wrote about my illness to let you know that you should never go to the extreme of being thin. If you're already caught up in not eating what's best and right for your body, get help. Believe me, an eating disorder as serious as anorexia or bulimia is way too powerful to beat alone. And they're more than stressful. Each can kill you. When you have death staring you in the face, it's pretty final. So my biggest stress is fighting to be healthy, one day at a time.

Amanda Wilson, 16

Love: An Annoying Fact of Life

Love can get annoying. The thing is, once you've known what love feels like, well, when you're without, you feel lonely, like a huge something is missing. Not having it can make you feel left out. And once you've got someone special, then your heart is always on guard, always checking in with your head to see if it feels just right, or not. "Does he love me? A little, or a lot? How do I know? What's the evidence, the proof?" Stuff like that. And, if someone is out to take love away from you, well, then, you're upset and hurting.

Don't get me wrong. Love isn't a bad thing, but it sure can be one of the most stressful experiences you'll ever have go through, as I discovered when I began to love Brandon.

I met Brandon on the first day of eighth grade. My friends and I were sitting in homeroom, just laughing and hanging out, speculating what the new homeroom teacher would look like. It wasn't a name we recognized from the school year before, though we had been told this teacher was once a teacher in our school. So we were having fun, joshing and joking around how the reason we hadn't noticed the teacher the year before was obviously because he was "just out of the loony bin." I was casually looking around when in walked a student obviously new to the school. Since he was new to the school, my friends pointed him out to me and said, "Hey, look who else must have been just released from the loony bin." Though I laughed along with them, I didn't let him see me do it; I was instantly smitten with Brandon.

I think he was with me, too, because he took a seat near me and the entire time in homeroom, he kept glancing in my direction. In homeroom each of us was given our new schedules for the semester, and given our newly assigned lockers. So I passed Brandon a note to ask if he had any clue where his locker was.

Within seconds he passed back a note and said, "No, but I'd love for you to help me find it." Well, you can bet I was more than willing. So after class, we hooked up, and I helped him find his locker. Then, he walked me to mine.

That's how our friendship started. We were great friends the entire year. I'd had a lot of good gal friends, but never boys who were this good of a friend, so it was really special. I could share everything with Brandon—hopes and dreams, and secrets, too. Nothing was off-limits—not the lives of our parents, our brothers or sisters, or good friends, too. We privately dissed those classmates whom we felt were the nerdy kids, as well as the "sane and insane" teachers. We shared jokes we couldn't tell to friends (for fear it might offend them). And best of all, even when we got upset at each other—for reasons we never understood—it didn't get in the way of our letting it go and getting on with our friendship. We were so tolerant with each other. It was wonderful.

In an eighth-grade way, I was in love with him.

Eighth grade flew by and our ninth year began. We lived quite a ways away from each other so we never did see each other over the summer, but we talked a lot by phone. So I was really happy to be back at school, back with my good friend. And overjoyed to discover that Brandon was in three of my classes.

It was a great first day, even if Brandon seemed quiet and a bit withdrawn. And then, on the way to our lockers just before lunch, he told me the news that made my joy stop forever. "My dad lost his job," he said quietly, "and we have to move away so he can find a better-paying job . . . we leave in three weeks."

I was so shocked. I remember thinking, "No, he's joshing with me." But I could tell it was real. In that terrible moment, my heart dropped down into my stomach. I was used to people moving. Already I had said good-byes to two best friends, but it didn't seem as devastating as having Brandon leave my life. Right there, in that hallway, dressed in my new back-to-school clothes, on the very first day of my high-school career, I cried.

I cried, and I didn't care who saw.

I knew I would have to stretch time and make every moment in the next three weeks last. Brandon had a different way of coping with it. He tried to distance himself from me, which made things worse. The fact that we no longer rushed to each other's side the moment a class ended didn't seem normal. And as if not talking about it would make it go away, we didn't talk about his leaving. Whenever it came up, we just sort of made light of it. Doing that only made it more stressful.

The day before he left, I decided to tell him how much I cared for him. I suppose he already knew, but I just needed to tell him exactly how much. It was sappy, sentimental and quite mushy, but Brandon listened. Happily, he told that he felt the same (only in less mushy terms). I felt as though my heart would burst.

The day before his departure, I had a get-together at my house for him—kind of an impromptu going-away party. It was a great party, until everyone began to leave. Finally, it was time for Brandon to leave. I said good-bye and have been crying since.

He left.

Life seemed so flat and lifeless without him. I'd lost everything: the phone calls that would sometimes go on until 2:00 A.M., trips to the batting cage together, our fiery religious debates. Even the time he dislocated my kneecap on his trampoline.

When he left, a huge part of me left, too. And it's the biggest, most terrible hole. I'm smart enough to know that I'll find love again, and maybe even one day see Brandon again. Just because someone moves across the country doesn't have to mean that person is out of your life forever. Who knows, maybe he and I will end up going to the same college together and even getting married. But the point is, even these prospects won't help my heart stop hurting today, and especially at nights when we used to talk by phone. Nor does it mean that I'll be just fine at the school dance without him—even if I'm asked to dance with a hundred other guys. Because I've known love for Brandon, well, I'm stuck having to face this hurt, and the only way out of it is through it. And that's a fact of life—but an extremely stressful one.

Tracey Grimm, 16

I Thought It Could Never Happen to Me

No, I reassured myself. *I'm not pregnant. I can't be pregnant. That would ruin everything. Besides, I'm taking "precautions."* It's the same message I repeated over and over in not so many different ways when I was "late."

"What are you going to do?" my mom asked. Too stunned to answer—not that I knew the answer to my situation—I just put my head down and cried.

My sister bought me a pregnancy test kit. I went to the bathroom and followed the directions on the box. Though it seemed like a lifetime of waiting, it only took two minutes for the two lines to appear. The results were clear: There was a baby growing inside me, relying on me to give it life and take care of it.

My younger sister looked at me and told me I was going to be a mommy. Those words seemed strange, but beautiful, too.

I thought—and hoped—maybe the test was wrong, so I made a doctor's appointment for two days later at the Mercy Clinic for pregnant girls. I didn't want to go to the clinic alone, so my friend went with me.

The bus ride to the clinic seemed hours and hours long. Suddenly life seemed very complicated. Wasn't I supposed to have a history test this morning? And wasn't I supposed to stop by the counselor's office and sign up for the SATs? And what about that overdue library reference book I absolutely promised to return today? Suddenly, these things seemed like everything I wished I could be doing that day—even though the day before I'd dreaded thinking they were there on my to-do list. But there on the bus, I would have gladly been doing those things. Instead, I was filled with so many urgent new to-do's—no, *must*-do's—that my stomach churned and my head ached. I just sat there feeling numb, huge tears clouding my eyes. I was too worried and anxious and stressed to even talk, or problem solve, with my best friend.

The doctor took me into a small room and gave me a urinal cup and told me where the bathroom was. I filled the cup and took it back to her. She put two little drops on the pregnancy test and the two lines immediately appeared. She told me she was going to give me an internal exam to see how far along I was.

I was almost six weeks along.

The doctor prescribed prenatal pills and gave me another appointment for four weeks from then. I was nauseous the entire ride home from the clinic, probably more from the condition my head was in than my body. I didn't want to think about anything, but no such luck. Millions of questions swarmed around and around. What should I say to Mom—though in my heart, I knew she knew I was pregnant. How would I answer her questions? And how would I explain my situation to Dad, and the thousand-and-one questions that followed? What would I say to Justin—and his mom who really liked me—and to his father who wasn't sure if he liked me? Would Justin be happy, or would he hate me now? Would he stay by my side, or would he leave? What should I tell the teachers—and the entire world at school? What would I say to the basketball coach?

I had questions of my own and worries of my own, and while I knew what was happening inside of my body was about me, suddenly my life was filled with needing to explain things to everyone around me. Everyone in the universe, it seemed, was now a part of life, or would be commenting about me—or my "condition." They'd talk about the baby. The "baby." The words seemed to float like a cloud, suspended, yet somehow anchored in the sky. *How did clouds stay up in the sky anyway?*

So many questions swarmed in my head, all I could do was rub my stomach, telling my baby I loved her and that, for now, that was all I knew for sure. Could I take care of her and give her a good life? I wanted to.

Finally, I got home. I was right, Mom already knew.

Then I told my boyfriend the news.

It came time for Justin to tell his parents, though we waited until after the Thanksgiving meal was over, so we didn't have to face the situation—and them—the entire afternoon. I felt for him; he was so scared to tell them.

When I was two-and-a-half months along, the *real* morning sickness started. I was sick day and night, and I couldn't eat anything. When I went back for my two-month checkup they said I was dehydrated and sent me to a hospital for an I.V. and an ultrasound to see if the baby was okay. The doctor said the baby was growing just the way she should. I was given medicine to help with the morning sickness because it was pretty bad.

Facing my friends was different than I expected, though I'm not sure what I expected. Of course I thought that good friends would cope okay, and some did, but some shied away from me. That was disappointing but I guess it was logical. My being pregnant changed everything. I really noticed this when, on our regular two-week slumber party, we girls would discuss things going on at school. Because we were such good friends, nothing was off-limits: We would talk about boys, who was dating so and so, and for those kids already going steady, well, we discussed that, too. We talked about who at school was getting kissed or having sex with whom. Real or imagined, we talked about it all. But suddenly, no one wanted to talk about sex because, of course, here I was, now the real-life consequence of it. And it wasn't like I was interested any longer in wondering who I was going to go out with, nor was I all that interested in going to the prom in my condition. I'd sealed my fate on boys and my future. Though they didn't say it, my girlfriends really didn't want me there at the slumber party: My "condition" had become a "party pooper" to them.

Though most everyone at school learned through the grapevine I was pregnant, when I started getting bigger, some of the kids looked down on me. While no one said anything, the look of disdain said enough. I found it to be a feeling as uncomfortable as carrying a growing baby.

I continued to go for a checkup every four weeks until I hit six months. That's when I went into premature labor. It was the most frightening experience I ever went through. Thankfully, they were able to stop it. It was too early for the baby to be born, and she would have been very sick if she had survived. From that point on, I had to go to the doctor every two weeks.

I am eight months along now. Everything has changed, and there are many things I'm unsure about. My life is still in flux—even though a lot of things have been decided for me—like where and how I'll be spending much of my time in the future. Is my life stressful? More than you can know, more than anybody can know. For sure, it's more than *I* can know.

Mandy Nosliw, 17

3

Teens and Stress: Are You Living in the "Land of Overwhelm"?

As you can tell from the stories in the last chapter, being a teen in today's times is not without its ups and downs, which create, in the words of teens, "the land of overwhelm." Virtually all young people—of every age and background—have worries and concerns that contribute to the stress and pressures they feel in coping with the many things going on in their lives. From acing the test to figuring out what sort of work or career you'd like to go into; from getting along with your parents to trying to decipher if that second glance from that special someone means he or she likes you (and if so, how much and for how long!) or was simply glancing in your direction, stress is "a way of life" for teens. The streets of Teenville are paved with stress, as sixteen-year-old Tandi Stevens found out after the party she planned with the hopes of getting to know a certain guy didn't exactly turn out as planned.

The Party . . . Turned Out Different Than I'd Planned

I sit alone in the aftermath
in a 1 A.M. world.
Empty soda cans, used paper plates,
candy wrappers, stains on the carpet.
Everyone's gone.
This isn't what I had planned.

Just a little casual party for friends
deliberately put together
for a chance to be in your presence.
Hoped you'd think I was cool, pretty,
worth getting to know
and want me to be your girl.

I could tell you enjoyed the party.
You came early,
stayed late,
talked with everyone,
laughed, danced and sang songs.
Then left with that other girl.

I sit and stare—at nothing in particular
too sad to laugh, too hurt to cry,
peeling off the sparkles I'd so carefully placed to adorn my skin.
I'd secretly hoped you'd find me cool, pretty,
worth getting to know.
Guess you didn't.

This room for my party,
once filled with laughter and all my huge hopes,
is now just an empty space

amplifying the ache of my lonely, broken heart.
It knows you didn't find me cool, pretty and worth getting to
  know.
And it's another—and not me—that you want to be your girl.

Tandi Stevens, 16

Is Your Life Stressful?

It's easy to feel for Tandi and to hear the sorrow in her heart.
Certainly our hearts wish her well. Have you ever found yourself in a similar predicament—one in which your expectations
didn't turn out as you'd hoped? Such times are sure to make you
feel disappointed, sad, even confused as to what went wrong.

You've been reading about the stresses of other teens. How
about you? What's going on in your life that makes it stressful?
Take a moment now to reflect and then describe what's stressful
about your life.

What makes my life stressful is . . .

_____

_____

_____

_____

_____

_____

_____

_____

Teens Discuss What Causes Teen Stress

Did you have an easy time writing about the big stress going on in your life, or did you have to stop and decide which of the many stresses was the main one to write about? If you're like most teens, you probably could have used several pages, explaining the stress and strain of your life as a teen. We asked teens nationwide (guys and girls of various ages and different backgrounds) to talk to us about what, in particular, they think makes teen life so stressful. Here's their take on the "top" causes of stress in "Teenville."

Carrie Linn, 16, Winter Park, Florida: "Most stressful is the balancing act: Being a teen means that you're always trying to meet the expectations of others—parents, teachers, activity coaches and friends—while wanting to do things your own way. You need to assert your own "voice"—I mean, teens have wants, needs and desires, too. And sometimes what others expect of you—from the things you're supposed to be accomplishing to the way you're acting or behaving—are in conflict. It's always a push and pull, a tug of war: You may want to make your own decisions, but you know that someone—and not you—is really in charge. All they have to do is dangle the power of a grade or the car keys over your head—and you know it's so."

Wanda Groff, 17, Chattanooga, Tennessee: "It's always being self-conscious—having acne, wearing braces, a constantly changing body, emotions bouncing around at will—and all are played out in the 'spotlight' so to speak. Everybody's watching. It's a time when being self-confident and giving off an air of self-assurance is necessary, but tough (and you're judging yourself, and hard on yourself, too). This sense of double-identity makes you feel out of sync with yourself, like you're not true to yourself. It's easy to feel bad about yourself: Because you know you're supposed to 'be yourself' and take your own lead—but you also know the consequences of not being one of the crowd—you can feel like a fake, a fraud, like you and your life is a big lie. Worse, you want to scream out about these things, but instead, sit on them, harboring them until you're sure no one can possibly know how you're feeling and by then, you're too mad at everyone for not reading your mind and knowing how upsetting this duplicity is to live with.

Greg Willis, 15, Toledo, Ohio: "I think the need to have friends dominates all the issues. A huge amount of time and energy is spent on trying to fit in and have others like you. Period. Without friends, you have no life. So figuring out how to get along with all the different personalities, and then learning the 'rules' for getting along is a really big stress in the teen years."

RaNelle Nelson, 16, White Plains, New York: "Hoping for love: You look around you and see a teen couple, and it just looks so cool to think that someone could be walking you to your class, saving a seat for you at lunch, always knowing you already have a special date for special events going on. You have someone to kiss you and someone to just be there. So when you don't have someone special, you feel that a big piece of life is missing. So teens are always hoping for a special someone. It's a constant search."

Nelson Becker, 17, Indianola, Iowa: "Being *happy* in a relationship is a really big stressor for teens. It's been my experience that you think you've found someone great to ask out, and then when you do, if you decide that person is really not right for you, well, before you can tell her that, she's told everyone in the world that the two of you are practically going steady or, she sort of locks in, even before the two of you have a real thing going on and have talked things over and know for sure that you want and expect the same things from the relationship. And since practically everything you do is scrutinized by your friends and classmates, you don't really have a chance to just follow your heart. Sometimes you date someone 'just because,' and it's a rut you get into or it's just more of a habit, a ritual you go through to be with somebody, but that doesn't always mean that it makes your life brighter or more spectacular. Worse, as a guy, if I ask out three girls for three different dates in a given month, I'll be labeled a runaround, and some girls will then no longer go out with me. It's not like my brother who is out of college and dates around. No one says anything or thinks anything about that, because he has more options for taking someone out and then, if he decides the person is not for him, he doesn't have to explain anything to anyone. It becomes the business of only the two of them. Dating in high school isn't that easy. It's a much more complicated thing."

Rianna Sharrit, 15, La Jolla, California: "The love thing—having love or not having love—is the most stressful. If you don't have someone special, you feel left out. But you quickly find out that finding someone to love isn't stress-free either. And, you come to understand that practically everything about love produces stress—whether finding it, keeping it, or breaking up or making up. And, you discover that you've got to make a lot of compromises and a lot of concessions if the relationship is to be fun. And, you hope that it is not going to be just chaotic—one that brings just constant upheaval. You look around and see that some of your friends are always sad or upset because they aren't happy about what's going on in the relationship. A lot of the ups and downs are too draining. Love can be a very stressful thing— both when it's great and when things aren't going so great."

Tyanna Peyton, 15, St. Joseph, Missouri: "Time demands are what makes things so stressful. Having too much to do and not enough time (or stamina) to do it is always an issue for teens. Everyone kind of forgets that having this mega-schedule is sort of a setup for doom-and-gloom from the beginning, because the truth is, you'd like to spend this supposedly 'best time of your life' sleeping. A teenager's body would like to sleep 'til noon. It's not like you wake up every day full of energy and just raring to go get things done."

Brad Bentley, 18, Alexandria, Maryland: "Personal power: Being a teen means you want to be in charge of your life, but more often than not, you feel like a puppet on a string. While on some days you feel like you are, on most days you feel as though you have no control over what happens, so it can be easy to just let others take control. But it ticks you off when they do, especially if they make choices for you and don't consult you first. As a teen, having any great amount of personal power is an illusion."

Betsy Little, 13, Sheboygan, Wisconsin: "Definitely, worrying about friends. Being a teen means that often you're concerned for your friends, especially for the things they're dealing with, like parents in the midst of a divorce, and especially those with big personal problems of their own, like doing drugs or drinking problems. For friends with problems of their own, you worry about them, but for the most part, you don't exactly know what to do or where to turn to get help for them—especially when most of the time you've been sworn to secrecy and so you find that you've promised a friend you won't reveal her problem—which can be as serious as bulimia, pregnancy, drug or alcohol abuse, or emotional or even physical abuse. It's very stressful to be a loyal friend, to want to help but feel powerless to help."

Scott Perry, 17, Syracuse, New York: "Money problems: Being a teen means you're always short on money. If you have a part-time job, you don't have as much time to be with your friends, and you have even less time for yourself given that there's always so much homework and things to do. Most parents pay for the basics and then some, but there are so many things you need money for—such as a special outfit for a date or something special, to go a school trip or special event like a dance or prom or go with a ski club, or even having those things that help you fit in with others. Most all of my friends—guys and girls—wish they had more money."

Janetta McGhee, 15, Salt Lake City, Utah. "A teen's life is filled with constant anxiety: keeping up grades, completing classroom and homework assignments, being able to answer questions in class; thinking you may not be as smart as you'd like to be; being uncertain about what college to go to and whether or not you'll be accepted there. There's also the worry that maybe college isn't going to be right for you and you'll just end up wasting time and money, and that maybe you should enter the job market once you're out of high school instead. Even then, you wonder what special skills—if any—you possess, but you're never quite sure how to find out for sure. It's a time of serious confusion."

Conrad White, 16, Rapid City, South Dakota: "Career and job concerns always make it to the top of the list for most teens. There is a great deal of turmoil over not knowing what to do with your life. You always hear, 'The sky's the limit,' meaning you can do anything, but knowing there are so many options doesn't make your decisions easier; in fact, it makes them much, much tougher. Sure you'd like to be president of the world, but what if it's your destiny to be Thoreau, or a surf bum. How do you know, and who's to judge?"

Marissa Hewitt, 17, San Bernardino, California: "One's family is always a big stress for teens. Making time to have fun and be close with each family member never seems to happen—but you know it's supposed to. Also, it's a huge emotional drain to be in an argument with your parents, as is being caught in the middle of parents who are separated or divorcing. Problems at home spill over to everything else you're doing—and to the way you're feeling. It's tough to separate yourself from the stress and strains going on in your family. Family stress becomes your stress, too. But it doesn't replace your own stress; it just adds to it."

Kevin Pauls, 18, Safford, Arizona: "Sorting out values. You're forever dealing with what you hear and know to be important and worthy values, but then you see them ignored and violated. And this happens not only in hypothetical situations like the movies or on television, but even by those in leadership positions who are charged with setting a good example for others. It's like there's right, wrong, more right and more wrong. While you'd like there to be a consensus on what's right and wrong, you learn that it depends upon the situation. So when someone asks you what you believe in, you find you're not quite sure. But, you'd like to be very sure."

VIRTUAL PRACTICE:
WHAT OVERWHELMS *YOU?*

After reading how teens characterize the stress of teen life, did you find yourself shaking your head while reading that list, thinking, "That's the way I feel," or "That's not one of my stressors, but it is for my friend," or "That hasn't happened to me—yet"? We all have an easier time relating to those who are in our own age group. After all, twelve-year-olds are more like twelve-year-olds than eighteen-year-olds, and eighteen-year-olds are more like eighteen-year-olds than they are fifteen-year-olds. You get the idea!

The following list shows what teens at each age find to be the things that trigger stress for them. If you are fifteen, you may want to skip ahead to the stresses listed by fifteen-year-olds and see how they compare to those you are feeling. Then, you might want to look at the "last year" and see how you've fared with the stresses you've "left behind." And you might also want to peek one year ahead—just to see what's coming up! After all, it's never too late to get a heads-up on being cool!

Common Stress Triggers: Ages 11 to 19

Age 11:

- ♥ Fear that I won't make friends
- ♥ Fear of losing a best friend
- ♥ Fear that a friend will tell my "secrets" to someone else
- ♥ Fear of not being able to keep up with others my age, such as not batting as well as everyone else on my baseball (or softball) team, or not doing as well as the others in my class

Age 12:

- ♥ Fear of being selected first (and having to lead) and fear of being picked last (seen as being disliked or unpopular)
- ♥ Fear of failing in school and not passing into middle school/junior high
- ♥ Fear that other kids won't find me likeable and worthy of their friendship
- ♥ Fear that others will criticize or make fun of my intelligence

Age 13:

- ♥ Not understanding the changes my growing body is undergoing (and wondering if they are "normal")
- ♥ Concern that my "moodiness" means that I am not as happy as I'd like to be—or as I'm "supposed to be"
- ♥ Fear of not doing well—most especially if others are

watching, such as being called on in class, or athletic competitions (like school sports)

Age 14:

♥ Not understanding the changes my body is undergoing (I wonder if I should believe what my friends say is the way things are "supposed to be")

♥ Fear that teasing by friends means that I am "disliked," unpopular

♥ Fear of the sexual feelings I am experiencing

♥ Concern about whether I am as happy as I am supposed to be

Age 15:

♥ Fear of others judging my body or my sexuality (such as in "tomboy" or "too sissy")

♥ Fear of exposing my changing and growing body (such as when shopping with friends, or showering in P.E. class)

♥ Fear of being challenged to a fight, or even getting in a verbal confrontation

Age 16:

♥ Fear of being disliked or unpopular

♥ Fear that another boy or girl will try to take my "sweet-heart" away from me, or share a secret of who I consider someone I'd like as a boy/girlfriend

♥ Fear that I won't ever get my driver's license, get to drive a car, pass a grade, get into college, find a job or a boy/girlfriend

♥ Fear that my family is not a "happy family"

Age 17:

♥ Worry about not liking school or finding it important

♥ Concern about my ability to get along well with others—boyfriends, girlfriends, classmates, teachers, parents, family members (or, that I compromise too much in order to be liked)

♥ Fear that I'm not in a "best family" (believing that other families are happier or are "more together" than my family)

Age 18:

- ♥ Fear of "not being okay"
- ♥ Fear of being made to feel insignificant by others (such as by teachers, or employers or employees at a part-time job)
- ♥ Fear of not ever being able to earn enough money for the things I want and need
- ♥ Fear that others will want to have control over me as I begin to live by values as I know them to be, and want consequences to be my own
- ♥ Fear of not passing all my classes to graduate with the rest of my classmates
- ♥ Fear of not knowing what to do when I get out of school
- ♥ Fear that my parents won't "let go" so I can go out in the real world as an adult on my own

Age 19:

- ♥ Fear that my parents won't be there for help, support or advice
- ♥ Fear of being on my own "for real"
- ♥ Fear that I didn't take school seriously enough and learn all that I wished I had
- ♥ Fear that I don't have the skills or knowledge I think I need to make it in "the real world"
- ♥ Fear that I won't make it in college or a career
- ♥ Fear that I don't have any friends left (because they've all gone off to college or work or moved away)

After reading through the stresses listed in your age group, consider how those stresses compare to your own. Then, using the space provided, identify other "stresses" you would like to add to the list. For example, I find it stressful:

♥ to be in an argument with a close friend—or my parents;
♥ when I've loaned money to a friend who refuses to repay it;
♥ when a friend tells a secret or betrays me in some way;
♥ when a rumor is circulated among my friends about me.

Stresses I would include:

♥ _____

♥ _____

♥ _____

♥ _____

♥ _____

♥ _____

♥ _____

♥ _____

In looking over the things you added, are you surprised to find that you didn't have too many things to list? If so, that's great. But if you are like most teens, you used up every line and maybe even needed more!

Cool Is Up to You!

Knowing that others are feeling some of the same things that you are can relieve some of the "fears" associated with wondering if you are "normal." This is good to know because while there many things you can do to lessen stress, you can't make all stress go away. However, you can learn how to manage yourself in relation to it, and throughout this book you'll find a good number of skills and techniques to help you do just that. But first, let's take a closer look at this thing called *stress*. The next chapter will help you understand more about what stress is— and isn't.

Part 2

Understanding the Many "Personalities" of Stress

We suffer more in imagination than in reality.
—Seneca, *Epistulae ad Lucilium*

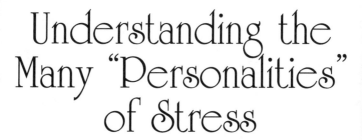

4

A Message from the Authors

Stress. We hear the word and use it a great deal, but what is it really? If someone asked *you* to define *stress,* what would you say? Maybe you associate it with events like taking a final exam; the adrenaline rush of being the focus of attention at an important competition in a sports activity; being on center-stage during a school play; or you've got the closing arguments in your school's debate club city championship. Maybe it's that sense of anxiety you have when you need to "face up," "square off," "confront" or "level" with someone, such as with a teacher or your parents because you've broken a promise or not followed through on a certain commitment. Maybe it's that sinking feeling of having an argument with a best friend or the nervousness of not being quite dressed and ready for the date of your dreams—who is knocking on your door.

While situations such as these can certainly cause an "I'm stressed" response, they are just that: a situation, an event, a happening. While you can't always control or change the event (it's your turn to get up and give that oral report in front of the class), how you respond is under your control. For instance, in the case of the oral report, you can be as prepared as you can possibly be; you can start your day by having a good night's rest, eating a good breakfast, and as an extra confidence boost, looking especially cool that day. *Stress,* on the other hand, is its own agenda: It is the body's *physical, mental and chemical reaction* to the circumstances you're facing. No matter what kind of stress-creating factor it is that you're facing—your first kiss, or facing a near head-on collision with a fellow classmate as you make a mad dash to get to class—the same reactions go off in your body. This is good: Your body readies itself to deal with the situation at hand. If, for example, you step off a curb and suddenly an unexpected car wheels around a corner and nearly hits you, it's highly likely that within the flash of a instant, your body will command you to leap out of the way.

And, of course, stress can overwhelm you to the point of not being effective. If, for example, you study for an important test, but on the day of the test you are not nervous about taking it, it's possible that you draw a blank, not remembering even the most easy and common facts! So, it's important to learn all you can about coping with stress in positive ways and not let it get the best of you.

Consider this unit the Cliff Notes on Stress. Throughout the next few chapters, you'll learn all about the nature of stress, its pros and cons, and how you can use stress to your advantage. You'll learn what you can do when your stress gets too high, and what you can do to create a little stress in your life so that things get exciting! And being the taste berry that you are, you know that information—like stress—is powerful!

5

What Is Stress?

If someone asked *you* to define *stress*, what would you say? Some teens define it as confusion, turmoil, even excitement. Perhaps LaToya experienced all three of these when the boy of her dreams became her first love, then dropped her for her best friend, and then dropped her now "ex" best friend because he wanted LaToya back, then. . . .

Stuck in the Crossfire

Kevin Larson, a guy I liked for nearly three whole months before he even noticed I was alive (even though I'd made it very obvious to him the whole time!) finally asked me out! He was my very first love.

I thought everything was just great between us. We were boyfriend and girlfriend for four months when suddenly he just dropped me for my very best friend, Karina Wells. My best friend! I'd seen that happen to others, but it never crosses your mind that it will happen to you. Well, it did.

When we broke up, I cried and cried. I was sad, mad, con-fused, miserable without him and indignant, too, and not above throwing a tantrum or two. But Kevin acted like he didn't care at all about my feelings. He paid no attention to me, just went on about his business, happy as a clam about his new girlfriend, my (and now "ex") friend.

Then, just two weeks later, just out of the blue, Kevin Larson broke up with his newest sweetie Karina Wells. This I found out when he handed me a letter as we passed each other in the hall one day. I was surprised to get a letter, and though I did my best to act like I could have cared less about receiving it from him, I made a straight beeline into the girls' restroom as fast as I could so I could read the words written by the love of my life—even if I was mad at him.

It was a great letter! Kevin told me that he loved me and only me and that he no longer wanted to be with Karina. I was thrilled of course, but still curious. I mean, did he really miss me so much and that was the reason he broke up with Karina—or did she dump him? To tell you the truth, while I was relieved to have him say he wanted me back, I was a little confused, too! I mean, while I was happy that he broke up with Karina, there was the thing about his having dumped me in the first place. And, there was the matter of Kevin wanting us to get back together. Should I just go back, be sweet and tell him how much I missed him, or should I make him work really hard to get me back? All the other kids at school knew the full story, so I couldn't just go back without a fight and lose my self-respect. Should I tell him, "No way! Get lost. You had your chance!"? These are all really important things to consider. And besides, one of his good friends, Rick Torres, had been making eyes at me like he's interested in me, and Rick is pretty cool. Going out with Rick would be a great way to get back at Kevin. But then, my heart belongs to Kevin. . . .

As you can see, it's a tough decision I have to make, one that is being battled out between my heart and my head. I'm stuck in the crossfire, and boy is it stressful:

My heart: "You see! I told you Kevin loves you! Now we can stop aching so much."

My head: "Be careful. You know he left you for another girl."

My heart: "Oh, don't worry about that now. What's important is that he wants you back. And besides, you know how good it feels to have him ask you to come back to him."

My head: "Go slow. Your turmoil is sure proof it may not be right."

My heart: "But he wants YOU, YOU, YOU! Be happy, don't worry!"

My head: "A week ago he wanted Karina Wells."

My heart: "But now he wants *you!*"

My head: "Kevin double-timed you."

My heart: "Yes, but he can be so romantic and sweet."

My head: "He may do it again. Why risk getting hurt again?"

My heart: "Oh, I'm sure he'll never do it again. He said he loves me."

My head: "He's proven himself as someone you can't trust."

My heart: "But I miss him. My heart hurts when I'm not with him. I want him back."

My head: "Take your time; think it over."

My heart: "If you don't act fast, Teresa Amos will snatch him up! You saw her flirting with him."

My head: "He is a big flirt. I'm suggesting you don't go back."

My heart: "But I love him."

My head: "You're doing just fine without him."

My heart: "Love is a wonderful thing. You know how happy it makes me. . . ."

What a seesaw! It's been thirty-eight hours and fifty-five minutes since Kevin Larson asked me to get back together with him. And I'm still very stressed out, not knowing what to do!

LaToya Jones, 17

STRESS 101: Everything a Teen Should Know About What Stress Is—And Isn't

Have you ever picked out a someone "special," only to have someone else decide to "select" that person, too, and edge you out? Talk about stress!

Stress? What is stress?

Most people think stress is having to confront a particular unpleasant or tough situation. Technically, these anxiety-filled events—such as taking a big test, taking your driver's license test, asking out a certain someone or having an argument with a good friend—are called "stressors." The "wear and tear" they cause us is the "stress." Regardless of whether the stressor is a biochemical insult (such as using drugs or alcohol); a physical injury (such as getting in a fight or falling and breaking your wrist); or confronting something you fear or someone who makes you upset, the body responds the same: It is thrown into a "stress reaction."

This reaction has three distinct phases, each one named after that which it does, basically, in response to the incoming stressor. These are:

(1) The Alarm Phase,
(2) The Resistance Phase, and
(3) The Exhaustion Phase.

Stress can be a good thing, then, primarily because it acts as a bell or siren telling you it's time to take notice, it's time to do something, to make a change, to cope, or adapt. That your body is equipped to "feel" stress is remarkable; our job is to use the signals our bodies send out to alert us to the stage of stress it's in, and do something about the level of stress our body is experiencing. Here's what you should know about the nature of stress so that you can do just that.

"Whaaaaat's Uuuup?"
The "Alarm Phase" of Stress

This first phase of stress alerts the body to the stressful encounter—warning it that it's time to make what we call a "fight-or-flight" response. In other words, the body gears up to take action. In stressful situations, messages from the brain trigger an outpouring of adrenaline from the adrenal glands. Circulation speeds up, more energy-rich sugar appears in the blood, muscles tense, saliva decreases, eyes dilate, senses become more acute, the thyroid is activated and the body's muscle function is strengthened. At the same time, blood cells are released from storage depots into the circulation, and the digestive system goes into temporary inaction. All of these reactions are designed to help the body gear up for action. You may recognize some of the following alarm reaction responses from your own experience.

1. Do you remember how your heart pounded when a speeding car wheeled around the corner, taking you by surprise and, luckily, just missed hitting you? In such situations, the heart speeds up and blood pressure soars, forcing blood to parts of your body that need it, thus carrying oxygen-rich blood to organs so they will be instantly fueled for action—including the brain, so it can make wise decisions quickly!

2. Can you remember trying to catch your breath after being frightened (like the time you were concentrating on an assignment or project and the wind caused the door to slam shut)? This reaction is caused by breathing faster to supply more oxygen for the needed muscles.

3. Remember getting your "second wind" the time your best friend was involved in a confrontation and you rushed over to help? Or were you once surprised by your strength and endurance during an emergency when you could tell from your dog's yelp that your pet might need your help?

The extra strength came from sugars and fats pouring into your bloodstream to provide fuel for quick energy.

4. Do you use extra deodorant when you know you're going to be under pressure, like going in to interview for a part-time job that you really want to get, or asking someone special for a date when you are unsure if he or she will accept? You perspire more when under stress. This is because perspiring is how the body tries to cool down. The cooler your body, the more efficient its energy.

5. Do you ever have a stiff neck after a long test or a really stressful day? In high-stress situations, muscles remain in a state of tenseness. Strained muscles are sore muscles.

6. Have you ever had "knots" or "butterflies"—or "eagles"!— in your stomach before taking an exam or making a presentation in front of your classmates? Because it's more important to be alert and strong in the face of danger than to digest food, your digestion slows so blood can be directed to your muscles and brain.

"The Coast Is Clear!" The "Resistance/Adaptation Phase" of Stress

Almost immediately following a stressful event, the body attempts to return to its normal balance. We call returning to "normal" *homeostasis,* a state of calm and normal functioning. In this phase, the body works to reverse the process described in the alarm stage, but only if it believes that the stressful encounter is over. If the danger is over, the body works to restore a state of calm by lowering blood pressure, heart rate, respiration and core body temperature. But if your body senses that danger is still present—you are still greatly worried or frightened—then the body replaces its temporary and emergency responses with more fixed ones. Muscle tension is a good example of this kind of "replacement" response. This is not a good thing because a great deal of energy and body nutrients (such as potassium and vitamin B) are depleted. Such nutrients are needed to not only keep you healthy, but also to help you fend off stress.

Here's how this works: Let's say, for example, you are home alone and hear a strange creaky noise in your house. This noise frightens you. Always working for you, your body gears up—your senses become keen, and your eyesight is sharpened—just in case you need to confront or flee the scene. Let's assume for a moment that the creaking noise continues every few minutes for the next couple of hours, making you so frightened that you decide to turn the lights on all over the house. You even go to your room, push your dresser in front of the door and sit quietly, your lamp in your hand in case the now larger-than-life "monster" decides to come down your hallway!

But now let's assume that while sitting in your room, you look up and discover that outdoors, the wind is blowing so strong that even the lamps in the street are swaying. Feeling relieved, you conclude that the creaking is obviously caused by strong winds—and this dispels the notion of anything sinister. Maybe you even laugh at the situation. For the rest of the evening, even though the creaking noise continues, you are no longer fearful. Having this information that you are safe, your brain triggers the "coast is clear" message, and your body returns to homeostasis, a state of relaxed normal.

But now let's assume that you never really are sure what is causing that frightening noise. If that were the case, you would remain in a heightened state of arousal—because of being fearful—and your body would stay in a state of tense alert. This is when the body moves to the third phase, the exhaustion phase.

"Give Me a Break!"
The "Exhaustion Phase" of Stress

When your body is under a period of prolonged and intense stress, it gets exhausted. Sometimes this is referred to as "burnout." Do you feel drained after a big test? What if the test went on for three weeks? You can only imagine how exhausting that would be. This same sort of wear and tear happens when you are constantly worried about something, even something that slowly brews—such as worrying about if your parents will get back together if they are separated, or if someone will find out that it was you who started a particular rumor or whether everything will go perfectly for your big party.

Prolonged stress can be dangerous over time because when you are under stress, your body uses your reserve of essential vitamins and minerals. Staying under stress for a long time means that these essential nutrients are drained from your body, and so your ability to withstand stress is lowered. If you are under stress for a long time (experts place this time period as anywhere from three weeks to three months), your supply of energy is used up, leaving you at risk for harming your bodily organs.

Since mind and body work in unison, when your body is tired, so is your emotional state of mind. One teen summed it up well when she said, "I was so exhausted from the constant stress I felt when my parents were divorcing that I reached a point where I felt drained and unable to 'get up' for my own school and personal life."

When you are in the midst of a long period of stress in your life, it's especially important to take care of yourself. Getting enough rest, eating the essential high-quality foods to restore your body and making sure you take the time to get the exercise your body needs to burn up excess stress, as well as relaxing the body so it can rejuvenate, are all very important steps to staying in good health (more on this in part 7).

VIRTUAL PRACTICE: *YOU* AND STRESS

Think of a time over the last few months when you experienced the *alarm phase* of stress. What was happening to cause the stress? _____

_____

_____

_____

How did you know your body was alerting you it was in this phase of stress? _____

_____

_____

_____

Think of a time over the last few months when you experienced the *resistance/adaptation phase* of stress. What was happening to cause this stress? _____

_____

_____

_____

How did you know your body was in this phase of stress?

_____

_____

_____

Think of a time over the last few months when you experienced the *exhaustion phase* of stress. What was happening to cause you stress? _____

_____

_____

How did you know you were in this phase of stress?_____

_____

_____

_____

How did you get your energy back?_____

_____

_____

_____

Cool Is Up to You!

One of the benefits of understanding the nature of stress is so that you can learn to use it to your advantage. Just as stress can be debilitating (such as stopping you from thinking clearly), you can make it work in your favor. How can you use stress in a positive way rather than letting it get the best of you? Knowing the benefits of responding to a stressful situation in a positive manner is a start. In other words, you can learn to be cool under stress.

Speaking of cool, when you're stressed-out, how does your body respond? How do you feel? How do you behave? The next chapter will help you examine the three ways stress shows up in your life—which is good to know. Being the taste berry that you are, you know how important it is that stress doesn't change your demeanor from cool to ghoul!

6

The Three "Side Effects" of Stress

While stress is a natural reaction of our body in response to the demands we make upon it, it's important that we always be aware of the amount of stress, strain and pressure we put ourselves through. Why? Because as you learned in the last chapter, too much stress can take a toll, and not just physically—such as feeling overwhelmed, burned out, or in an extreme case, by getting an ulcer or suffering other health breakdowns. Stress also affects the way we feel (emotions) and the ways in which we behave. Health experts confirm that "side effects" of stress are threefold: physical, emotional and behavioral. As you can see in the story below, the stress and strain seventeen-year-old Gerard Hamilton felt in his efforts to deal with "goddess" Cassandra affected him in all three ways! Read for yourself to see if the stress he felt by "the Goddess" brought out the cool, or ghoul, in him!

The Trouble with a Goddess

Cassandra Allen is practically a goddess—she's that cool. What's more, she is smart and funny and beautiful and nice to everyone—even kids who aren't popular like her. I've been secretly in love with Cassandra for almost a whole semester now, and hoping there would come a time when I got the chance to ask her to go out with me. Asking a girl for a date, especially a girl like Cassandra, can be tricky because she's the sort of girl who has a waiting list practically a mile long of guys who want to date her. For the last two months she's been dating one of the most popular guys in school, Manny Ellison. Before that it was exchange student Jake Lidstrom, and before that, a "serious" relationship with Neil Garza. But she's done with all of them! So finally, I saw my chance. Cassandra wasn't dating anyone and wasn't even interested in anyone else (I got this on good authority from my younger sister, who got it from Cassandra's younger sister). Best of all, the Christmas formal was fast approaching and surely she would want a date to the Christmas formal. Not that Cassandra wouldn't be able to get any number of guys to ask her to go to the formal—like I said, she's a goddess.

When you ask out a girl like Cassandra, you have to plan things carefully, look for the right moment and say the right thing—because once you get a "no," you pretty much lose confidence to try again. Cassandra and I had a few classes together, and we share some mutual friends. She and I talked a few times a week, but usually there are tons of people around her, so that's definitely not a good time to ask. What could be worse than rejection in front of a gazillion classmates?

The "right moment" meant asking her when no one else was around. I did know her schedule and where her locker was located, so, two weeks before the dance, I spent every spare school-hour minute watching for the time when she was alone so I could ask her.

I was so busy keeping track of her that on some days I actually didn't eat lunch, since I'd hang pretty close to the back of the cafeteria line so that I would have a chance to be near her and see her come in so that I might get a chance to sit at her lunch table or something. I guess it's a good thing that the stress I was feeling meant that I lost my appetite, since on some days she never did show up for the lunch line, and they closed the doors while I still stood outside waiting for her.

All this was pretty exciting, but nerve-wracking, too. Still, I considered it well worth it. I'd spent hours practicing what I was going to say and how I was going to approach her. My plan was that once the time was right, I'd stop to say "Hello" as I was strolling by, then pull a pack of gum from the pocket of my shirt and offer her a piece (I thought that was a great touch: you know, just to make it all seem casual). Then I'd say: "Hey, Cassandra. What'cha up to? Want a piece of gum?" I'd be gallant as I handed her the stick of gum. She'd smile, I'd smile and then I'd say, "How would you like to go to the Christmas formal with me?" I'd practiced the words so they would have a warm but "no pressure" tone. (You don't want to make a goddess feel pressured.)

I must've rehearsed the scene in my head a hundred times. The problem was that right moment never presented itself. The wait was torture, and I was getting anxious: The Christmas formal was fast approaching. The stress of it all was really wearing. I found myself daydreaming in class, and not really concentrating on my studies. It even spilled over with my friends, as I discovered one day when Joel Burrows, one of my best friends, came up to me and asked if I'd hurry and go with him to the school library to help him check out a book he badly needed for his next class. Because he owed a late fee for a book he'd checked out the week before, the librarian wouldn't let him check the book out under his own library card. Well, normally I'd just go do it for him, but from the corner of my eye, I'd just had a Cassandra-the-goddess sighting. She was out in the school courtyard—alone—just looking through her notebook. Thinking "now's *the* moment!" I was suddenly faced with my best friend needing an urgent favor. "You're always needing something!" (which isn't the case at all) I barked unfairly.

Joel looked surprised and kind of hurt. I looked up, and poof! Cassandra was gone. My friend left, too, and that upset me as well. By Wednesday I still hadn't seen her alone again, and by Thursday, I had a headache at the end of the school day, and my shoulders and neck were actually aching.

The next day, I finally got another chance: Cassandra was actually alone at her locker! How long would it last? My heart began to pound, my pulse was zipping along like hummingbird wings. I scanned the area—no one was approaching Cassandra in the distance—this was it! I set out on my practiced "stroll." When I got to Cassandra, just as rehearsed, I said, "Hello, Cassandra." Cassandra glanced at me and smiled absently, then continued digging in her locker, "Hi, Gerard. Gosh, I can't find my civics book!" She swiped her hair from her face and continued searching her locker. "What am I going to do? It's just gotta be in here somewhere!" she huffed. I hadn't really practiced for coming up with answers, nor for asking out a goddess who was obviously feeling upset.

What to do? Remembering my props, I went to pull my pack of gum from the pocket of my shirt and offered her a piece. Remembering my lines, I asked, "Whatcha' up to? Want a piece of gum?" I tried to be gallant as I handed her the stick of gum. She turned to look at me again, this time her expression baffled, as if wondering if I was deaf. Wouldn't you know, as I stood there with my hand outstretched with the gum that way, I got so nervous that I started to shake—right where she could see the tremors in my hands. "Gum?" she asked, then shook her head—whether in refusal of the gum or in wonder at my stupidity, I don't know. Trying to regain lost ground and look cool and nonchalant, I went to flick a piece of gum from the pack—and all the pieces flew out on the ground. Now I was sweating—literally and obviously. I dove to the ground to pick up the gum and accidentally spilled the contents of my backpack—books crashed and pencils rolled.

Remembering how I'd once pictured Cassandra opening her mouth gracefully and placing the gum in it, instead her mouth was open all right—but in a kind of "is he for real?" expression. She stooped down to help me pick up my stuff, looking genuinely concerned for my sanity. "Gerard, are you okay?" she asked, her missing civics book momentarily forgotten (I told you she was nice).

I sighed and confessed, "I wanted to look cool."

"You wanted to look cool?" she repeated and then laughed. Then, she smiled, and out of nowhere, the scene I'd practiced for this moment returned to me as I smiled back at her and then she said, "If you really want to be cool, why don't you ask me to the Christmas formal? I've been hoping you would, but I'm not going to wait for you much longer."

"Yeah. I mean yes. Sure. Great! Okay, then."

"Good," she said, "so let's talk about the details after school tomorrow. I've got squad practice tonight and tons of homework."

It was that simple—all that worry, drama and disaster and in the end I got the answer I'd waited forever to hear. I wish I'd known that was how it was going to turn out before I made myself a nervous wreck. But that's the trouble with a goddess, you never know just what she's going to do—or say.

Gerard Hamilton, 17

How to Recognize the (Physical, Emotional and Behavioral) Signs and Symptoms of Stress

Gerard's dealings with a "goddess" make it clear that trying to get a date with a special someone can have some side effects (check out some of Gerard's symptoms in the following section).

What causes these symptoms? Health experts have found that stress triggers chemical changes in the brain and alters the body's chemical balance, all of which has an effect on the way we think, act and feel. Depression, for example, has been associated with low levels of two neurotransmitters: serotonin and norepinephrine. These may be big words, but ask anyone who has ever been "blue," "in a funk" or "depressed," and they'll no doubt describe a time of great stress.

Stress can result in muscle tension, headaches, stomachaches, feeling irritable, not being able to concentrate and even in low feelings of self-worth. Some of the common symptoms of stress are listed below.

Symptoms of Stress
- ♥ headaches
- ♥ continued feelings of being annoyed or irritated
- ♥ low energy or bouts of high energy
- ♥ dramatic change in food cravings
- ♥ feeling like a victim, feeling "trapped"
- ♥ outbursts of temper
- ♥ pains in the lower part of your back or neck or shoulders
- ♥ feeling "blue," or lonely
- ♥ lack of interest in things once enjoyed (such as time with friends)
- ♥ heart pounding or racing

♥ jumping from peaks to valleys of self-esteem
♥ nausea or upset stomach
♥ inferiority feelings
♥ sleep difficulties (too much/too little)
♥ difficulty making decisions
♥ loss of concentration
♥ feeling hopeless

A good way to look at the effects of stress is to break them into three distinct categories: physical, emotional and behavioral. Pinpointing these stress reactions is yet another clue for you in learning how to deal with the stress and strains in your life. For example, if you know you're going to get a tension headache just before taking a big test, using a quick muscle relaxation exercise can help you avoid some of the tension. In the coming units you'll learn a great many exercises designed to help you effectively cope with stress. Right now, let's look at how Gerard said the incident with the "goddess" affected him.

How stress affected me:

Physically	Emotionally	Behaviorally
I got headaches.	I got nervous. (I'd often stutter.)	I didn't eat.
I lost my appetite.	I felt insecure.	I couldn't concentrate.
My hands got shaky.	I was irritable.	I was short-tempered.
I began to sweat. My muscles tensed. My heart pounded.	I felt scattered.	I snapped at my friends.

VIRTUAL PRACTICE:
HOW DOES STRESS AFFECT *YOU?*

How about you? How does stress affect you? Read each of the following three categories, and place a checkmark beside those that apply to you. Then, on the lines provided, list other ways stress exerts power over you.

The Physical Side Effects of Stress

How stress affects me *physically:*

___ My muscles get tense.

___ My hands get cold or sweaty.

___ My stomach feels as if it is churning.

___ I have difficulty sleeping.

___ My heart beats rapidly.

___ I have sudden bursts of energy.

___ I am extremely tired.

___ I lose my appetite, or eat too much.

♥ _____

♥ _____

♥ _____

♥ _____

♥ _____

The Emotional Side Effects of Stress

How stress affects me *emotionally:*

___ I get nervous.

___ I cry.

___ I want to strike out or hit something.

___ I feel sad.

___ I giggle a lot.

___ I worry excessively and can't stop thinking, "what if?"

___ I am irritable or feel depressed.

___ I feel bad about myself.

___ I daydream a lot at school (or have bad dreams at night).

___ I get angry easily, sometimes even to the point of being explosive.

___ I lose interest in my appearance.

♥ _____

♥ _____

♥ _____

♥ _____

♥ _____

The Behavioral Side Effects of Stress

How stress affects my *behavior:*

___ I have difficulty concentrating.

___ I substitute food, drugs or alcohol for coping.

___ I become grouchy, irritable, even mean.

___ I cover up by not being honest about something.

___ I get into arguments or fights with others.

___ I deliberately do sloppy work (not caring about how it is done).

___ I procrastinate.

___ I smile a lot to cover up my feelings.

___ I ignore my feelings.

♥ _____

♥ _____

♥ _____

♥ _____

♥ _____

Cool Is Up to You!

While some amounts of stress can help us feel creative and move us to action, too much can cause us to feel overwhelmed, even debilitated. So you'll want to know what you can do to use it to your advantage. That's why knowing how stress affects you physically, emotionally and behaviorally can be useful information. Does even a small dose of stress gives you a tension headache? If so, use that symptom (the headache) as feedback that you need to find better ways to cope with your stress. If the smallest amount of stress makes you frustrated or upset to the point of avoiding what you need to do, that, too, is useful information: You need better skills so as to be sure stress isn't taking a toll on your life.

Obviously, you can't make all the stress and pressures of life evaporate, nor should you ignore them. Coping effectively is the key. How do you cope when stress comes your way? In the following unit, you'll get a chance to find out—which is good to know. Being the taste berry that you are, you know that being able to deal with the constant ups and downs of life as a teen can spell the difference between staying in Teenville, or being tossed headfirst into the "land of overwhelm"!

Part 3

How Do You [Re]act When You're Stressed-Out?

If you're all wrapped up in yourself,
you're overdressed.

—Kate Halverson

7

A Message from the Authors

When you're face-to-face with a stressful situation, how do you react? Are you cool and confident under stress, or does it change your demeanor from cool to ghoul? Think about that for a moment. Let's say you're in school, and you're moseying down the hall on your way to your last-period class. It's been a long day and you're tired, and this last class isn't necessarily your favorite subject. You just wish the school day was over and that you were on your way home where the refrigerator, your pet and favorite TV show await you. You look down at your watch and take note of the fact that you have exactly fifty seconds to get to class—and experience tells you it'll take a full minute to get down the hall, turn left at the library, down that corridor, take a right at the science lab, and whew, finally you'll be there. The thing is, you *have* to get there on time; you simply cannot be late. Another tardy will surely take a toll; even with all your persuasion and charm, it won't work for you today because you've used up all the teacher's patience with your being late to class. You take off on a near full run for class!

What are some of the possible results of the stress of feeling you'll be late? Possibility one: Panicked and consumed with thoughts of some of the most terrible outcomes of your being late to class—like getting a lowered grade after a certain amount of tardies (which, by being late today, you will most certainly qualify to be a recipient); like your parents not allowing you to use the car during the week if your grades drop; like not making the honor roll—you bump into a group of students in a huddle, causing one of them to drop the books and notebooks in her arms. Now having to help your classmate pick up her dropped things, and knowing this upset has sealed your fate on being late for class, you get even more frustrated—and consider skipping class altogether!

Possibility two: Having set your course to get straight to class and focused on each and every little detail, including steering clear of the students in the huddle (as well as slowing your speed to "power walk" as you pass the teacher standing outside his classroom talking with a student), your mad dash pays off. You arrive on time, albeit panting. Smiling ear to ear—and happy that the stress of the moment has stirred up enough of your body's endorphins to keep you awake during the class—you take your seat, beaming and energized to boot.

Of course, there are other ways this scenario could play out, but you get the idea! Here's the good news: You get to decide how you react. While a situation creating stress isn't always under your control, how *you* respond is.

So how do you act and react to stress? Are you overwhelmed by it, or instead, exhilarated by it? In this unit, you'll get a chance to find out—which can be good to know. Being the taste berry that you are, you know how important it is that when stress is staring you in the face, you handle it like the cool pro!

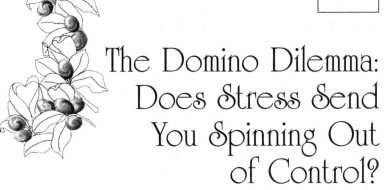

8

The Domino Dilemma: Does Stress Send You Spinning Out of Control?

There is no such thing as a stress-free life—especially in Teenville. Nor is it possible to stop—even change—some of the stressful times that come our way. If you have a huge test in the next class and you are simply not prepared, and are overtired from getting back late on the bus from your school game, you probably can't do too much about being tired and that test waiting for you. You'll have to do the best you can. So while you can't always change the stressor, you can focus on *you* and your reaction to the situation at hand. In this instance, for example, you can encourage yourself to do the best you can, and maybe even explain your situation to the teacher and see if he or she will allow you to take the test at another time. Maybe the teacher will allow this, and maybe he or she won't.

Managing yourself is an important concept in that if you don't intervene, things can get out of hand. Have you ever set up a row of dominoes, and then triggered them into falling? Stress can cause a similar effect in that one stressful event (when not stopped) can trigger and provoke the next stress reaction. While having one domino trigger a chain reaction might be good when it comes to the row of dominoes, it's not what you want to have happen in the face of stress, as fifteen-year-old Rob Lawson found out in the next story. Because his snooze alarm didn't go off one morning, he found himself in a landslide of stress. Let's check in with Rob to find out why his stress dominoed its way from running late to running rampant.

You Snooze, You Lose!

I set my alarm for seven o'clock in the morning, but when it went off, I hit the snooze button, thinking I'd catch five more minutes of sleep. Well, the snooze alarm didn't go off!

When I looked over and saw that it was 7:45, I couldn't believe it! I skipped breakfast so I could run to catch the bus, but I missed it anyway. Luckily, my father hadn't left for work yet, so I asked him for a ride to school. He wasn't too happy about it because it meant he would be late for an appointment he had set up. We rode to school in dead silence.

By the time I got to school, the five-minute bell had already rung, so I had to go to the office to get a late pass. I hadn't asked my father to write a note for my being late, so I sat out first hour in the principal's office. By now, things were really starting to snowball. Since I was absent from my first-hour class, I missed my science test. My teacher said I couldn't make up the test since I had an unexcused absence. When I went to my locker to get my books for my second-hour class, my math book was missing. My locker-mate, Barney Johnson, had picked up my book instead of his own. I was frantic. I hadn't turned in my math assignment the day before, and Mr. Cohen warned me not to let it happen again. My overdue math paper was in the book Barney had, and I had no idea where he could be, so, rather than face the teacher, I decided to skip math class! The math teacher took attendance, and because I wasn't reported on the absence list the vice-principal called my mother at work to tell her that I wasn't in school. When I got to third-hour class, my friends teased me about my whereabouts during second hour. I was in no mood for their humor. "Why don't you just worry about yourself?" I snapped, "Who do you think you are, a truant officer?" Being upset with my friends always makes me feel bad.

Standing in the lunch line, I noticed Barney Johnson. "Hey, Johnson! You took my math book, you idiot!" I called out. Barney yelled back, "Get off my back, you jerk!" At the end of my rope, I shoved Barney against the wall, my fist raised ready to hit him—when who should appear but the vice-principal! Surprised to see me, he ordered me to get away from Barney, informed me about the call he made earlier to my mother and took me to the office. Knowing my mother had been told that I wasn't in school made me feel even more stressed out. I knew she was going to call my father and tell him, too. Since I wasn't allowed to leave the office because I was in trouble for fighting, I wasn't able to make a call from the hall pay phone, either.

Finally, the school day was over. What a nightmare. And I still had to face my parents! I learned the hard way that when you snooze, you lose.

Rob Lawson, 15
from Taste Berries for Teens

What to Do When Stress Takes Over

As Rob found out, when one event collides and crashes into the next, your stress begins to resemble dominoes tumbling. Instead of letting your stress snowball to a point where it's controlling you, try to control your stress. Here are three important things to do.

1. Admit you're out of control. Don't collide from one reaction to the next, trying to deny that you're not feeling out of control—or trying to pretend that nothing is wrong.

2. Decide to get back in control. Make a decision to regroup and look for the solution. Stop and gain a new perspective, then commit to a better course of action.

3. Deal with the stress going on in this moment. Look for the next indicated step and then take it. Don't project and worry about those stressors you'll be facing in the future— stay in the here and now and do what you have to do.

VIRTUAL PRACTICE: HOW TO KEEP YOUR DOMINOES (LIFE) FROM FALLING APART

Write about a time when something similar to Rob Lawson's experience happened to you, when the "cycle of stress" was under way and rolling out of control. _____

_____

_____

_____

_____

At what point did you know your stress was "out of control"?

_____

_____

_____

_____

What did you do? _____

_____

_____

_____

_____

Who did you turn to for help and support? What did you ask of that person?_____

_____

_____

_____

_____

What do you think you could have done differently so that things wouldn't have become as stressful? _____

_____

_____

_____

_____

At what point could you have "rescued" things for yourself, and thus gotten *back* in control?_____

_____

_____

_____

_____

What "price" did you pay for being out of control? For example, did it land you in trouble with anyone? If so, with whom?_____

_____

_____

_____

_____

What did you do to get yourself *back* on track? What did you learn as a result, and how can you use this information the next time you feel out of control?_____

_____

_____

_____

_____

Cool Is Up to You!

Understanding how one event leads to another is an important step in getting back in control when things begin to spin out of control. This is also important information for you in knowing what to do, and when. And of course, putting in place those skills that help you "regroup" sends a message to you (and others) that you can manage yourself in stressful situations. This, too, is an important part of the picture of whether or not you see yourself as capable in managing yourself in relation to stress.

Building a storehouse of positive experiences from which to draw helps you face the next stressful situation with confidence. Maybe this is why some people actually like stress—so much so that they welcome stress into their lives with open arms! How about you? Do you thrive on stress? Some taste berries do, as you'll see in this next chapter.

9

Extreme Edge: Do You "Thrive" on Stress?

Not all people shy away from stress; some welcome it! How about you? Do you feel like the more intensity in situations, the better? Do challenges like a deadline or a jam-packed schedule gear you up for action? Do you like "extreme edge" events such as in-line skating, kick boxing or bike racing? Are you excited by goals, motivated by stress?

If you like the thrill of "edge events," you may be what experts in the field of stress refer to as a "stress-seeker." Certainly this is a trait that holds true for *National Geographic*'s Boyd Matson—and fifteen-year-old Joshua Thomas (in the story below), who would like to follow in his footsteps—literally. Joshua is definitely looking forward to some adventurous—and stressful—times!

Globe-Trotting, Jungle-Braving, Tundra-Probing: Boyd Matson!

When I grow up I hope to be like the globe-trotting, jungle-braving, tundra-probing Boyd Matson! As the host of *National Geographic Explorer*, Boyd Matson's whole life is like one big adventure after another—and he gets paid a lot of money for it!

Just look at all the wild animals he gets to play with: snakes, bears, bats, mountain lions, chimpanzees. And his job includes traveling everywhere in the world—the Sahara Desert, Chile, New Zealand, Patagonia, the Sierra Nevada Mountains, the Amazon, New Guinea, the Arctic. My very greatest hope is to travel like that when I grow up. Everywhere he goes is an adventure. He went cave-diving in underwater caverns in Wakulla Springs, Florida, and climbed Africa's highest mountain, Mount Kilimanjaro in Tanzania. In the Dominican Republic, he swam with humpback whales. In Hawaii, he stood on the rim of the active Kilauea volcano.

He's always facing extreme-edge, thrilling adventure—like the time he hand-fed sharks in the Bahamas, or the time he was charged by hippos and elephants in Botswana. Once he actually rappelled into the Devil's Sinkhole in Texas, which is filled with six million bats. He's even journeyed across the outback in Australia with no food or water. All the things he gets to do are so cool.

Besides having all that fun and excitement, Boyd Matson also gets to help the planet in a lot of ways, such as helping biologists tag polar bears in the wild, piloting the Sustainable Seas Expedition's experimental one-person submarine, and joining crews from around the country to fight wildfires in Florida.

Imagine living a life of adventure, traveling all over the world while doing an important job that's a real taste berry to the planet—just like Boyd Matson. It's exactly what I hope for out of life!

Joshua Thomas, 15
From More Taste Berries for Teens

Extreme Edge: The *Thrill* of Stress!

Stress-seekers thrive on pressure, competition and risk. These are the individuals who say they do their best when "under the gun." In fact, they sometimes wait until the last minute so as to create a deadline—because they like the "now or never" intensity. Rather than being overwhelmed by stress, they are motivated by it. They may even drift through a project half-heartedly if they start far ahead of time, not putting their focused all-and-all into it. But, knowing "this is it" compels them to apply themselves. While doing things in this way creates a lot of stress for some people, for others a stress-filled agenda is an atmosphere that helps them feel alive and inspired and that motivates them into action.

Are you a stress-seeker? The following quiz will help you know for sure.

VIRTUAL PRACTICE: ARE YOU A STRESS-SEEKER? HOW TO KNOW IF YOU ARE

The following checklist will help you see if you are someone who thrives on stress. Read each of the statements and then using a rating of 1 to 4 (4 = Always; 3 = Frequently; 2 = Sometimes; and 1 = Never) rate yourself as to how you typically react in each situation.

___ 1. Do you tend to put things off until the last minute and then have to "bear down" to get them done?

___ 2. Are you "at home" or comfortable in those situations where there's pressure, competition or risk?

___ 3. Have deadlines or competition been a driving force behind many of your accomplishments?

___ 4. Do you feel exhilarated or energized while working toward a difficult task or reaching a big goal?

___ 5. Do you enjoy being in situations that are new, unfamiliar or different from what you're used to?

___ 6. Do you tend to see obstacles as challenges rather than headaches?

__ 7. Are you constantly looking for ways to improve your-self, such as to get better grades or to improve your performance in sports?

__ 8. Do you prefer friends who are risk-takers rather than those who "play it safe"?

__ 9. Do you often compete, challenge or make a bet with yourself?

__ 10. Do you like to "come down" or "calm down" shortly after a tension-producing event?

__ 11. When you're looking for things to do, like planning your weekends and having your "vote" in where and what will be done for family vacations, do you suggest activities that include a lot of action?

__ 12. Do you like activities that include a certain amount of competition or risk (for example, activities like rock climbing, racing or dirt-bike jumping)?

What Does Your "Score" Mean?

What does your total score mean? If your score is between 36 and 48, you are a stress-seeker who enjoys excitement and exhilaration. You actually look around for and create a high-stress level to propel you to action. You like stress. You *thrive* on it!

If your score is between 24 and 35, you probably like things to go smoothly; you like harmony and strive to keep things in perspective, to balance your life in order to stay on an even keel. A score between 12 and 23 indicates that you are likely to avoid stress and seek security instead. You prefer not to be charged with emotion and find such conditions drain and sap your energy.

Is being a stress-seeker a negative or positive? Actually, it is neither. Being a stress-seeker is a part of your personality. And of course, if you are stress-seeker who finds the stress you are looking for, hopefully you can also deal with it. What could be more stressful than attracting stress but then not using this "tempo" to your benefit? Likewise, if you are someone who likes things smooth, easy and trouble-free, that's not a negative either. It's just the way you prefer it. So what's the benefit in knowing if you are a stress-seeker? When you know you are stress-seeker you can then accommodate it! If you wait for the last minute to get things done, for example, then when it's time to "bear down" get to it!

Cool Is Up to You!

Stress can be exciting! Certainly the person who is a stress-seeker uses it as a motivator. Being motivated and successful in meeting the challenges of stress are what keep stress in check—which prevents it from snowballing into a landslide of stress. The good news is that while you can't always prevent stress, you can manage yourself in relation to it. In this next chapter, you'll meet two teens who find themselves in a similar situation—each one handling things differently. It's a very good example showing how stress can get the best of you, or, how to be a taste berry even when you're "locked out."

10

Stress—An Individual Matter: Only <u>You</u> Can React as You Do

Our friends Sherry and Monica have similar personalities, yet they react so differently in stressful situations. For example, both girls are usually very shy and reserved. Yet when Sherry is "stressed to the max" she gets really quiet and even withdraws from wanting to be around others. On the other hand, when Monica is stressed-out, she moves out of her shyness and lets you know about it—often getting edgy, irritable and even loud.

As with most of us, how we respond to stress is an individual matter, as you'll see as you read about a stressful experience that happened to two teens in Tacoma, Washington—Leah Matheson and Karen Billings. Both eleventh-graders arrive at school early one morning. Pulling into the parking space for students, Karen spots her good friend, Tina Bruner. The girls get out of their cars, call out hellos and walk to the school building together, talking about their plans for the weekend.

A few minutes later, Leah Matheson arrives in the same parking lot, hoping to get to the library as quickly as she can so that she can look up a reference book. She has an important test in Mrs. Willit's class this morning, and hopes to do well on it. Leah is quite sure the test will contain questions from a particular chapter in the reference book, and she wants to review the chapter. Leah hurries into the building, makes several quick stops and then heads for the library.

Meanwhile, Karen goes along with her friend, Tina, to her locker, and after Tina gets the books she needs, the girls head off to Karen's locker to retrieve the books she'll need. That's when Karen realizes that in her hurry to get to school, she's forgotten her backpack! About this time, Leah finds the reference book she is looking for, sits down at a table and reaches into her backpack with the intention of reviewing some of her class notes centering around the reference book. She searches through her papers, but cannot find the notes. Then she realizes that when she packed her backpack this morning, she forgot to pick up the study notes, which she'd laid on her bathroom sink so she could review them while she brushed her teeth.

Since each girl lives close to school and has ample time to return home, pick up the items she needs and still make it back to school without being late—each makes the decision to return home to get what she needs. Small problem: Neither girl can locate her keys! But even though each girl faces the same problem, each one responds differently to the situation—the *stressor*. As is the case with stress, each girl's *response* to the situation at hand determines the *stress* level she feels. But let's have them tell their own story.

Not Two of a Kind

Leah Matheson: "While still in the library, I reached into my purse to retrieve the keys, only to discover they weren't there. Discovering they were gone, I frantically raced around, asking all my friends if they had seen my keys. 'Nope,' they all replied calmly, and then went on with their business—as if a major crisis wasn't at hand! Their calmness only added to my frustration. I ran around searching every inch of where I'd been, looking wildly in every room I'd been in—the rest room, the library (I looked on every bookshelf twice!) the rest room yet again. Then,

I stormed to my locker and pulled everything out of it, recklessly tossing out every single item, shaking out the books (as if a set of keys could be slipped inside of them). I'm sure I looked like a total madwoman.

"Next, remembering that I had bought some juice from the hall snack dispenser, I actually clawed through the trash can, thinking I might have accidentally thrown my keys away along with the juice carton and napkin. They weren't there—and by this time I know that *I* looked 'trashed.' And so much time had gone by that even if I did find my keys, I'd never be able to make it home and back in time for my first-hour class. Totally frustrated, I headed for my class. Unable to even think of anything other than locating the keys, I forgot to get the books I needed from my locker before my next class—even after having spent all that time pulling it apart. Not only did I feel unprepared for the test the next hour, because I was so upset and scattered, I couldn't concentrate and just knew I'd do poorly (and the next day when the test grades were posted, my worst fears were realized).

"My stress showed in other ways, too. That morning—and for the rest of the day, too—I was demanding and impatient with my best friend, totally resenting that she would rather stand in the back hall in a lip-lock with her boyfriend than help me, her frantic friend, search the garbage for my keys. Then I was a grouch to my teachers because I was so worried about my keys and wished that I was looking for my keys instead of sitting in class. I ended up getting a headache and a nauseous feeling in my stomach. My whole day was shot."

Karen Billings: "When I noticed my keys were missing—something I'd gone through before—the first thing I did was to remind myself not to get too "nuts." I always lose my cool when I get that way, so I decided instead to spend my energy finding my keys. I retraced my steps, considering the most likely place they could be. I told myself what I knew to be true—it would all work out one way or another. I'm not saying I didn't feel any stress—I just put my stress to work honing in on finding my keys. After checking every possible place they could be, I returned to my car to see if by chance the keys were still in the ignition. They were. But now there was a new problem: The car doors were locked!

"Now that I knew where the keys were, I started thinking of all the ways I could solve the problem. It seemed to me that the best way to resolve my dilemma was to call my mom at work to see if she could bring me an extra set of car keys over the noon hour. While I was a little disappointed that I'd be using my lunch hour to retrieve them (especially since I had planned on sitting with friends in the cafeteria for lunch), I didn't totally freak out. Though I regretted the inconvenience that it would cause my mom (and how it would interrupt her noon-hour plans), I didn't become upset. And I didn't run around looking like a buffoon. I went to first-hour class, made the necessary apologies for not having an important assignment turned in on time, and rather than make excuses for myself, told the teacher what had happened. It's not the greatest thing to get by for a half-day without your backpack when your homework and books are inside of it—not to mention my note to my boyfriend and my lip gloss— but it's not the end of the world. I had to explain to my teachers in the classes where I had homework assignments that were in the backpack; probably because I was honest and sincere about it, they gave me a break and let me bring my homework in the next day. The good news is that even though my free time with friends over lunch may have been shot, my whole day wasn't.""

Cool or Ghoul? It's a Personal Thing

While two individuals may experience the same stressful situation—such as accidentally locking their keys in their cars— the choice of how to respond is an individual one. Leah and

Karen's different *responses* to the stressful situation of needing their homework and backpacks—and the keys to their cars to be able to get the things they needed—illustrates an important point: It was their *responses* to their situation—and not the situation itself—that determined how much stress each experienced.

And even Karen, who responded with relative calm, admitted, "I've locked my keys in the my car before. I panicked, ran around like a chicken with my head cut off, and basically stressed myself out to the point of having a bad day for the rest of the day. I know I looked as if I had the words 'Stressed-Out!' stamped on my forehead. And I'm sure my friends were just waiting for steam to come out of my ears! But I don't act like that anymore. I've discovered that my being stressed-out doesn't help me resolve my situation any sooner and, if anything, it makes it worse."

VIRTUAL PRACTICE: ARE YOU COOL (OR A GHOUL) WHEN STRESSED-OUT?

How do you respond to a stressful event? Do you get frustrated and go into a whirlwind of panic-stricken and futile activity? Or, do you use your stress as a call to action, as a sign to get busy and resolve the problem at hand?

If you were to assess your overall response to stressful situations, how would you say you respond?

When I'm facing a stressful time, I usually: _____

_____

_____

_____

Maybe you found that easy to do, especially if you focused on the sorts of things that make up the bulk of your stress, such as feeling that your life is too hurried and that you'd like more hours in the day so as to have enough time to do all the things you'd like to do. But you're a teen, which means your world is going to be expanding and getting more complicated (and fun, too). Try your hand at seeing how you'd respond to new and different "stressors."

Read each of the following scenarios and imagine yourself in each. The goal is for you to think about your *typical reaction* to a stressful event.

1. You've left an important assignment at home and there is positively no way the teacher is going to let you off the hook for not producing it. You're standing outside the classroom, having just discovered your "problem." How would you respond to the situation at hand? _____

_____

_____

_____

_____

2. You just remembered you forgot to feed and water your best pal, Rover, your golden retriever. It's a very warm day and expected to get much hotter. It's 11:00, and you won't be home until after practice today at 5:30 (nor will your parents be home until then). How would you respond to the situation at hand?

_____

_____

_____

_____

3. You're on your way to school in your parents' car when you get a flat tire. You've got an important quiz first period and you know you're sure to be late. How would you respond to the situation at hand? _____

_____

_____

_____

_____

4. The one person in the entire school who you've been wishing to go out with asks if the empty seat next to you in the library—the one with your notebook and books all spread out on the desk before it—is taken. You say "no" and start to move your stuff out of the way, only to accidentally knock most of it on the floor. How would you respond to the situation at hand? _____

_____

_____

_____

_____

List two things you could do to be even more "cool" even when stressed-out.

♥ _____

_____

♥ _____

_____

Cool Is Up to You!

As seventeen-year-old Kelly Anne Warren from Corvallis, Oregon, said, "Figuring out I didn't have to let everything 'get to me' was a real breakthrough—and a huge relief!" Sounds like Kelly Anne has learned that each of us gets to choose—at least to a large degree—how we're going to react in times of stress.

The following unit will help you learn some important thinking skills, what we call "joggin' your noggin" skills—that can help you stay cool and think your way through a stressful situation. And you know how important it is to stay cool while living in Teenville!

Part 4

Coping Skills: How to "Think" Your Way Through Stressful Times

If a person sits down to think, he is immediately asked if he has a headache.

—Ralph Waldo Emerson

A Message
from the Authors

"If I had a little more money, I'd have a little less stress. And if had a lot of money, I'd have no stress!" commented seventeen-year-old Tony Butalla in a recent workshop we conducted for teens. "How so?" asked Sharon LaCross, a sixteen-year-old girl who sat next to Tony in the workshop. "Well," he explained, "having more money, I could afford all the things I want and need, like buying my girlfriend a promise ring and getting a car of my own. I'd get some totally great clothes, go on the ski trip to Lake Tahoe with my school's ski club over Christmas break, and I'd go do the things with my friends that I can't afford to now—like Noah's Ark Conservancy Theme Park, a place some of my friends hang out as much they can. I'd get the most incredible sound system for both my car and for my room at home. And you can bet I'd add to my already extensive CD collection. I'd get a new and faster computer system; a cell phone; a new surfboard and a dirt bike. Oh yeah, money could wipe out a lot of my stress in life. I wish I were as rich as Bill Gates (Microsoft founder and owner, considered the richest man in America), that way, I'd have absolutely NO stress at all."

As Tony was going through this list, many of the teens were nodding in agreement, perhaps thinking money is a very nice thing to have in ample supply. Since money can alleviate some of d needs, perhaps Tony would have fewer problems, other things would crop up and create stress. As sixteen-year-old Michael Fuller informed him, there are many things that happen in our lives that no amount of money can fix: "There's a guy who goes to my school whose parents give him many of the things you'd like to have. But still, his life is as stressful as anyone I know. As an example, getting good grades is tough for him and he's always worried about whether or not he's going to get into college. He's really sweating passing the SATs because it's a pretty tough test for anyone, and he knows it's going to be particularly tough for him. And though he has the money to treat himself and his girlfriend to nice restaurants and movies and things, it doesn't stop them from getting into arguments. Money doesn't seem to make their relationship run any smoother than most of the teen couples I know, and in fact, I'd say it's rockier than most, or at least it seems that way to me. They're always upset with each other and break up every few weeks. Then, whenever they've broken up, he gets really stressed-out. Money can't prevent him from having hurt feelings or an aching heart. Nor can his terrific allowance keep him from worrying about how to keep his face from breaking out so much (he really does have a bad case of acne and he's very self-conscious about it—like most teens with acne). He worries about the amount of sweets he eats, which he really has to watch because he has diabetes. Believe me, the guy has just as much stress as anyone—even with all his money."

Point well taken. As Michael knows, there are many things that money can't buy: A stress-free life (in Teenville) is one of them. And, of course, Microsoft's Bill Gates's life is anything but free of stress!

We work with teens throughout the nation, and we know firsthand that for teens stress is a common occurrence. Activities like getting good grades, planning ahead for college and beyond, getting your driver's license, upsets (and make-ups) with friends, coping with school life and home life—all are stressful, to be sure. Be cool. Cope.

Throughout this book you'll learn a good number of skills to help you manage stress as you make your way through stressful situations. This next unit begins your skill section on how to do just that, specifically focusing on how to "think" your way through stressful times. In the workshops we conduct for teens on managing the stress, strains and pressures of teen life, many of you began to fondly refer to these skills as "noggin skills," a term we've since adopted. So in this unit, we'll help you use your "noggin" to think your way through stress—such as when you want to change a negative mood to a positive one so you don't create any more stress than what you're already dealing with, or when you see that you're heading for a collision course and you know it's in your best interest to redirect the stress at hand in order to be cool.

The good news is that you *can* manage the stress, strains and pressures of Teenville. This unit is sure to "jog your noggin" on how to be a taste berry who can do just that!

12

"Joggin' Your Noggin" Skill #1: The A + B = C Test for Clear Thinking

Sixteen-year-old Jon Branson, whom you'll meet in the following story, had finally talked his mother into letting him ride to school with his best friend. What luck! One morning when riding to school with his buddy, Paul, he agreed to go with him to "check out the girls at Madison High." As destiny would have it, there he met the girl of dreams. He and the girl looked at each other, and it was love at first sight! Soon jaunts to Madison High were regular occurrences—as were his late arrivals to his own school! A feud with the school, his mother, his buddy—and Destiny—ensued. As you can guess, the jam he got himself into resulted in a lot of stress—of his own making.

When stress closes in on you, it can be a good time to practice *"Joggin' Your Noggin" Skill #1: The A + B = C Test for Clear Thinking*. This "slow down, let's think about what's happening" basic thinking skill helps you look squarely at what's going on, and then choose a response that's going to produce the best results. This way, you're sure to stay calm and cool under pressure and work your way out of the mess-of-stress you're in—or soon to be in. It's a "heady" technique that helps you make sure you don't create even more stress for yourself.

As for Jon, he's in a big mess, and he's going to have to act fast to get himself out of it. His best bet is to think clearly and not dig himself in deeper trouble than he already is in. If he doesn't, his "Destiny" may just be fated for a new beginning elsewhere! See for yourself!

A Date with Destiny

Of course, I just knew when my friend Paul got his car, we'd be even better friends than we already were. When you've got a car, practically everyone wants to be your friend, but Paul and I have a lot in common, so I'm his best buddy. When you get a car of your own, you can pretty much name who you want to be your friend, but I knew he'd want me to hang around with him even more than I already did. So two weeks before he was going to close his loan and "take possession," I started doing every-thing around the house and yard Mom asked me to do, because I needed the brownie points all accumulated and ready to work their charm when I planned to ask her if I could start riding to school with my buddy. He lives about five minutes from me. (Picking me up is a little out of the way for him, but not much when you consider that we are such good friends.)

It worked! Mom said, "No problem! As long as you get to school on time and riding with Paul doesn't distract you from being a good student."

Well, you can imagine how happy I was that my life was beginning to feel like I was growing up! But I would have never known that Paul getting that shiny old Cougar would be what would deliver me into what poets call "a date with destiny"! It all started one morning when Paul arrived about ten minutes earlier than he usually does. He honked his horn out front, and I ran out the door without a clue that I was about to have an awe-some "chance happening"—one that comes along maybe once in a lifetime!

Paul and I had ridden to school together for almost two weeks now, and boy was it a lot of fun. Sometimes we'd head straight for school, especially if we wanted to check out the cheerleading squad and "Go Gang" pep squad on the day of the school game or special sports assembly. But on other days, we'd hang out in front of the 7–11 with friends, swing by McDonald's for a fast bite to eat, and sometimes we'd just cruise like the cool dudes we were. I tell you, catching a ride to school with Paul improved my life considerably. It also made it way more fun. But on this day, my life was about to change, and I didn't even know it! Luckily, I'd chosen to wear my new Tommy shirt and my best pair of jeans; I was looking good, and so I was feeling pretty good, too. (It always helps your mood if you feel you're looking good. It just sort of gives you that extra bit of attitude.)

On this particular destined day, I hopped in the car, fastened my belt and greeted my friend. "How ya' doing, dude," he replied. "Hey, how about we cruise by Madison and check out the girls?" Madison is the high school across town from ours. "Cool," I said. I mean, who wouldn't want to check out girls anywhere, and Madison had a reputation for having some pretty cool girls—but then, that's the way most girls other than the ones you go to school with seem. But I was totally up for Paul's suggestion. With Paul's new car, my life was definitely picking up; I was finally doing the things high school is about. Wheels, freedom and now checking out the girls at another school. "Oh yeah!" I replied. "We're on it!" and off we went to Madison High.

I glanced at my watch and knew we wouldn't have time to do more than drive by the school. Still, I was not about to discourage such a chance to "see and be seen"! This was the life, riding to school with my buddy, free to make any stops along the way—including stops to check out the girls! Oh yeah!

"Hey, there's Jessica Waite!" Paul pointed out from among a group of girls talking on a nearby lawn. Jessica went to school with us in junior high before she moved and transferred to Madison. Paul always had a "thing" for Jessica. Suddenly, I understood more about Paul's motives when it came to his brilliant idea to check out the girls at Madison. Paul tapped on his horn, rolling down his window so Jessica could get a better look at him. All the girls in the little group squinted over toward the car, and Paul waved and called out, "Jessica!" You could see recognition dawn on Jessica's face as she smiled and waved back. She said something to the other girls and two of them joined Jessica as she came over to Paul's car. "Hi guys," Jessica chirped. I could see why Paul had a thing for her. She was definitely cool. Paul put the car in park and got out. Well, of course, I got out, too. I walked to his side of the car, leaned against it and shoved my hands in my pockets—my pose deliberate so as to look "cool." While Paul talked to Jessica, I was more than content to take in the spectacular sight of all these girls. But a guy has to be slick about those kind of things—you can't look like you're checking them out or anything.

"I haven't seen you in forever. What are you doing here?" Jessica asked.

"Just cruising," Paul answered.

"Is this your car?" Jessica asked, and Paul nodded a proud, "Yep."

"Cool," Jessica complimented. His chest got a little puffed up at her praise, something I totally understand. Just then Jessica realized we didn't know her friends, so she introduced us, "This is Patty and this is Destiny—Patty, Destiny, this is Paul and Jon, friends from my old school." I casually reached out a hand and said "hi" to Patty. I was about to do the same with Destiny when my eyes met hers—large green eyes, like pools of turquoise. They were *soooo* mysterious—as if I could swim into them. For me, it was love at first sight! A guy doesn't really know what it is until it happens to him, nor is such a thing easy to describe—other than it feels as though you've been hit over the head with a tree; you're that sure that it's love. "Hi, Destiny," I said, my voice hardly sounding like my own. I was in total awe of her.

"Hi," she said softly and then smiled. I could tell she was a shy girl and I hoped she wasn't some other guy's girl—but I knew even if she was, I was going to vie for her. But then, noticing from the way she breathed that her heart was pounding as fast as mine, I could tell she fell in love in that very same minute. It would seem impossible to believe that the moon and stars aligned so right. I mean, my friend wants us to cruise by Madison High (no doubt to try and run into Jessica), and I meet the girl of my dreams. That's incredible enough, but the even more perfect thing is that I was pretty sure that she was very interested in me, too.

By now, being in love as I was, I could hear Paul and Jessica talking, but it sounded like mere background noise. I couldn't make out a word they were saying, nor did I want to. All my attention was on Destiny—and hers was all on me. Though I'd never thought about a soul mate before, I was sure that I'd found mine. "So, what grade are you in?" I asked, just so I'd be saying something and she'd know I was interested. (I mean, I pretty much knew she was a junior like me and Paul and Jessica.) "I'm a junior," she said, her voice like music to my ears. I kind of scooted further down from Paul and Jessica and Patty, as I talked to Destiny—about nothing, really. But our eyes said a lot. Destiny followed me, slowly, to the other end of the car and we stood there—talking about school and music and movies. Just then the bell rang and jarred us from our magical unspoken conversation. "So, we'll probably swing by here tomorrow morning. Will I see you around?" I asked.

"I always get to school the same time," Destiny said sweetly. "Same time, same place?"

"You bet," I said, knowing that nothing would stop me from being here in this very place the next morning. Then, she was off with Jessica and Patty to class. I don't even remember getting in the car, but miles down the road, with Paul going on about his chances with Jessica, I announced, "We've gotta go back tomorrow."

"Oh yeah!" Paul assured me. "Did you see the way Jessica was looking me over? She's interested to be sure. I can tell when a girl wants to know more." I breathed a huge gulp of content. I'd see her again tomorrow. I glanced at my watch and saw that we were going to be late, but I couldn't get too stressed about it. I mean, what's being a little late to school when you've just gotten a date with destiny?

Jon Branson, 16

Stress Affects Your Destiny, Too!

When you've finally found your "date with destiny," it can be a positively giddy, thrilling, extremely awesome and good thing. But for Jon, if he doesn't come up with a way to find time for Destiny and getting to school on time, then driving with his buddy over to Madison in the mornings is going to create a date with a destiny of a different nature—like with the attendance clerk at his school for being late. To say nothing of the date with destiny he'll have when it comes to answering to his mother for breaking his promise with her to get to school on time. Doing what you're supposed to affects your destiny, too. As for Jon, he's got some explaining to do—and this would be a good time to think clearly and rationally. Jon's desire to see Destiny in the mornings and his wish to keep his promise to his mother are colliding right now.

With stress closing in on his heels, it's a good time for him to practice the A + B = C Test for Clear Thinking. This basic *thinking skill* helps you stay calm and cool under pressure and is very helpful in getting you out of the mess-of-stress, as well as in helping to assure that you don't create even more stress for yourself. Jon, for example, is going to have to take responsibility for getting to school late that morning. He's also going to have to think very clearly about how he can make amends—and not dig himself in deeper. If Jon doesn't get things straightened out and on track he is likely to find himself riding to school with his mother again. (And since it's highly unlikely his mom is going to swing by Madison High in the mornings, his "Destiny" may be looking for another guy!)

Thinking Clearly—And Logically—Can Help You Stay Calm and Cool Under Pressure (and Maybe Even Out of Trouble!)

There is a *direct* relationship between what you think and what you're likely to do as a result (your behavior). And, as you've no doubt learned firsthand, how you respond (or react) to an incident sets the tone for what happens next, which can affect whether or not your stress goes away (or at least is minimized)—or whether it snowballs into even more stress. You can think of this chain of related events as the A + B = C effect:

A (your thinking) + B (your behavior) = C (the probable outcome of the situation).

Keeping in mind that what you *think* determines your *behavior*—which can influence what happens next—let's check in on Jon to watch this formula in action as he faces up to one of the consequences of his being late to school—answering to his mother.

Incident:

Jon's mother: "Jon, I know how much you like going to school with your friend Paul. When you asked me if you could ride with him, you assured me you wouldn't be late to school. However, the school called me because you've been late getting to school twice in the past week. Starting tomorrow, you'll need to start riding to school with me again."

Jon thinks about what's been said. There are any number of ways he could think about this (the "A" part of the equation). Here are two possibilities.

A-1: Jon's thinking:

"Mom knows how much I'd rather ride to school with Paul than with her. If she cared about whether or not I was popular with my friends, she would let me ride to school with Paul. She's not being fair. I wish she'd get off my back."

A-2: Jon's thinking:

"I wish I had kept a better handle on getting to school on time. I knew getting to school late would have consequences. And, I promised my mom I'd get to school on time when I started riding with Paul, and I didn't live up to my word. I'm disappointed in myself for not getting to school on time."

The "B" part of this equation is: *What you're thinking influences how you're likely to respond—your behavior.* Let's look at how Jon's thinking influences his behavior in each example:

A-1: Jon's thinking:

"Mom knows how much I'd rather ride to school with Paul than with her. If she cared about whether or not I was popular with my friends, she would let me ride to school with Paul. She's not being fair. I wish she'd get off my back."

B-1: Jon's behavior:

Glaring at his mother Jon accuses, "You're not fair! I have no life of my own, and now all my friends will think I'm a geek and it's because of you." He then storms out of the room and into his bedroom, slamming the door behind him.

Obviously thinking that it's his mother who is responsible for keeping him from riding to school with Paul, Jon decides to be upset with her and feels angry. This is not clear (or logical) thinking. If anything, he should be upset with himself for failing to live up to his end of the bargain to get to school on time. Instead, his feelings of being upset are focused on his mother. Yet it is Jon who is responsible: He didn't live up to the requirements (getting to school on time) to ride to school with his friend Paul.

Let's look at how this plays out when Jon thinks clearly and logically.

A-2: Jon's thinking:

"I wish I had kept a better handle on getting to school on time. I knew getting to school late would have consequences. And, I promised my mom I'd get to school on time when I started riding with Paul, and I didn't live up to my word. I'm disappointed in myself for not getting to school on time."

B-2: Jon's behavior:

Owning his mistake, Jon then apologizes to his mother: "Mom, I know I promised I'd get to school on time, and it's my responsibility to do that. I'm sorry. I really want you to trust me and to feel that I'm mature enough to ride with my friend to school and still be to school on time. I hope that you'll give me another chance to prove that I can ride with my friend and still be to school on time."

The "C" part of the equation is: *Your* behavior *is highly likely to influence the probable outcome of the situation.* Jon's storming out of the room, for example, probably isn't going to work in his favor, and quite possibly will produce even more stress for him!

B-1: Jon's behavior:

Glaring at his mother Jon accuses, "You're not fair! I have no life of my own, and now all my friends will think I'm a geek and it's because of you." He then storms out of the room and into his bedroom, slamming the door behind him.

C-1: Probable outcomes:

- ♥ Jon must ride to school with his mother instead of his friend from here on out.
- ♥ Jon is placed on phone restriction, and he cannot even call Destiny to tell her why he is no longer coming to see her.
- ♥ The school places Jon on restriction for his tardiness.

See what happens when Jon is thinking clearly and logically.

B-2: Jon's behavior:

Owning his mistake, Jon apologizes to his mother: "Mom, I know I promised I'd get to school on time and it's my responsibility to do that. I'm sorry. I really want you to trust me and to feel that I'm mature enough to ride with my friend to school and still get there on time. I hope that you'll give me another chance to prove that I can ride with my friend and still be to school on time."

C-2: Probable outcomes:

- ♥ Jon's mother is proud to see Jon take responsibility for his actions and compliments him for being so mature and owning up to his actions.
- ♥ She tells him that he must ride with her for the next two weeks and then, at that point, they can evaluate his riding with his friend.
- ♥ Jon's mother allows him to keep his phone privileges.

Putting the "A + B = C" Clear Thinking to the Test: Will Jon Pass the Test?

When Jon's *thinking* about having to ride with his mother isn't clear, logical or rational, it works against him. He feels persecuted, upset and resentful. There are bound to be stressful ramifications for talking to his mother disrespectfully and storming from the room (which quite probably created even more stress for him). Just because Jon is thinking clearly and logically doesn't necessarily mean his mother will allow him to ride with his friend Paul to school beginning tomorrow (though it might!), but it will lead to a more effective way to reduce the stress at hand.

It may be wishful thinking on our part, but we're betting that Jon's mother accepts his apology and, being proud of him for taking responsibility for his actions, tells Jon he has one more chance to prove he can ride with his friend Paul and still get to school on time!

VIRTUAL PRACTICE: SKILLS TO SHARPEN YOUR "A + B = C" THINKING CLARITY

Here's an exercise you can use to apply this "clear thinking" process to steer you through a tense or stressful situation.

A stressful situation I'm currently facing: _____

_____

_____

_____

_____

_____

_____

_____

My thoughts about how to handle this situation:
A. My clear and logical thinking:

♥ _____

♥ _____

♥ _____

My thoughts on how I should behave in this situation:
B. How I'm choosing to respond (my behavior):

♥ _____

♥ _____

♥ _____

What I think are likely outcomes of this situation:
C. Likely outcomes:

♥ _____

♥ _____

♥ _____

Cool Is Up to You!

Thinking clearly reduces not only the stress of the moment, but also reduces the possibility that you'll behave in ways that will create even more stress for yourself. In the next chapter, we'll examine how you can look on the bright side of things, even if it's your nature to see the glass half-empty—a sure-fire way to get yourself on everyone's list of taste berries!

13

"Joggin' Your Noggin" Skill #2: How to Be a Positive Thinker

Understanding that your thinking has an immediate bearing on the way you're likely to respond to an incident at hand is an important first step in managing stress. The choice is literally yours: As the old saying goes, "You can see the cup half-full or half-empty." In other words, just as you can convince yourself that things are "doom and gloom," so can you convince yourself that things will turn out in a beneficial way. How? Make a decision to see life from the cup-half-full point of view, as Kelsey, in the example below, chose to do.

"Oh, great! Just great!" Cheyenne groaned, looking like true tragedy had struck. "It's starting to rain, and the newscast says it's going to rain throughout the weekend! There goes our plans to play miniature golf."

"Hey, great! Think of it this way—*because* of the rain, everything is going to work out just great for us!" her friend Kelsey countered, a huge grin lighting up her face. "Now we can go see the new Brad Pitt movie instead. It's only on until Saturday. Plus, we can still play miniature golf next weekend. Rain for this weekend couldn't be more perfect timing!"

While Cheyenne focused on the negative and experienced the stressful feelings of frustration and disappointment, Kelsey chose to see the positive, the *possibilities* the turn of events created. Those who are able to find the positive in situations are often referred to as *optimists*. Being an optimist is not an inherited trait, it's a learned response. Perhaps you have heard someone say, "I can't help the way I feel, it just happens." This assumes that your thoughts, feelings and behaviors are independent of each other—and are not something you have any say over. However, the opposite is true. You *can* change the way you perceive your feelings: This is good to know!

Strive to be as positive as you can be. Jamie, in the story below, is about to learn how such thinking can reap rewards!

The Night the Power Went Out

My parents were in a huge argument, and I was really hurt and upset about it. I didn't know who I should talk with about how I was feeling, because for one, I didn't want any of my friends to find out how bummed-out I was. So while talking on the phone to my best friend Nikki, I started crying. When she asked me why I was crying, I told her I was just stressed-out about school stuff. "Hey, why don't you ask your mom if you can come over to my house and stay the night?" (She only lives three blocks from my house.) Though I knew I wouldn't tell her about my parents' situation, I was looking forward to just getting out of the house. So I asked my mom, and at first she said I could go. I was in the middle of packing up my schoolbooks and putting together an overnight case, when suddenly the power went out in our entire neighborhood.

Mom quickly got out some candles and, bringing one to my room, told me that because of the power, I couldn't stay with my friend. Then she told me that I needed to look in on my grandfather, tell him about the power going out, and stay with him in his room until it came back on. (Repairpersons were already working on restoring power.)

I was really disappointed about not being able to go to my

friend's house, and not all that excited about now having to go sit with my grandfather who had recently moved in with us (because his health was frail and he could no longer care for himself alone). My grandfather is nearly eighty and, while a very sweet man, it's not like we had much to talk about. But I knew he would be frightened alone in the dark, so I did as my mother asked.

I went to his room and informed him that the power had gone out in the neighborhood and that I'd stay until it had been restored. He seemed quite happy, and I assumed he was being his polite and sweet self. Then he said, "Great opportunity."

"What is?" I asked, not at all sure what he meant by "great opportunity."

"To talk, you and I," he said. "To hold a private little meeting about what we're going to do with those two—your mom and dad, and my daughter and son-in-law. And what we're going to do with ourselves now that we're in the situation we're in."

"But we can't do anything about it, Grandpa," I said, surprised that here was someone with whom I could share my feelings—and with someone who was in the same "boat" as I was.

"Oh," he said, "we may not be able to talk sense into them, but we can talk about how we're going get through it, and we can help each other work through it. Do you think we can?"

And that's how the most incredible friendship between me and my grandfather started. Sitting there in the dark that night, we talked about our feelings and fears of life—from how fast things change, to how they sometimes don't change fast enough. We talked about so much. Not only did I come to know him better, but I discovered that Gramps would be my lifeline to comfort and soothe me when I felt overwhelmed. That night, in the dark, because the power had gone out, I'd found a new friend, a friend with whom I could safely talk about all my fears and pain, whatever they may be.

Suddenly, the lights all came back on. "Well," he said, "I guess that means you'll want to go now. I really liked our talk. I hope we can do it again. Maybe we'll get lucky and the power will go out every few nights!"

Jamie Dykes, 14

Seeing the Bright Side of Things Can Help You Redirect Stress

Obviously, Jamie's grandfather and Kelsey have learned to see things as bright as they can possibly be viewed. Looking at life this way—making a point of finding the good in situations—is a great way to redirect the negative energies of stress. Certainly, Jamie and her grandfather turned that dark evening into brighter days ahead. And while Cheyenne's first response was to view the rain as ruining her weekend plans, it took only a minor change in plans to go with a great weekend.

Looking for the positive is a real asset when faced with a stressful situation. Try not to "make mountains out of molehills."

Do You Have a Tendency to Make Mountains out of Molehills?

It's easy to exaggerate feelings about the latest crisis. The thing is, while every molehill can look like a mountain, things aren't always as do-or-die as they first appear. Try this exercise. In the space provided, describe one of the biggest "worries" you had during this last year._____

_____

_____

_____

Are you looking at your "worry" and thinking, "It sure *seemed* worse at the time than it does now"? Sometimes we think things are more catastrophic than they really are. But in the end, many things aren't as bad as we imagine them to be. Many times resolution is easier than you might think. See for yourself. Using the "worry" you described, did your "prediction" happen or not?

How did things turn out in the end? What actually came true?

Outcome: _____

_____

_____

_____

When the Molehill *Is* a Mountain!

Usually "mountains" are never as daunting as they look, but consider for a moment that the worst did happen: The molehill really *did* turn into a mountain. Did you survive it? If you had hoped a special someone was going to ask you to the prom and he (or she) didn't, did you survive not going to the prom with that person? Weeks later, were you on to new worries, new concerns and maybe even a new "special person"?

Was there ever a time when you were afraid to return a library book because it was *verrry* overdue? Did you really get into all that much trouble when you finally returned it? Did your parents stop loving you or your friends stop being your friends? Probably not. The key is to see that your worries and fears, while real, are not the end of the world.

Deciding that the world won't end is a real breakthrough.

VIRTUAL PRACTICE: HOW TO *ALWAYS* SEE THE CUP HALF-FULL (AS OPPOSED TO HALF-EMPTY)

Describe a big worry facing you right now.

My #1 worry right now is: _____

_____

_____

_____

Now, imagine that it's one year later, and you are reading what you've just written down as your most pressing worry right now. Keeping in mind how your past worries have turned out, how do you think you will feel about this problem in one year?

A year from now, I predict this is how I'll feel: _____

_____

_____

_____

When it comes to skills for seeing the cup as half-full or for not making mountains out of molehills, a great place to begin is with the words you speak. It helps if you don't put yourself down by saying negative things about yourself. Doing so only makes you feel worse. Don't say things like "I'm so stupid," or "No one likes me," or "I just know I'm going to flunk that test!" These comments only bring you down in negative thinking and don't serve you well in getting to work on changing things. For example, if you tell yourself you are not a good student, you will probably find school stressful; this will contribute to your not liking school.

On the other hand, when you send mostly positive messages to yourself, you are more likely to influence things in a positive way. This is the first step in changing a poor situation to a more positive one. There is an expression that goes: *When things are objectively bad, they may seem subjectively worse.* This means things often seem worse than they are. A useful tool for coping with stressful situations is to remind yourself that there is light at the end of the tunnel. Tomorrow will come. You will be okay. Then, pick yourself up and coach your way through the stressful encounter.

Here are some helpful phrases for you to tell yourself to help you through stressful times. Read through each one of them and, in the space provided, add others that can support you in reducing stress.

Preparing for Everyday Stress:

For example, you are about to take an exam or to ask out a special someone, or you're running late getting to work after school.

Say to yourself:

♥ *Be calm. Just think about what I have to do. I need to put my energy towards that.*

♥ *No negative self-statements: Just think rationally.*

♥ *I'll just do my best and let go of the rest.*

What else could you say?

♥ _____

♥ _____

♥ _____

Preparing for a Confrontation:

For example, you are about to face your parents or teachers about a promise you didn't keep, or you accidentally grabbed your locker-mate's book and you know she needed it and she's going to be upset with you.

Say to yourself:

- ♥ *This could be a rough situation, but I know how to deal with it.*

- ♥ *I can work out a plan to handle this.*

- ♥ *Keep your cool.*

What else could you say?

- ♥ _____
- ♥ _____
- ♥ _____

Preparing to Meet a Big Challenge:

For example, you are going to take your test for your driver's license or it's the big day of your pep squad or basketball tryouts.

Say to yourself:

- ♥ *I can meet this challenge.*

- ♥ *Relax. Take a slow deep breath.*

- ♥ *There are a lot of wonderful things going on in my life; this is only one event, don't make it more than it is.*

What else could you say?

- ♥ _____
- ♥ _____
- ♥ _____

Preparing to Cope with "Overwhelm":

For example, you are in the middle of a day that includes three final exams, and a job interview after school; or you're in charge of the prom committee and the big day arrives, and everyone is coming to you with questions on what to do and what goes where, and you still have to get it all done in time to get home and get dressed for the big event.

Say to yourself:

♥ *Take a deep breath and exhale slowly.*

♥ *Focus on what is happening now; what is it I have to do.*

♥ *I can make it through this.*

What else could you say?

♥ _____

♥ _____

♥ _____

How to Change a Negative Thought to a Positive One

Okay, you want to be a positive person, but there is this negative thought pestering you, trying to get the best of you. So how do you make it go away? You change it to a positive one. Changing or "rewriting" the way you think about something is a good way to stop focusing on the negatives and the "what ifs." Instead, focus on what you can do to change the situation in a positive way. How? By applying these three steps.

Step 1: Visualize a yellow stop sign whenever you start to get negative. In your mind's eye, make it big and yellow with the huge letters, STOP! This stop sign acts as a signal for you to stop thinking a negative thought and to replace it with a positive one.

Step 2: Reframe the thought, changing a negative thought to a positive one.

Step 3: Give yourself direction, one that points you toward a positive action.

EXAMPLE

1. **Negative Thought:** "I don't have any friends."
2. **Reframe to a Positive Message:** "STOP! I do have friends. But though I'd like to be friends with Amber, she doesn't seem to want me as a friend. Still, Jenaye is a very good friend to me, and I have a lot of other friends, as well."
3. **Direction for Positive Action:** "I'm going to focus on being a good friend to my friends, and stay open and friendly with the goal of making even more friends."

Your turn. What is a negative message you're in the habit of telling yourself? _____

_____

_____

_____

Reframe to a Positive Message: _____

_____

_____

_____

Direction for Positive Action:_____

_____

_____

_____

Cool Is Up to You!

It takes a little practice, but you can change the way you think. Almost as quickly as that negative thought comes to mind, you can replace it with a positive one—and avoid all the stress that comes with negative thinking. But, yet again, it's up to you to do the brain work in thinking the cup is half-full. And speaking of "brain work" the next chapter shows you how you can keep your cool when trying to work your way through a stressful problem, even when you're faced with trying to be cool with friends, and look really, really cool when a special taste berry is checking you out!

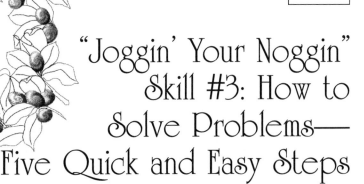

14

"Joggin' Your Noggin" Skill #3: How to Solve Problems— Five Quick and Easy Steps

Have you ever been stressed-out making a decision, especially when all the solutions looked good to you, or they all looked "doom and gloom"? Or maybe the problem was so intense there didn't appear to be *any* solutions. In the story below, sixteen-year-old Sabrina van Arnem found herself in a predicament: Her parents had given her permission to spend the night with a friend, Sonja, but with the understanding the girls would be at Sonja's all night. But Sonja changed their plans, lining up a ride to the movies for them with her older brother. What luck! But what a dilemma! On the one hand, Kyle Thurman, who Sabrina had a crush on, would meet them at the movies and Sabrina wanted to go, but on the other hand, she didn't want to be in trouble with her parents and risk getting grounded for life. What a bind!

If you find it stressful to make good decisions, not to worry, this chapter will show you how. But right now, let's check in with Sabrina who has her own set of problems.

Sonja and Sabrina—And Omigosh! Kyle Thurman!

My friend Sonja is a lot of fun. When she invited me to spend the night at her house on Friday, I really wanted to go. My parents can be strict about me being out overnight, so when I asked them if I could go, they had to know my exact plans, which included dinner and an at-home evening at Sonja's. Then, of course, they wanted to be sure that we would be "properly supervised" (my parents are big on that term). Well, I checked with Sonja, and she assured me that her mother was going to be there. After I passed this news along to my parents, they gave me permission to go.

That evening, my parents dropped me off and went on their way to have dinner with some friends. I waved good-bye to them and went to the front door. Sonja answered it with a huge grin. "You are not going to believe our good luck!" she screamed. "My mom had to go on a last-minute business trip to some boring old trade show and she won't be home until tomorrow morning!" Sonja clapped her hands, then threw a fist across the air as she shouted, "Yes!" and added, "My brother said he'd drive us to the movies! Is that so cool?" Sonja had an eighteen-year-old brother—true, technically he was an adult, but I knew my parents wouldn't see him as being suitable as someone who could "properly supervise" me and Sonja.

Now I was really stuck in a huge bind: My parents and I had an agreement. I didn't want to break the trust I had with them, yet I really wanted Sonja to think I was cool; I also wanted to go to the movies. Besides being fun, Kyle Thurman was going to be there. Kyle is so cute and I've had a huge crush on him forever—every opportunity to even just glimpse him is golden.

When it comes down to being entirely honest, I have to admit when it came to reasons I shouldn't go, there was more than just that I didn't want to disappoint my parents. I'm a good-enough kid, and I have a conscience and all, but experience has taught me there's a price to pay when I do something against their rules—and it's always a price I hate paying! For example, once I didn't tell them all the facts about a school ski trip. I figured they wouldn't like a few things about the trip: one being the fact that it was coed; and two being that only one chaperone was going to supervise nearly twenty kids (and that chaperone was Ms. Kiernan, the P.E. teacher's aide, who is only twenty years old herself). So those are the facts I didn't divulge. I figured what they didn't know couldn't hurt them. But my parents have a way of finding out everything—it's almost spooky. When my parents found out I had been less than forthright about the coed, one twenty-year-old chaperone facts, they got themselves booked on the trip as chaperones! You can imagine how embarrassing that was. Then, for the next two weeks they took away my phone privileges. You can see why I can never be quite certain that they won't find out. It's a huge risk. Still, there was Kyle, my image and standing with Sonja, and the movie I really wanted to see. . . .

I tell you, it was like I went from happily knocking on the front door looking forward to just hanging out with Sonja at her house all night to—wham!—instant stress! What should I do? My parents were out with their friends, so I couldn't call and check with them about the new plans until much later in the evening. By then it would be way too late to go to the movies. If I went without their knowing, I'd be in big trouble. Yet, here was this perfect dreamed-about moment to be with Kyle Thurman, and my friend, Sonja, who is very popular. I was totally confused—and stressed to the max.

Sabrina van Arnem, 16

Solving Problems Effectively—Or, How to Decide Between Mom and Dad and Sonja—Or a Kyle Thurman

Having a problem that you don't know what to do about is very frustrating, especially if you happen to act impulsively or make a rash decision, one that not only doesn't solve the problem but makes it worse. To solve a problem you have to identify the problem, search for sound solutions, try them out, then evaluate the consequences of your proposed solution.

Here's a simple but very effective five-step process to help you develop an organized approach to problem solving, one that involves asking yourself the following questions:

1. What is the problem?
2. How can I solve it?
3. What are the consequences?
4. What is my plan?
5. How did I do?

Here's the five-step problem-solving approach and how Sabrina used it to resolve her dilemma.

1. **What is the problem?** (Sometimes the problem is always readily apparent, as is the case with Sabrina. If the problem you are trying to solve is very complex, just keep asking yourself, "What else is the problem?") Here's what Sabrina identified as her problem:

I accepted an invitation to an overnight stay based on certain criteria and assured my parents of these plans. Sonja has changed the plans without notifying me, and I can't locate my parents to get permission regarding the changes. Without their permission, I'm sure to be grounded. Trust me. But, Kyle— what an opportunity . . .

2. **How can I solve it?** (Here you should come up with as many possible ways you can think of to solve the problem; basically, this means asking, "What could I do to make the problem go away?") Here is how Sabrina worked through this part:

Action #1: I could go along with Sonja's new plans without telling my parents.

Action #2: I could wait until my parents are home to contact them about getting permission to accept the new plans.

Action #3: I could tell Sonja that the new plans sound interesting but that I can't go, because I've told my parents one thing, and I'm certain they wouldn't approve of the new plans.

Action #4: I could tell Sonja that she's a poor friend to put me in this predicament.

Action #5: I could leave a message on my parents' answering machine, telling them of the change in plans, and go off to the movies—and be with Kyle!

3. **What are the consequences of each proposed solution (action)?** (Not all solutions work equally well. After you've generated as many possible solutions to the problem as you can, assess the potential outcome of each proposed action by asking, "If I do that, what would happen?" Remember, thinking through potential outcomes can save you from experiencing even more stress!)

Here is how Sabrina worked through this step:

Action #1: I could go along with Sonja's new plans without telling my parents.

Consequence #1: I'll break the trust me and my parents have established.

Action #2: I could wait until my parents are home to contact them about getting permission to accept the new plans.

Consequence #2: It will be too late to go, and everyone will be in a bad mood from waiting for my decision.

Action #3: *I could tell Sonja that the new plans sound interesting but that I can't go, because I've told my parents one thing, and I'm certain they wouldn't approve of the new plans.*

Consequence #3: *I'll take the responsibility for my decision and run the risk that my friends will mock me.*

Action #4: *I could tell Sonja that she's a poor friend to put me in this predicament.*

Consequence #4: *Sonja will feel offended, and it'll put a strain on our friendship.*

Action #5: *I could leave a message on my parents' answering machine, telling them of the change in plans, and go off to the movies—and be with Kyle!*

Consequence #5: *My parents will most certainly feel taken advantage of and probably will say no to overnights in the future. Plus, I may be grounded for life!*

4. **What is the plan?** (After considering all the consequences and which ones you are prepared to accept responsibility for, decide what you are going to do. Then, make a plan and commit to the plan.) Here's what Sabrina decided:

I'm going to tell Sonja that though the new plans sound interesting, I won't be able to accept them without first checking with my parents. I'll tell Sonja to go to the movies without me if she wants to, but that I don't want to take a chance on breaking the trust my parents have in me.

5. **How did I do?** (After you've followed through with your decision, evaluate how you did and make some value judgment about it. Was your decision a good one? What were the consequences of your decision?) Sabrina said this was the outcome of her decision:

I liked my decision. It worked. It helped me keep the faith with my parents. And, though I didn't know it at the time, as it turned out, my friend Sonja was relieved not to have to follow through with her own revised plans, knowing that her mother, too, would be upset when she learned of the incident.

VIRTUAL PRACTICE: HOW TO BE A PROBLEM-SOLVING SLEUTH

Using the situation below, apply this five-step approach to deciding how to best solve the problem it presents.

Invited to the "Party of the Year"

Sixteen-year-old Amy gets invited to the biggest party of the year. It's at a senior's house, and all the upperclassmen will be there. "Great!" she thinks—until she realizes that party falls on the exact same day as her ten-year-old sister's birthday. Amy's family has been planning on taking her little sis, Margo, out to dinner with some of Margo's friends, and then coming back to the house for a surprise party, complete with birthday cake and presents. Amy's parents have asked her to be in charge of greeting guests and to "store them away" so that little Margo is sure to be surprised. Amy definitely wants to be there for her little sister's surprise party—but not quite as much as she'd like to be at the upperclassmen's party!

1. What is the problem? _____

_____

_____

2. How can Amy solve it?

Action #1: _____

_____

Action #2: _____

_____

Action #3: _____

_____

3. What are the consequences of each proposed solution?

Action #1: _____

_____

Consequence #1: _____

_____

Action #2: _____

_____

Consequence #2: _____

_____

Action #3: _____

_____

Consequence #3: _____

_____

4. What do you suggest Amy's "plan" be? _____

_____

_____

_____

5. If Amy follows your suggestion, how do you think things will turn out? _____

_____

Okay, you know the drill! Write down a problem you are currently facing, and then, the sleuth that you've become, use this approach to "solve" it!

1. What is the problem? _____

_____

_____

_____

2. How can you solve it?

Action #1:_____

_____

Action #2: _____

_____

Action #3: _____

_____

3. What are the consequences of each proposed solution?

Action #1: _____

_____

Consequence #1: _____

_____

Action #2: _____

_____

Consequence #2: _____

_____

Action #3: _____

_____

Consequence #3: _____

_____

    4. What is your plan? _____

_____

_____

_____

    5. What is the likely outcome of your plan? _____

_____

_____

Cool Is Up to You!

When you take the time and effort to weigh out the consequences and come up with a plan to solve your problems, you're certain to create less stress for yourself. The decision, the time, the effort and the rewards are all yours! In the next unit, we'll look at some other coping skills, those you can use to "talk" your way out of a stressful situation.

Part 5

Coping Skills: How to "Talk" Your Way Out of a Stressful Situation

When I was one and twenty,
I heard a wise man say,
"Give crowns and pounds and guineas
But not your heart away;
Give pearls away and rubies
But keep your fancy free."
But I was one-and-twenty,
No use to talk to me.

—A. E. Housman

15

A Message from the Authors

Have you ever been in a stressful situation and then made it even worse because of something you said—or didn't say? Have you ever had the right words, but then "bashed" what could have been a good thing—and all because the tone (or the attitude in which you delivered the words) were all wrong? Have you ever just assumed that you knew what another person was thinking? Have you ever been totally wrong about it? Have you ever been sure of how someone felt—without ever hearing it from them? Sometimes we add to the stress of a situation (or create it) by the way we express ourselves. Or fail to listen.

One of the most potent forms of communication is "listening attentively." Listening attentively means attending fully to the words someone is speaking and to the feelings that person is expressing. Just knowing someone cares enough to really listen to what you're saying and feeling can ease the stress of a situation—and avoid the stress of unnecessary misunderstandings. Consider how Chad "saved the day" when his brother, Brian, walked into the family study where Chad was working on the computer. Seeing his brother was using the computer, Brian huffed, "Man, I can never get my homework done around here! Everybody hogs the computer!"

Upon hearing these words, Chad considers saying, "Who are

you calling a computer hog, you creep?" Knowing this will only add to his brother's frustration, instead Chad says, "You sound pretty stressed-out. Are you upset with me, or do you need the computer?"

"I have a humongous assignment due tomorrow!" Brian responds. "And I don't want to do it, but I'll get an F if I don't."

Now with a better understanding of where Brian is "coming from," Chad volunteers, "Do you want to use the computer now? Because if you do, you can have it. I'm not working on anything urgent."

"That'd be great. Yes, I need to use it," replied Brian. "And hey, I'm sorry for kinda sounding like a jerk. Do you need a little time to finish up what you're working on?"

"No. You can have it now, bro. I'm done with my homework. Need help on anything?"

This exchange is a good example of how keeping cool in the face of someone else's stress can actually defuse their stress. And, of course, it helped that Chad didn't add to the fuel of an already stressed-out brother by using sarcasm of his own. Here are four important reasons why listening attentively can defuse stress.

1. **Listening attentively defuses stress because the other person feels heard.** Having someone trying to understand your position is calming and soothing, as Brian discovered when Chad showed empathy toward Brian—which alleviated some of his frustrations.

2. **Listening attentively defuses stress because it increases understanding—and reduces misunderstandings.** Chad's listening and questions made it clear that, yes, Brian was frustrated about something—but he was not upset with Chad. Brian was stressed-out by the amount of homework he had to do and with the short amount of time in which to do it.

3. **Listening attentively leads to conflict resolution.** Learning why someone is stressed allows you to decide if there is anything you can do (or wish to do) to resolve the problem. For example, if Chad's need to use the computer was also as urgent as Brian's, the two boys could talk about what they could do to work things out.

4. **Listening attentively defuses (and can prevent) defensive behavior.** When you are actively paying attention to someone, it reduces the chances that the listener is going to be defensive. Instead of snapping, "Don't be such a jerk. I have just as much right to the computer as you do!" and feeling upset and stressed himself, Chad chose to listen to what his brother was really saying, and learned the situation is not personal—it's not about him.

Make a point of being a person who communicates effectively. Here are four listening tips that can help you *minimize* stress and are sure to make you really popular with others!

1. **Don't fake attention.** Even if you decide that what the other person has to say is not of consequence, don't fake attention. If you fix a stare or look around, the other person can tell, and as a result, can feel rejected. Stay tuned.

2. **Don't interrupt.** Wait until the other person has had the opportunity to say what he or she has to say before you begin to speak. Your "listening actions" show how interested you are in hearing the other person out, in wanting to understand.

3. **Listen between the lines.** Listen to the content, but also pay attention to the needs and motives behind the words. The speaker's words may not always contain the entire message. The changing tones and volume of his or her voice have meaning, too, as do facial expressions, gestures and body movements. If you are not sure of what is being said, or if body language and content of message seem to say

different things, ask the person to repeat or clarify his or her point. This helps you evaluate *your* understanding of what has been said.

4. **Listen without judging.** No one wants to be in the company of those who are more than willing to hand out a judgment. You want the other person to feel that he or she can come to you with a triumph to be shared or a problem to be discussed—and know that you will listen with an open, unbiased mind. Practice doing this, and you will see that it creates an environment of trust and leads to each of you better enjoying each other's company.

Try these out and see for yourself how they improve and enhance your relationships with others.

This unit is about communicating effectively: how to use not only our ears, but also our words (and the style and tone in which we use them) to short-circuit stress. Here are the "essentials":

♥ *Good communication is a "two-way" deal.* Even if you think you know what the person is going to say (because you have great mind-reading skills), allow the other person to express herself. Tell yourself that the other person has a *right* to share her views and that these might very well be different from your own—and that's okay. Decide that even if the other person has a completely different perspective, opinion, view or "take" than you do, that doesn't make that person wrong, or right. Nor does it make you wrong or right. The goal is to allow expression. Rather than to shut that person down (because he or she, or you, have opposing views—or like-minded views and therefore you already know all there is to know on the subject), say, "Tell me how you came to believe what you do, and then I'll share my views with you. This way, we can better understand where each other is 'coming from.'" This open-minded style of

communicating is a low-stress way to converse with someone because it conveys "You have a right to your views, just
as I have a right to mine," and "I'm open to hearing your
side of things." Try it out: Your parents have just informed
you that they are setting your curfew earlier than you'd like
it to be; you're debating an important issue with friends;
you are discussing grades with your teacher. If you are an
effective communicator, you'll discover people will listen to
you and respect you for what they perceive to be your
"mature manner."

♥ *Get a read on what's being said before you add your "two-cents'
worth."* When someone is talking, rather than butting in and
expressing your views right away, or being so busy formu-
lating what you're going to say that you really aren't attending to what is being said (and maybe even missing the body
language—which is also an important cue to what is being
said), first listen to what's being said. And, while the other
person is speaking, be patient and display patience. If you
convey impatience, the other person will feel that you've
rejected what he or she is saying, and be upset that you've
already formed an opinion without knowing for sure what
he or she is going to say. Feeling neglected and misunder-
stood—or condemned as being wrong—the person might
even walk out on the conversation. By tuning in to what
someone is saying, you can save yourself (and maybe the
other person as well) the stress from having to deal with
misunderstandings and hard feelings that are sure to result
if you don't. And, of course, you know what has been said,
so that you can then know what to say, or do, as a result.

♥ *Speak clearly and assertively.* Say what you mean and mean
what you say. Be direct and straightforward and do this in
a courteous way so that others will not be put off or turned
off by your "attitude." Should that happen, it's possible the
other person won't want to hear what you have to say, nor

honor your wishes. Being assertive means being heard—without using intimidation, or being intimidated.

♥ *Own what you say.* No matter how tempting, do not repeat rumors or hearsay. Make it clear that your words are your own personal feelings or viewpoint. For example, say: "I feel . . ." or "In my opinion . . ." or "As I see it . . ." Communicating in this way will get you a reputation as someone whose words can be trusted. Practice this. You will find it very rewarding—and personally esteeming.

♥ *Don't overreact.* It's easy to get baited into an emotionally charged conversation, especially when your convictions, beliefs or values are challenged. From that moment on, emotional filters keep you busy thinking up arguments of defense and negating those of the speaker instead of listening to what he or she has to say. Be calm and cool. Your goal is to stop stress from snowballing and getting out of hand.

♥ *No "dirty fighting."* Say what you intend to say, but don't demean the other person in the process. If the other person tries to pick a fight, simply repeat what he has to say. For example, if he or she shouts, "You never listen to what I have to say!" then you say, "You feel I never listen to what you have to say?" By "parroting" what the speaker said, you let him or her know that you heard what she had to say. By maintaining your cool in these tense situations, you will let the other person know that you are there to have a civil conversation, and a two-way one. If you do this, you will find that, in most cases, the other person will follow your lead of patience and poise—otherwise, you may find yourself in a yelling match. And here's another benefit that is sure to follow: Many times this approach will cause the other person to calm down and even apologize!

You can learn to be a good communicator. Maybe you already are. Or maybe you aren't. Maybe you've grown up with others (parents, siblings, friends) whose style of relating to others is to tease, shout, ridicule, or make light of what they're saying by laughing it off, or by expecting the other person to just know what's on their mind (and then be upset when this doesn't happen). By seeing and witnessing these inappropriate and ineffective ways of expressing oneself, maybe it's become your style of communicating, too. If so, know that it doesn't have to be. This next unit will show you how communicating effectively can help you be a true taste berry, even at life's most stressful times.

16

"Self-Talk": How to Talk to Yourself When Stress Sets In

Seventeen-year-old Brianna Reed is an aspiring actress who has her heart set on winning the leading female role in an upcoming production of *Romeo and Juliet*. Imagine her delight—as well as her anxiety—when she learns that Todd Knowles, her very own secret Romeo, is trying out for the leading male role. Brianna knows that she needs to be calm, but just the thought of Todd makes her heart race. She knows that she has to concentrate on getting into her role, it's important to her future as an actress, yet the sight of Todd can make her mind go blank. What is Brianna to do?

It's obvious that Brianna needs to take a deep breath and think clearly about pulling off a stellar audition as Juliet. Have you had days like this—times when you need to think clearly, make a plan and then rev into action to make sure the energy of the stress you're feeling results in positive action, and not just knots—and butterflies—in your stomach? Most teens do.

"Thinking out loud," commonly called *self-talk* (a technique you'll learn about in this chapter), can be used to guide yourself through a tense or difficult situation. It's a simple but sure way to focus your attention on what needs to be done *this very minute*. Rather than being "scattered" and "all over the map," you concentrate on the task at hand.

What should Brianna do for the big day when she'd like to help Romeo swoon? You'll have to read her story to help her out!

Juliet—And Her Romeo

Ever since I heard about the drama club's upcoming production of *Romeo and Juliet*, I'd been rehearsing for the role of Juliet. More than anything I want to be an actress—a serious actress—and what's more serious than a leading part in Shakespeare? Every night, after all my homework was done, I'd get out the script, memorize lines and practice performing them in front of the mirror. I was in the middle of my best mirror-performance yet, when my mom came to my room to tell me that my friend Cassie was on the phone. Really excited, Cassie said, "You won't believe this! Todd Knowles is trying out for the role of Romeo!"

Todd Knowles! Todd is the undisputed, positively *most* sexiest, the most handsome, the most buffed, the coolest guy in our school. Cassie knew I had a huge crush on Todd, and above all else in life I wanted to him to notice me. I wanted to go out with Todd even more than I wanted to become a serious actress, which says a lot, because becoming a serious actress is my passion.

"For sure?" I questioned.

"Yes, for sure," Cassie assured me. "I got it from his sister, Tara. But there's more. Didn't you say you were scheduled to read for Juliet right after school tomorrow? Welllll . . . that is the exact time that Todd is scheduled to read for Romeo, too. What that means is that you're going to read opposite Todd!"

My heart started racing—words failed me. I couldn't believe it. What if I got so nervous I'd forget my lines? He'd think I was dumb. And what if we did the kiss scene—tomorrow?

"Is this like too perfect? This is your big chance. Can you believe it?" Cassie gushed. "Of all the other guys reading for the role that you could've been scheduled to try out with, you get Todd Knowles. What luck!"

Of course, I was thrilled . . . I really was . . . but I'd been preparing to get the role for a play that would begin rehearsals in two weeks—however, I hadn't been preparing to actually read with and maybe even kiss Todd tomorrow afternoon.

"Cassie, thanks for calling. But I have to rehearse. Gosh, what if I forget my lines? What should I wear? I just have to be perfect. What if my hair decides at the last minute to have a bad hair day? What if I trip walking up on the stage? What if I didn't emote? What if Todd kisses me and I faint?"

The "what ifs" were endless. Even trying to rehearse was futile after that, because I couldn't focus at all. I could hardly sleep that night. But the next day held even more stress. It was like anticipation and dread at the very same time. Finally 3:15 rolled around, and it was time for me to try out for the role of Juliet. There I was and there was my Romeo, Todd Knowles.

I can only say all my fears were foolish. My hair was great, I didn't trip on stage and I said my lines like a true serious actress. We actually kissed—well, not a French kiss, but still a kiss. And yes, I did get the role of Juliet—on stage, and off!

Brianna Reed, 17

How to "Sweet Talk" Your Way Out of a Jam

The night before her audition, Brianna needed to think clearly about all that she should've done in making sure the next day came off the best it could. What did preparation for the big day with Romeo include? You can bet that Brianna had to do some talking to herself—some "thinking out loud."

"Thinking out loud" is the same skill or technique you use when winding your way through a maze. Think about the process you use to talk to yourself as a way of guiding yourself to the end. If you made a wrong turn you simply stopped, looked ahead, and then tried a new direction. That's the point. A methodical step-by-step way of thinking through what you are going to do, and then self-correcting when you've made a wrong turn, is very helpful when you are in a stressful situation. Here's how Brianna applied the thinking-out-loud skill to her predicament.

"Okay, tomorrow is the big day. I'd better get organized, starting now. I don't want to leave everything until the last minute in the morning. No need to be any more stressed than I already am.

"First, I'll check on my black skirt to see if it's clean. Here it is. Great, it's clean. I'll wear the striped sweater with it. It's a great look. Looking my best always boosts my confidence.

"I don't want to be rushing around in the morning, so I'll hang my clothes on the back of the door with my black shoes and everything else I'll be wearing, and they'll be ready for me to put on right after I shower in the morning. I'll spend a little extra time on my face tonight, I'd like it to glow tomorrow. I think I'll put on a facial mask while I'm preparing. That always makes me feel extra pampered.

"I want things to go smoothly tomorrow morning, so I'll go check on what there is to eat for breakfast. I'll need to be thinking and feeling my best so I want to make sure I eat a healthy breakfast. Since I'm slow getting started in the morning, I'll get to bed a half-hour earlier than usual, so that I can wake up a half-hour earlier in the morning and still feel well rested.

"I will definitely reset my alarm clock to give myself plenty of time to spend on getting ready so I won't feel so hurried. I'll *study my lines in front of the bathroom mirror one more time before I go to bed and once again in the morning. Being sure that I've done all I can to feel and look my best should help me sleep easier tonight . . . so when Romeo looks for his Juliet tomorrow, I'll be as ready as I can!"*

VIRTUAL PRACTICE: TALKING YOUR WAY THROUGH A STRESSFUL SITUATION

You can use the Thinking Out Loud skill to steer yourself through almost any stressful situation. Here's a scenario for practice (though you may want to simply jot down a real-life dilemma you're facing, and work through it). If you found yourself in the following predicament, what would you tell yourself to get yourself through it without adding more stress to an already tense situation?

Tuesday—And Late!

You have just arrived at school ten minutes later than usual. The five-minute tardy bell has just sounded. You need to go to your locker to get your books, set up an appointment with your counselor, stop by the library to return a book that is due this morning, go by the office to turn in a permission slip in order to be excused on Friday for a dental appointment and buy a lunch ticket. In short, you have much to do in a relatively short time.

"_____

_____

_____

_____

_____

_____

_____

_____

_____

_____

_____"

Checkpoint: Did your thinking-out-loud dialogue go something like this?

"I have only five minutes until class. That means I'm going to have to concentrate on what I must get done right now. Let's see, since I'm right here, why don't I go to the office first? Why don't I get the permission slip my mom wrote this morning? Here it is. Good, that's done. Okay, I was going to talk to the counselor but I'd better do that during lunch time. I'm afraid that I'll be late if I do it now. I'd better get the lunch ticket then, too. Okay, the office visit is completed so I'll swing by the library next. There's Johnny Watson. Gosh, I'd love to talk to him about last night's soccer practice. I'd better not, I just don't have the time. How am I doing? Hmmm, three minutes to go. Good, the library book is returned, now off to my locker. Let's see, 35 right, 15 left, turn it all the way around, and 25 right. Oops, I'm hurrying too fast. I went right by 25. Okay, slow down, let's try this again: 35 right, 15 left, turn it all the way around, now slowly to 25 right. Great. Okay, there's the book I need. Let me think, do I need anything else? Oh yes, I was going to have Mr. Winfield look over my Science Fair project before I get it typed up. I'll take that with me now. It will save me a trip later in *the day. How's my time? Great, still one minute until class. I'm not going to be late. Nice going!"*

As you can see, coaching yourself along can really help you keep calm and to stay on track toward what ought to be your next move.

Cool Is Up to You!

Teens tell us that once they try out the self-talk skill, they use it again and again. Perhaps this is because it's quick and easy to apply in those situations in which they find themselves harried or scattered. At such times, self-talk provides direction and guidance, allowing you to focus in on the crisis at hand. Try it for yourself. Self-talk is a great technique—but here's a helpful hint: Don't move your lips or you'll look geeky, and you're too cool for that! And speaking of moving your lips, in this next chapter you'll learn how to say what you mean, and mean what you say, which is also a sign of a "cool" taste berry!

17

Saying What's on Your Mind—Without Shouting, Pouting or Running Away

There are times when you need to communicate how you feel, what you think is important, and what you can and will and won't do. And you want to do this in a way that others will hear and accept. It doesn't do you any good to yell, nor does it do any good not to say anything at all and hope people guess what your needs are. They will likely guess wrong, and your needs will not be met. It also doesn't do much good to hope that if you are just nice to people they will somehow know what it is you need and give it to you. This usually doesn't work either. Not getting your feelings, thoughts and needs across clearly can create stress for everyone involved—most especially you. Certainly this was true for sixteen-year-old Curt Lindholm when he found himself in class with a project he thought was out of line with what he believed in. The thing is, he wasn't sure what to do about it. Given that he really liked his teacher and knew and respected her reputation as a creative educator; and given that he didn't want the other kids in the class to think he was putting them down for his not wanting to participate in the project; and given that his mother had enrolled him in this after-school class so that he could stay at school the hour until she was off work and could come and get him . . . well, you can only imagine Curt's reluctance to "make waves" and "cause everyone grief." Assertive skills to the rescue! If Curt had been more assertive, he could have kept a stressful situation from being even more stressful. See for yourself! Let's check in on Curt and his dolls.

Little Dolls

A few years ago, my parents enrolled me in an art class after school. In this course, we would do all sorts of arts and crafts projects, which I usually really enjoyed. One day in this class, we were going to make little dolls that were about one-inch tall. They were very simple dolls. At first I just thought it was a little sissy to make dolls, but everyone, even the guys in the class, got busy assembling the pieces, so I did, too. Then the teacher told us these dolls were good-luck charms that we could keep in our pockets and use when we felt we needed some extra luck—like during tests. Supposedly, if we held or rubbed the doll while we took the test, we would get a better grade.

I was brought up to believe that doing something like this was worshipping an idol—something that was completely against my religious beliefs. So making these good-luck dolls seemed very wrong to me. I knew I had to refuse to make them, but I didn't know how to tell my teacher that I wanted nothing to do with making an "idol." I didn't want the teacher to be upset with me, I didn't want her to think that I was belligerent, and I didn't want to be dropped from the class because I refused to do what was asked of me. So instead, I told the teacher that I needed to go to the office to call my mom. The teacher looked confused, but said, "Sure. There's only a few minutes left of class, so I guess I'll see you tomorrow."

So I gathered up my things and went to the office, where I called my mother and told her about the dolls. My mother said to wait in the office, and she would come right over and get me. Sitting in the office, my tension multiplied each minute I had to wait (which wasn't all that long, but it seemed like forever). The longer the wait seemed, the more I hoped everyone—the teacher, my mom and the others in the class—wouldn't be upset with me or think I was only trying to "make waves."

By the time my mother arrived, the workshop class was over, but she still went to my classroom, where my teacher was cleaning up from the class. My mom talked with the teacher and explained why I didn't want to make the good-luck charms. "No problem," the teacher said. "Curt doesn't have to make the dolls, I'll find another project for him instead." And then the teacher explained that in the future, if there was ever a project that conflicted with something I believed in, I should feel comfortable telling her about it, because she never wanted me (or any of her students) to feel forced to do something that went against their beliefs. I was surprised that the teacher was agreeable to my not doing the little dolls project. It was good to learn that if I had told the teacher about my feelings in doing the doll project, she would have understood and assigned me another project. I wouldn't have had to ask my mother to stand up for my beliefs in my place, and she wouldn't have been inconvenienced by making the trip to school.

I also learned that speaking up is important to learning what others think: What may seem very natural to one person can seem "weird" or "strange" to someone else. For example, the next day when I began working on the new project the teacher had assigned me, the girl I sat next to, May, was adding the final touches to her little dolls. When she asked me why I wasn't working on the same thing as everyone else and I told her making them was against my faith, she looked very surprised. Then, she told me it was *because* of her faith that she didn't see the little dolls as idols, but rather, as reminders that God was there even in the little things and for the little worries we had. May said she couldn't wait to finish her little dolls, because she was looking forward to carrying one around in her pocket. She had even asked the teacher if she could make two other dolls, one for her sister and another for a best friend.

May's views didn't change what I believed, but it helped me understand that different people can believe different things and for different reasons. It was good to learn May's views on this project: Maybe it explained why others hadn't objected to the project as I had.

Talking about things helps us learn about each other, as well as think about new ideas. I mean, what if sharing with my classmates had helped give them a new point of view, and they'd thought about it and decided that making the dolls was creating "idols"? Having said something could have been important in that respect, too. Other people can't know how we feel about things unless we say something. So now I feel more confident talking about how I feel about things and why. When you think about it, it's the only way others know what's important to you.

All in all, it takes courage to stand for your beliefs, and make the decision to act according to your values—without worrying about how others might judge you. When you do this, you help others find the courage to do the same. If I'd been assertive in expressing myself that day, I could have accomplished all that. And, no one would have thought I was making waves at all, just clearly expressing myself.

Curt Lindholm, 17

What Part of "No!" (or Yes) Did You *Not* Understand?

Curt sounds like a gracious and considerate young man, but by not expressing himself, by not saying what was on his mind, he created even more stress for himself. Had he been assertive, Curt could have resolved his dilemma almost as soon as he discovered he didn't want to commit to the project. Then, he would've had to worry what others thought of him. As he learned, others don't resent you for speaking your heart at all, and in fact, because they then understand "who you are" and what you stand for, usually they'll readily accommodate your needs. Certainly his teacher would have.

One important reason to learn how to assert yourself is so that you can confidently face situations that would usually produce frustration and stress. Being assertive does not mean being rude, but rather, it gives you the power to assert your rights without using intimidation or being intimidated.

Here is some very useful information to help you understand the difference between communicating in a style that is passive, aggressive or assertive.

Passive, Aggressive and Assertive Behavior: Do You Know the Difference?

Perhaps you know people who have learned that by shouting, pouting, ridiculing and being intimidating they can get what they want. Psychologists call this "aggressive" behavior. Just by looking at them you can see they are in "high stress" mode and create a lot of stress in others around them.

Perhaps you know people who are the sweet, likable "I'll-do-anything-you-want" types. This is called "passive" behavior. But not being honest about their needs, and always setting them aside to make someone else happy, can cause a lot of stress.

Being assertive means taking responsibility for your needs and doing so in a way so that others will listen and not be offended or "turned off" by what you're saying. It means giving them the opportunity to respond in return. Being assertive means developing a style of communication that is direct, self-expressive,

self-respecting and straightforward. It means to value yourself—
to act with confidence and speak with calm authority.

Being assertive is the most effective way to communicate with
others, and it assures the least possible amount of stress.

Let's look closer at the characteristics of each of these
behaviors.

The Passive Person

The passive person appears to be a calm, complacent individual who never makes waves and is always responding to the
needs of others. The problem is that the passive person usually
"keeps score," and just when you least expect it he or she blows
up. The stress of all that denial of his or her own needs is just
bottled up inside. When the person does react, incidents from
weeks, months and even years ago are brought up! Plus, when
the passive individual reacts, the situation is usually blown out
of proportion.

Passive Paula: Paula was asked by her friend Sue to go to the
library and check out a reference book that Sue needed to complete a research project for her English literature class, even
though getting the book was Sue's responsibility and not
Paula's. Paula agreed to do it, even though she didn't want to.
The following week, Sue asked Paula to return the book for her.
The next Tuesday, Sue asked Paula to call a mutual friend with
the message that Sue wouldn't be attending a friend's birthday
party. With this, Paula finally exploded. "Why don't you do it?
I'm sick of doing favors for you. What do you think I am, your
errand girl?"

Sue was shocked at Paula's outburst. She had no idea that
Paula was displeased with her. After all, she had never complained before and, in fact, had seemed more than willing to do
whatever Sue had asked of her.

The Aggressive Person

At the other end of the spectrum is the aggressive person, who would like to control others, but doesn't use much tact in doing so. They may justify their tactless behavior by saying "Well, at least everyone knows where I stand!" or "I just tell it like it is, and let the chips fall where they may!" They get their needs met—usually at the expense of others, and often that expense includes others being humiliated or hurt.

Aggressive Agnetha: Agnetha saw that Jake, the boy she liked, was interested in Kristin. Agnetha was determined to put an end to that—Jake was hers, whether he knew it or not. When Kristin was at her locker, Agnetha marched up to her, looked her in the eye and ordered, "Stay away from Jake." Unprepared for Agnetha's hostility, Kristin questioned, "Jake?" Her stance intimidating, Agnetha snapped, "Don't play dumb. You stay away from him. Jake is mine." Leaning forward, she slammed Kristin's locker closed and turned and stormed away. Kristin had almost no interest in Jake to begin with—now, although she was intimidated by Agnetha, her interest in Jake had risen. What's more, when Jake heard of the incident (which, of course, was the talk of the school), he was all the more sure he wanted nothing to do with Agnetha.

The Assertive Person

Statements that affirm what you are feeling and what you need are assertive. Communicating effectively means that you are direct, straightforward and courteous in the way you relay your message.

Assertive Angie: Angie and Tyanne had three classes together. During each class, every day, Tyanne borrowed a pencil. Almost every day, Tyanne forgot to return Angie's pencil at some point and needed a new one the next day. It was no big deal at first—after all, it was just pencils. But after awhile,

Tyanne's lack of responsibility bothered Angie. The next time Tyanne asked for a pencil, Angie met her eyes and said clearly, "I feel like you're taking advantage of me by borrowing a pencil every day and never returning it. I'll lend you a pencil, but I want it back at the end of class." Tyanne hadn't even realized how habitual her pencil borrowing and losing had been, now aware of it and how it had bothered Angie, she said, "You'll get it back. You're right, I've been really bad about losing them without getting them back to you. It won't happen again."

Five Cool Tips on How to *Best* Be Assertive

Here are some important tips for being assertive:

1. *Eye contact:* The assertive person uses direct eye contact. This doesn't mean staring someone down and not blinking, it means looking at the other person, keeping eye contact throughout the conversation.
2. *Posture:* Sitting or standing straight, not hunching over, and not hiding in the corner of a room all indicate assertiveness.
3. *Voice:* Speaking up and not mumbling—but not yelling—is
 · being assertive.
4. *Words:* It's common to see people make assertive comments and then ruin the effect by either dropping or raising their voices at the end. For example, you might say to a friend in a firm voice, "I want you to be more truthful with me." This by itself sounds fine. However, if instead of waiting for a response you ask, "Okay?" you are destroying the assertiveness of your statement. Make your statement, and then know when to stop talking.
5. *Responsibility:* Own what you say. Make *I* statements, such as "I feel," "I like," "I wish," "I would appreciate," "I need."

VIRTUAL PRACTICE: ARE YOU PASSIVE, ASSERTIVE OR AGGRESSIVE? UNDERSTANDING WHAT AND HOW YOU COMMUNICATE

Being assertive lets others know your ideas and feelings while respecting theirs as well—these actions and behaviors are sure to reduce stress. Would you say that your style is more likely to be assertive, aggressive or passive? Here is a simple multichoice quiz to help you decide.

Read each situation, and then choose the response that is most like you, and circle it. Don't cheat yourself! Just go with your first instinct of what you'd say or do—even if it's a response you'd only utter under your breath! Remember the goal—to help you decide the patterns of communication that you tend to use most. By being totally honest with yourself, you are more likely to get a good sense of the way you respond to others, so that you know if you are okay with that, or if you'd like to make some changes.

1. Your mother has asked your older sister to be in charge of you and your little brother until she gets home from work. Your sister asks you to turn the television off and begin your homework, as you know you are supposed to do. Which of the following are you likely to say:

   (a) "But I would like to see the end of this show. I promise to turn it off at the end. Please? Pretty please?"
   (b) "The show will be over in only six minutes, and Mom did say I could watch this one show. I promise to get on my homework in a few minutes."
   (c) "Stop acting like you're my mom!"

2. A girl asks to cut in front of you in a line. You don't want to let her cut in. What do you say?
   (a) "Who do you think you are, a member of the royal

family? Get to the back of the line like everyone else!"
   (b) "I'm sorry, but no. That wouldn't be fair to all of us who've been waiting our turn."
   (c) You step aside, looking a little put out and mutter, "Well, I guess so."

3. You are watching TV when your brother/sister comes in; your sibling wants to watch a two-hour special on TV. He/she walks over to change the channel. What do you do?
   (a) You say, "Excuse me, but I'm watching this. It will be over in fifteen minutes, you'll be able to watch your program then."
   (b) You jump from your chair towards him/her and the TV and shout, "Hands off, you little jerk! I'm watching my show right now!"
   (c) You let your sibling change the channel but sigh and complain, "I really would've liked to watch the last fifteen minutes of my program."

4. A classmate asks to copy your answers to a test. You don't want him to. What do you say?
   (a) "Forget it, pea brain. Why don't you try cracking open a book instead?"
   (b) "I'm not even sure if all my answers are right. I mean, you can go ahead and copy them . . . but they might not be right."
   (c) "No, I can't do that for you. Not only does cheating not feel right to me, I could end up getting an F myself if we got caught."

5. The teacher asks the entire class to stay after school because someone was talking. You don't want to take the blame for something you know isn't your fault. What do you do?

(a) You raise your hand and when the teacher calls on you, you say, "It doesn't seem fair that we all have to stay after class. Is there any way a different solution could be worked out? Maybe the people who were talking could come forward and agree to stay after, instead of all of us paying for their mistake?"

(b) You yell, "Whichever of you motor mouths were talking, you should be the ones staying, not me! I wasn't doing anything wrong. And when that bell rings, I'm out of here! I don't care what anybody says." When the bell rings, you stand up and walk out of the room, ignoring the teacher's calls for you to get back in your seat.

(c) You look unhappy and say nothing.

6. Your sister wants to borrow your favorite CD and take it with her to a friend's house. Because you have observed that your sister is careless with her own things, you are afraid she will not care for your CD and it might get scratched or lost. What do you say?

(a) "Oh, just go ahead. You always use my stuff anyway."

(b) "No way! Let's get this clear: You can never borrow my CD, or anything else of mine for that matter. I don't want to end up with all my stuff trashed like yours."

(c) "To be honest, I'm worried about it getting ruined. You have trouble taking care of your own things. So, I want your promise that if I let you borrow it you will take care of it and bring it home in the same condition it was in when you left the house with it. If you can give me that promise and keep it, then I'll take a chance and let you use the CD."

7. You are watching a TV movie. It is scheduled to end in five minutes. Your dad/mom comes in and says you must go to bed immediately. What do you say or do?

(a) You shout, "You're so unfair. You're always looking for

ways to pull a power-trip!" and then you storm from the room.

(b) You nod unhappily, then glare at your mom/dad's retreating back as you get up and go to bed.

(c) You explain, "There's only five minutes left until this movie is over. I've watched it from the very beginning. May I please watch the last five minutes?"

8. Your mother tells you that you must baby-sit for your sister this evening. You have already made plans to go to a school play with a friend; your mother had already given you permission last week to do that. What do you do and say?

(a) You whine, "Okay, I'll do it—even though I really wanted to go to that play."

(b) You snap, "You said I could go to the play, and I'm going."

(c) You calmly remind your mother of last week's conversation, "Mom, maybe you've forgotten that you gave me permission to go to the school play last week—all my plans have been made and my friends are counting on me going with them. I'd be happy to baby-sit any other night this week."

9. What would you do or say if another person is calling you names?

(a) Ignore the person and hope he or she eventually gets tired of it and stops.

(b) Threaten to punch the person if he/she doesn't stop.

(c) Tell the person, "I really don't appreciate it when you call me names; it hurts my feelings and I'd like you to stop."

10. You don't understand a problem the teacher has just explained. What would you do or say?
    (a) You raise your hand and say, "I'm having trouble understanding that problem. Could you please explain it again?"
    (b) You say nothing and hope that you can figure it out by yourself later at home.
    (c) You don't raise your hand, but you complain out loud, "This is stupid. What do we have to know this for anyway?"

Okay, it's time to check your score.

Answer Key

1) a = passive; b = assertive; and c = aggressive.
2) a = aggressive; b = assertive; and c = passive.
3) a = assertive; b = aggressive; and c = passive.
4) a = aggressive; b = passive; and c = assertive.
5) a = assertive; b = aggressive; and c = passive.
6) a = passive; b = aggressive; and c = assertive.
7) a = aggressive; b = passive; and c = assertive.
8) a = passive; b = aggressive; and c = assertive.
9) a = passive; b = aggressive; and c = assertive.
10) a = assertive; b = passive; and c = aggressive.

Scoring. If you got six or more "assertive" answers—great! Give yourself an A! If you got three or less "passives"—good for you! If you got less than two "aggressives," that's good news as well. Of course, being assertive is the goal, so the more you got, great!

If you feel you need to work on reducing stress by being more assertive, you may want to go back and reread the last chapter, as well as look into taking a class or seminar on effective ways to be assertive. Maybe your school offers such a course, or check your community college (which often offers this sort of curriculum).

As always, "practice makes perfect." Sometimes it helps to practice on paper, writing out what you want to say. Not only does this help you sort out what you want to say ahead of time, it also helps you commit to the words.

With whom would you like to practice being more assertive?

_____

_____

Why do you want to be more assertive with this person? ___

_____

_____

Cool Is Up to You!

A teen in our workshop, fifteen-year-old Alex Masters, made this comment, "Being a teenager is a juggle of two main battles. The first is with your parents: With them it's hard to say what you mean and still get your privileges. The second is with your friends: With them it's the battle to have their acceptance while still being yourself." Getting what you want and need from friends and family is just the beginning when it comes to learning how to be assertive.

Assertiveness, like all aspects of communication, can be developed with practice. In the next chapter, you'll learn a great way to practice by "role playing": How, by playing and exchanging roles with the help of a parent or friend, you can reduce stress by being prepared with the best possible solution for several different ways that the situation could unfold. What a taste berry!

18

"Role-Playing": How Rehearsing What to Say Can Help You Get What You Want

Have you ever gotten yourself "stuck" in a situation—one in which you wanted out, but it took some explaining, and you stressed out because you didn't know what to do or how to do it? That's the case for seventeen-year-old Brenda Walters, who accepts a date with Larry—and then decides there is no way she's going to follow through on going out on the date, and so she decides to "ditch him"! That's not a very nice thing to do! The good news is that a friend helps her find a really creative way to get herself out of the bind she's in, and prevents her from getting herself in even more trouble—but you'll have to read her story to find out what he did to help and how it worked. We will tell you his plan involved a nifty little skill called "role playing."

By allowing you to evaluate the pros and cons of proposed solutions beforehand, this technique involves asking others to help you work your way through a potentially stressful situation. That way, by rehearsing strategies to the solutions you choose, you get to decide whether you'll be able to commit to a certain course of action. Let's check in on Brenda to find out how she (and Brad) found a better solution than "ditching" Larry.

"Ditching" Larry

At my school, Spring-Fling is a big deal to attend. Everyone goes, especially since all the junior and senior guys play "host." Spring-Fling is more of a have-a-date event than a singles thing. As the day of the big event approached, I found myself without a date. I was hoping that Ben Tripp, a really cool senior, would ask me to go with him. Sometimes when Ben passes me in the halls, he'll give me a certain look, so I know he's interested in me. But Ben Tripp had done nothing but give me that look; there was still no invitation to be his date at Spring-Fling. So on Wednesday, two days before the dance, when Larry Welch asked me to be his date, I said I'd go with him instead.

Now, Larry is a nice guy and all, but he's someone who fits the "he has a nice personality" category. You know what that means: He's not your "to-die-for" date, or at least he wasn't mine. Still, I really wanted to go to Spring-Fling, and it was unthinkable to show up alone. Going with a group of girls was a dead give-away that you couldn't get a date, so that was a no-no, too. So, I accepted Larry Welch's invitation.

But by the end of the next day, I wished I hadn't. I mean, what if Larry Welch expected me to dance with him and only him the entire evening? And what if Larry got the idea that because I went to the dance with him, he and I were "dating"? What if Ben thought that because I was with Larry, that Larry and I were dating? As you can see, I simply had to get out of the date with Larry Welch. The problem was I really didn't have a good reason to break the date, other than that I shouldn't have accepted it in the first place. An even bigger problem was that I didn't know how to tell Larry. I didn't have the nerve to tell him face-to-face.

"So, what are you going to do?" my good friend Brad asked me when I told him about my predicament.

"I'm just going to pretend I'm not at home when he comes to pick me up!" I answered.

"Speaking from experience," Brad replied, "that's a pretty cruel way to learn you no longer have a date! And besides, there's a better way to undo a date."

I was sure I knew what he was going to say, so I argued, "Brad, I'm afraid that if I call him up, I'll back down from telling him I've changed my mind—and then I'll be stuck!"

"You don't really know what Larry's going to say," my friend responded.

"What do you mean?" I asked innocently enough. Boy, did I get an answer.

"I'll show you. Pretend I'm Larry and you're phoning me. Go ahead." Even though I felt silly, I put an imaginary phone to my ear and said, "Hi, Larry."

"Hi, Brenda!" Brad said in return. "Now say something, like 'I'm calling about the dance tomorrow night.'"

So I said, "I'm calling about the dance tomorrow night."

Taking on Larry's personality, Brad responded, "I can hardly wait! My dad said I could borrow his car instead of using my old beat-up one. And guess what, Brenda? I'm taking us to dinner before the dance, and I bought this great new shirt and sweater in your favorite color! It's going to be so much fun. I'm really looking forward to it. I'll pick you up at 6:30."

"You see, Brad," I shouted. "That's exactly why I don't want to call Larry. Because I wouldn't want to disappoint him—at least while I was on the phone with him—I'm sure I'll say, 'Oh, okay,' and then I'll still be stuck going out with him. I'm not going to take that chance, and that's that. I'm sticking with my plan to leave my house before Larry arrives!"

"Not so fast," Brad told me. "That's one possible scenario, but there are others. Come on, one more time, pretend you're phoning me."

And so I did. "Hello, Larry," I said once again. "I'm calling about our date for Spring-Fling."

"Oh, Brenda," my friend Brad replied. "I'm glad you called. I'm really sick. I won't be able to go. I'm really sorry to back out at such a late date, but I have strep throat, I'm running a fever and taking medication." Well, you can imagine how surprised I was at Brad's words, because it presented a different view. I mean, maybe Larry would get sick or would want to back out of going—which would be okay with me!

"Hey, that went pretty well," I told my friend Brad. "Now, how do I make sure Larry gets strep throat?"

"Very funny," said Brad. "But there are still a lot of other ways that things could play out. C'mon. Let's try it one more time."

"Okay," I agreed. "Hello, Larry. I'm calling about our date for Spring-Fling."

"Yes, what about it?" Brad asked, then paused, obviously forcing me to say something first this time.

"Well, I can't go with you," I blurted, "and I was hoping you might make other plans."

"Oh, I'm sorry to hear that, Brenda," my friend Brad replied. "I was really looking forward to going. Are you sure I can't change your mind?"

"Yes, I'm sure," I said. "I really have to say no. I'm sorry."

Sounding disappointed but accepting it, Brad said for Larry, "Okay, Brenda. Well, since we won't be going to the dance together, would you be okay with my asking Karen Hood to go with me? I know she's a friend of yours, but I really would like to go out with Karen. I've been too shy to ask her, but just yesterday her sister told me that Karen was hoping I'd ask her to Spring-Fling. It all sounds very complicated, but if you wouldn't be upset, I'd love to ask Karen."

In short, I was surprised at the possibility that Larry could respond to my backing out in a number of ways.

I found the little exercise with Brad helpful because it gave me the confidence to handle a situation that I not only knew would be hard to deal with, but also knew I could easily mess up. And when Brad said, "If you want a real eye-opener, Brenda, we could reverse roles. You play the part of Larry and I play you." That's when I realized that if I were to put the shoe on the other foot—put myself in Larry's place—I wouldn't want him to stand me up. So I decided to treat Larry exactly the way I'd want to be treated if the same situation were reversed. I'd want someone to give me time to make other plans, and to be honest, I wouldn't want someone to go out with me if they really didn't want to. I called Larry; he took it much better than I had first imagined. He was disappointed, but he didn't act totally devastated or anything like that. I was kind about it—and we stayed friends.

Brad really helped me learn to say what's on my mind, but without hurting someone else in the process. In my case, Larry had done nothing wrong. I was the one who wanted to back out of something I'd committed to. As Brad said, standing Larry up would have made him feel rejected and humiliated. That's not a very nice thing to do. The approach I thought I was going to use gave him no time or chance to make other plans. And so it was my friend Brad who taught me one of the most important things ever about being a friend. Not only does the way you communicate make a difference in how good your friendships are, it can also make you a taste-berry friend—which was what Brad was to me, and ultimately, what I was to Larry. I'm happy to say that Larry and I are not only friends, but are now good friends, too.

Brenda Walters, 16
from More Taste Berries for Teens

Have You Ever Been in a "Larry Welch" Situation?

Brenda really didn't want to hurt Larry, and felt the stress of knowing that she would. And surely the turmoil of avoiding Larry and then hurting him would have been sure to cause her yet more stress (to say nothing of Larry). She would've also been going through the stress of worrying about the worst possible scenarios, rather than taking action to prepare for actually having the conversation that would break the date. Role playing helps you rehearse strategies to the solutions you choose, and then to decide whether you will commit to your choices. Whether you tend to be more aggressive or more passive in situations where it could feel stressful to say what's on your mind, role playing helps ease the stress of the situation. Perhaps just as important, role playing allows you to see that there are any number of ways that the situation could take place. This helps reduce the stress of dwelling on the worst possible scenario.

VIRTUAL PRACTICE: REHEARSING . . . TO GET YOUR WAY

Rehearsing can help build your confidence in handling situations that could have stressful outcomes. By exchanging roles, you build confidence in your ability to assert yourself. This kind of preplanning reduces the stress in the situation by lowering the risk that you will be overwhelmed at the time of confrontation. It also provides you with an opportunity to really look at and assess your understanding of the situation, and then it helps you use your understanding when you are under stress.

Here's a scenario for practice. As you read it, be thinking of all the possible ways the conversation could unfold.

Your Favorite Band . . . in Concert

For months you and your best friend have been planning to go visit her cousin the weekend of spring break, but now you've found out that your favorite band will be in concert in your town that very same weekend. You'd really rather go to the concert. You're really stressed about this situation because you know how much your friend is counting on you to be with her. You simply have to get out of going with your best friend to her cousin's—but, of course, you want a stress-free resolution.

Using the space below, describe three possible ways your conversation could play out:

Test run #1:

You: " _____ "

Friend: "_____ "

You: " _____ "

Friend: "_____ "

You: " _____ "

Friend: "_____ "

Test run #2:

You: " _____ "

Friend: "_____ "

You: " _____ "

Friend: "_____ "

You: " _____ "

Friend: "_____ "

Test run #3:

You: " _____ "

Friend: "_____ "

You: " _____ "

Friend: "_____ "

You: " _____ "

Friend: "_____ "

Now apply this skill to a real-life situation in your life. Describe a sticky situation in which it would be helpful to "rehearse" some of the possible ways things could turn out. You might also think about who would be the best person to help you play it out, be it your mom or dad, teacher or friend.

A sticky situation I'm in right now is: _____

_____

_____

_____

Three possible ways it could play out:

Test run #1:

You: " _____ "

Other person: "_____ "

You: " _____ "

Other person: " _____ "

You: " _____ "

Other person: " _____ "

Test run #2:

You: " _____ "

Other person: " _____ "

You: " _____ "

Other person: " _____ "

You: " _____ "

Other person: " _____ "

Test run #3:

You: " _____ "

Other person: " _____ "

You: " _____ "

Other person: " _____ "

You: " _____ "

Other person: " _____ "

Cool Is Up to You!

Role-playing and rehearsing your conversations with others can reduce your stress level and build your confidence in affecting the way things turn out. Seeing a stressful situation from several angles can make the situation seem easier to handle. This is the real beauty of asking others for help and support. And speaking of support from others, this next unit will show you just how much—and how many—people are there for you during times of stress. Think of it as your own team—stress-management team, that is.

Part 6

Reaching Out to Others:

Who Are the Members of Your Stress-Management Team?

The key is to keep company only with people who uplift you, whose presence calls forth your best.

—Epictetus

19

A Message
from the Authors

Having people in our lives who care about us, root for us, and help us feel significant, loved and loving plays a big part in feeling that we can make it through stressful times. Our interdependence with others, and the support we feel from them, helps us feel okay about ourselves—and less diminished—when our lives are burdened by stress and we feel overwhelmed, even on the losing end, by it.

This is true even at those times when there is little to nothing you can do about that which is creating stress for you. Things like taking a very big and important test or having a heavy heart because you've just been turned down or rejected by a special someone, or a group of your friends have planned a get-together—and didn't invite you—are stress-filled times in which all the love and support from others is not going to make the stress go away. So how can others take the sting out of the stress you're feeling? It is precisely because there are times when a stressful situation is yours and yours alone that your support system can prove to be most necessary in helping you summon up the personal courage to get through it. That others care about us, and are there to listen and to comfort us, can help us feel that our stress-filled situation is not the end of the world. Feeling "anchored" and "grounded" is to feel bolstered by knowing

193

when the world is falling down on your head—and you feel like running out from under it—there will be others you can turn to. And best of all, they won't think any less of you for needing support and comfort at this time.

From family to friends, teachers and coaches, to pets and the face in the mirror, the numbers of those who care about you is, quite possibly, bigger than you may imagine it to be. In this unit you'll have an opportunity to look at how extensive your "support system" is and learn ways in which those who root for you (true taste berries!) can help make the stress and pressures in your life feel less crushing, less potent and less important than they seem.

The more people you have to turn to, and the more you feel connected to these taste berries in your life, the greater the likelihood that you will to turn to them for comfort, support and direction when the chips are down; when the day at hand deals you a bad hand; or when you're simply being too hard on yourself.

Drawing upon the strength of this most valuable and loving asset—your support system of "taste berries"—begins by knowing who is in your camp and on your side. And speaking of taste berries, don't forget to include the person peering back in your mirror! So get your pen and pencil handy; it's time to explore and compile your stress-management team.

Reaching Out: You Don't Have to Go It Alone

Are you going through a tough time right now? Are you facing a situation that feels overwhelming? Are you unsure what to do or who you can turn to for help? Sometimes we face situations that are too overwhelming to go through on our own.

It's important to know that you don't have to face tough situations alone. In fact, you definitely shouldn't! But you may have to be the one to reach out and let others know that you're needing their help. Getting help is an important first step in coping with the stress you are facing. Share what you're going through and ask for the help and support that you need. Fortunately, sixteen-year-old Lara Jesiek did—via the Internet—and connected with Jason, a person who lived more than a thousand miles away. Though they never met in person, Jason was a real help, encouraging Lara to get the help she needed to cope with the stress and challenges she was facing in her life. Find out why Lara dubbed him her "Prince."

My "Prince"

My eleventh-grade year was a really tough time for me. My father's company transferred him from our town in Michigan to a town in Alaska to start a new division within the company. So my family moved to Alaska in August, just before the school year began. In addition to moving halfway across the world, my mother seemed more unhappy than usual. My parents had been having a lot of problems for the last several years, and it seemed like they were always fighting about something. But the move added to the unhappiness my mother was already feeling in her marriage, and after the move, she and I started to argue about a lot of things, too.

But I was unhappy for other reasons: I didn't like my new school, and I really hadn't met any classmates who were good, true friends—or at least not as good as some of the friends I'd left behind in Michigan. Plus, I seemed so far away from the plans I once had of going to a college in my home state of Michigan. Back at my old school, a counselor had helped me plan what courses I needed to take in order to get accepted into the college of arts and letters at Michigan State. So everything I'd worked for in ninth and tenth grade was with that goal in mind. It made working for good grades seem worth it. Now, living in Alaska—where my family would be for God-knows-how-long—if I went to school in Michigan, I would be considered an out-of-state resident, so I'd have to pay out-of-state tuition. Out-of-state tuition is almost double what you pay when you live there, so now going to Michigan State isn't possible for me because I can't afford it. Now I didn't have any idea about where I would go on to school, and worse, I had no desire to figure it out. So whereas before I had a plan where I could see where I would be in a couple of years, now I could no longer envision my future. Without this dream of going to Michigan State, getting good grades seemed pointless.

Everything seemed pointless. And hopeless. My desperation finally got to the point that I attempted suicide.

I took an entire bottle of pills. It was a terrifying experience: The walls began to ripple and the ceiling looked as if it were going to tumble in on me. I couldn't stand, let alone walk. For nearly three hours, hot tears ran down my very burning cheeks. I hurt so badly and felt so sick! Though I didn't die, it did scare me.

I got over the sickness from the pills, and no one ever knew I tried to end my life. My parents just thought I had the stomach flu. I'm sure they never considered that their daughter could ever want to take her life. Nor did they understand how lonely I was. But how could they? I hadn't said anything about the way I was feeling. For the next few months, I went through the motions of life, day by day, always the same. Feeling hopeless. And useless. Nothing mattered. But worse, I didn't know why nothing mattered, and I didn't care. Then one day our family got a computer and online service.

That's when I met my "Prince."

One day an instant message showed up on the screen. "Hello!" it said, "I read your profile and loved it! I see you love Aerosmith! I do, too! Wanna chat?" I replied in a heartbeat! "Yes! My name is Lara. What's yours?"

"Jason. Nice to meet you, Lara!" And that began a friendship so pure and true; it was to be a friendship that genuinely saved my life. For nearly four months we talked online almost daily, and sometimes, though not very often because of the expense, we talked by phone. Jason lived in Pensacola, Florida. The distance between us didn't keep us from "chatting" online nearly every day. We talked about our friends, our parents, our goals and our dreams—everything. We learned so much about each other, every detail, from what we wanted for our lives to our favorite song: Aerosmith's "I Don't Wanna Miss a Thing." Jason e-mailed me poems and stories. He introduced me to books I would never have read if not for the fact that he said they were worth reading. Then, we'd talk about the books, and their philosophy, and what we got out of them. We each shared what we believed—about everything from spirituality to art. We exchanged opinions on politics and even the answer to the world's problems. Other days we'd feel less "deep" and instead share our favorite jokes—or the funniest thing we had ever seen.

Most of all, we told each other precisely what we were feeling and what was going on in the "here and now" of our daily lives. It's funny how someone who you've really just met—even thousands of miles away—can know you better than the people you've known all your life. That's how I felt about Jason. It's funny how sometimes even a face you've never seen can honestly become your very best friend—a friend who can even save your life. Jason saved mine.

At first, having Jason in my life, I didn't feel depressed. But over time my depression returned. Like a shadow that loomed larger and larger, it began slowly and soon shrouded my whole existence once more.

I even contemplated suicide again.

And I told my Jason about it. "No," he said. "I understand life can feel unbearably tough and lonely, but if you reach out, you will find someone who will help you through. Suicide is never the answer. Don't ever, ever think those thoughts again. I'd be sad without you. You make my life bright. I look forward to every day, to every chat we have together." To those who have someone tell them all the time they are loved and wanted, it may sound strange for me to say that I feel lonely. Even though my parents tell me they love me, I am still a girl who feels lonely.

But so much of that went away with Jason in my life. When I thought no one cared or loved me, my "Prince" convinced me someone did. He wasn't there for me in person, like for a hug, but he was a true friend. And while I know that you have to learn to love yourself and want to live for yourself, I've also learned that sometimes the desire to live and even the ability to love yourself can begin with someone else loving you first—like a true friend.

Jason made me promise that I'd never try to take my life again, and he made me promise to get help. I promised him, and I kept that promise. Now I'm seeing a counselor one day each week. The counselor has helped me work through my depression, and like Jason, she encouraged me to reach out to others, too.

Over the past months, I've made new friends at school, friends who I have a lot of fun with and who I can talk to when I'm feeling down or facing something stressful. Through the help of just one friend, I now have many friends. It's awesome how it worked that way.

I credit my "Prince" Jason with saving my life. He is the light that helped me make my way through the dark. It's been about a year and a half since this happened. Jason and I haven't met yet, but one day I know we will. And when I do, I will look him in the eye and tell him he is my best friend!

Lara Jesiek, 18

Royal Treatment—You May Need to Ask for It

Lara kept her pain bottled up for a long time and then, luckily, she decided to stop doing that. Finally, and not a moment too soon, she reached out for help to let someone else know how she was feeling. And that's a first step: Don't keep painful feelings to yourself; don't pretend that everything is all right if it's not.

Six Positive Ways to Cope with Private Pain

Reach out and ask for the help and support you need. Do you know who to turn to? When the stress and strains are simply too big for you to handle alone, consider the following sources. Each can help you alleviate the stress of the inner turmoil and pain you're feeling, and help direct you to the help you need.

1. **Tell your parents.** Even if you think they will be upset, even if you feel you have let your parents down, tell them anyway. After all, your well-being is almost always their

number-one concern, so brave their reaction and know that in the end, your parents usually are the ones who know what's best for you and will do all they can to help you. Once your parents are on board, they can help you see it through to the end.

2. **If you can't tell your parents, confide in someone you trust.** Should you be facing struggles that seem overwhelming, rather than suffer alone or resort to doing things that are self-destructive, confide in a best friend or a trusted adult. This especially applies when facing physical or sexual abuse, suicidal feelings, eating disorders, depression, pregnancy or using drugs or alcohol. Parents, teachers and other professionals (such as school nurses or counselors) were once teens (and many are the parents of teens), so they can understand what it feels like to be unsure of yourself and to have fears and anxieties about coping with life in general. Talking eases the burden and allows you to express your feelings. It's a first step in making the load of stress lighter.

3. **Join a "support group."** Support groups, whether teens helping teens, or adults helping teens, can be an excellent way of coping with the stress and strains of teen life. Be sure to ask your school nurse, counselor or principal if your school provides "Peer Counseling," a program where teens in schools are trained to help teens. Check to see if your school has this program, or a similar one, in place.

4. **Seek the help of a professional counselor.** A professional trained to help those in crisis can help you in troubled times. A counselor will not tell you how to live your life, but he or she can help you learn to handle stress that is simply too big for you to handle alone. Ask your parents or school counselor to help you find one. If you're looking for a counselor without their help, begin by looking in the social services section of the yellow pages for the various agencies

that assist teens. Look for the numbers that refer you to the best source. You can also turn to the Suggested Readings and Suggested Resources sections at the end of this book for sources of support, including hotlines.

5. **Let your faith comfort you.** Faith is a potent source of comfort in times of stress. Whatever your faith, feed your heart and soul by studying the doctrines of your religion and applying their meaning to your life. Believing you can draw on the strength and power of a loving and caring power—especially in your darkest and most stressful moments—is the essence of faith.

6. **Be extra good to yourself.** Especially when life seems particularly stressful, it's time to be extra good to yourself. In addition to getting help from others, get adequate rest, eat properly, and get the exercise your body needs to burn off tension. This is a good time to be patient with yourself, and to do things like practice your relaxation skills, listen to soothing music, talk with your friends and hug your pet. You know what a good person you are to others; be sure to be that for yourself, as well.

VIRTUAL PRACTICE: DO YOU KNOW WHERE TO GO TO GET HELP?

When the stress of life seems overwhelming to you, who are the first three people you would turn to?

1. _____

2. _____

3. _____

Consider that you are or a good friend is facing a stressful predicament such as those listed below. Check off what you would consider to be the best sources of help and support in each.

1. You (or a good friend) suspect you are pregnant. Sources you could turn to:
   ❒ parents
   ❒ Planned Parenthood
   ❒ school nurse
   ❒ family doctor
   ❒ peer counselors at your school
2. You (or a good friend) recently lost a very special someone, a friend, your grandmother, a pet. Sources you could turn to:
   ❒ parents
   ❒ clergy (rabbi, priest or minister)
   ❒ school counselor
   ❒ family doctor
   ❒ peer counselors at your school
3. You (or a good friend) need help saying "No" to drinking or drugs. Sources you could turn to:
   ❒ parents
   ❒ peer counselors at your school
   ❒ school counselor
   ❒ Narcotics Anonymous
   ❒ counseling center at your (or their) mother's or father's place of work
4. You (or a good friend) are having a difficult time with your body image and your weight. Sources you could turn to:
   ❒ parents
   ❒ community weight-loss centers (such as Weight Watchers)
   ❒ school nurse
   ❒ bulimia and anorexia hotline
   ❒ peer counselors at your school
5. You (or a good friend) are always sad. Sometimes, you even think about suicide. Sources you could turn to:
   ❒ parents
   ❒ Alateen
   ❒ suicide prevention hotline

❏ school counselor
❏ peer counselors at your school

Answer key: In each case, all are sources you can turn to! Of course, there are others, too, some of which are listed in the Suggested Readings and Suggested Resources sections at the back of this book. Can you think of any others?

Cool Is Up to You!

Getting the help you need can be the first step when it comes to coping with the stress you are facing. Just because you're growing up doesn't mean you have to have all the answers. Growing up is stressful for everyone; it's okay to say, "I need someone to talk to about this." And then, of course, accept the love and support and use them for your good. Family, friends, professionals and hotlines for teens—all can offer the help and support you need to make it through stressful times. But you're the one who has to let them know you need their support and assistance.

In the following chapters, you'll discover how extensive your support base is and the taste berries who are there for you in stressful times.

21

Family: Members of the "A" Team

"I love you because I know you so well. I love you despite knowing you so well." Have you ever heard or seen this phrase? It's cute—but meaningful, too. Someone who loves you "warts and all" can be a real asset in times of stress! And who knows you better—inside and out—and still loves you through it all— than family members? The members of families are almost always our number-one fans, as well as our first line of defense in weathering stress. While there certainly can be exceptions, no matter how bad things may seem, those who love us are going to be with us through thick and thin, on our side and in our camp—even when things get tough, and even though we ourselves may not necessarily be at our best.

Perhaps the most important way family members help us cope with the stress and strains of life is this: The love we give and get from our families is important to our feeling *wanted, needed and loved*—attributes that in the face of life's stresses and strains shield us from feeling alone, without support, even helpless. And while some families may have poor skills in showing love and support—while others have wonderfully positive skills, such as the Buell family in sixteen-year-old Craig Buell's next story—for the most part, our families have the ability to see us through tough times. It's an important consideration.

Psychologists say that teens who have a strong bond with their families, those who feel "anchored" to family, are better able to cope with stress than those who do not. Of course, this does not mean that families are perfect or that family life is without conflict and some stress and strains of its own. Certainly the stress Craig felt was intense and lasted several years. But his situation illustrates how families each have their own unique qualities and their own set of stressful challenges, and shows that just as families can fall apart under stress, they can also pull together to support each other through tough times and incredible challenges.

It's heartening to learn that the most potent way to combat stress is by developing loving bonds with your family—which is a pretty cool thing to know considering that your family are taste berries on your team—for life!

Anything but Normal

I'd always thought that I wanted to be (or even just feel) a *little* different from others my age, just something to stand apart—at least a little. Maybe I felt this way because I was so like everyone in my school and in my neighborhood. I was just one of your average run-of-the-mill, common kids, just one of the group, an ordinary, normal, regular sort of guy. I thought it was a boring existence. Even my family was the typical, "all-American Family." But then something happened, and suddenly my family was anything but "normal" or "all-American." Though it started with a doctor's prognosis when I was little, it didn't dawn on me that I got my wish to be "a little different" from all my classmates—or anyone my age, for that matter—all in a moment's realization.

I was only five when my mother returned from an eye exam with news that she didn't need glasses; she needed surgery to remove a tumor that was attached to her pituitary gland. Unfortunately, the tumor was the size of a golf ball and could not be totally removed. After her surgery, the doctor advised her to stay in bed for six weeks. During this time, my grandmother came to stay and help my father keep our family's daily life running smoothly. But even with her there, we really missed our mother: We all sort of coped, trying to do for ourselves what our mother had done for us. And we all did our part helping our mother, doing things for her—like taking her meals to her bed and being extra quiet while she was resting so she would get well really soon.

After the sixth week, my grandma left, and each family member took on a little more responsibility to keep things going on as normally as possible. Little by little, Mom did get better, or at least it seemed like she was getting better.

Then, when I was about ten, doctors discovered that the tumor had grown even larger. My mother started radiation treatments to try and stop the tumor from growing, so she wouldn't lose even more of her eyesight. Once again, my grandmother appeared, taking on the role of family caretaker. Once again, we each pitched in to do our part, and hoped our mother would get well—the sooner the better!

But this time, my mother didn't seem to get well—and she just wasn't her usual healthy and happy self. The radiation destroyed her pituitary gland along with, hopefully, the tumor. Now she napped every afternoon and had no energy at night. This was the first time that I realized that there wasn't anything "normal" or "all-American" about my family anymore; feeling terrible was beginning to be "normal" for my mother. Headaches and lack of energy were her most common symptoms, and more and more, there were a lot of little things she could no longer do, like cooking, for example. While my dad took over as head chef, he just can't cook like my mother. No one can cook like my mom, and I really missed all the special things she once made for us—

homemade lasagna, for example! Our family sort of "limped along" (as my dad would say when people asked us how we were doing).

There were other things that were not "normal" as they had once been—like the new ban on all friends coming over to the house, because my mother needed so much rest. It was hard to accept that my house would never be the one where all the kids could come and hang out—like Zach Myers's house, for example. His parents let everyone come over, their doors are always open, and all the kids play pool in his family room—*his* mom even sets out snacks. So while I understood the compromises we made because of my mother's failing health, I resented them, too. There seemed to be no end to them. Even our family's yearly ritual of going away on a trip together, which included everyone getting to vote on where we were going, changed. Now Mom's health was what mattered most. Would she be comfortable? Would it be safe to take her there—was there a hospital or a medical facility nearby (in case she needed emergency care)? Now it was my father—and not my mother—who was "scout leader," a scout master who had to care for my mother as well as us kids. Our family motto: "Ready, set, charge" was replaced by, "Honey, have you taken all your pills?" Yes, there certainly was a change in our family from once "normal" to now "different" than the other families I knew.

Perhaps *memories* of our trips together underwent the most radical change. Where we once took more pictures than we could possibly use to fill the family album, now we took select pictures, and tried not to photograph our mother when she wasn't feeling her best. Of course, her not being in the photo made her absence really noticeable. Some of the photos were so sad to look at that we didn't even show our mother some of them for fear they would make her self-conscience or sad, like some of the ones we took right before this really bad incident last summer. Compounded by the tumor and having forgotten to take her pills that day, my mother suffered heatstroke. Mom was sort of moaning and making no sense, holding her head as she sat on the ground. My dad took all the water bottles we were carrying and dumped them on her head—and then she recovered and sat in the shade. Needless to say, the photos that were taken that day were sad reminders of a time when, once again, someone we loved so much was so sick.

It's been six years since I was ten and my mother began her radiation treatments. Our whole family's life changed so *drastically.* We certainly aren't your typical family anymore. Given my mother's health condition, and given that we all love each other as we do, we keep making the changes that help each of us cope with our lives—like being involved in lots of school activities, having a lot of friends and dating, too—while still taking care of my mother's special needs. There is no doubt that our family will continue to change: Much of our lives and activities are centered around how my mother is feeling, which varies all the time.

But *I've* changed, too. I have a better understanding of life— and what it does and doesn't mean to be "normal." I have to admit that there were times when I was resentful of every- thing—especially my life—revolving around my mother's "health needs." I don't feel that way any longer. She has been an ill woman and a lucky one, too. If my mother continues the treat- ments she needs, though her health may not improve, she will live—hopefully to a ripe old age. So for our family, her health care needs are routine, just "the way it is" and in a word, "normal."

And, I guess you could say I'm "maturing." I've certainly grown into being more understanding and compassionate of my mother's circumstance. Over the last couple years, I've become more aware of the challenges my mother faces with the lack of a pituitary gland, her dependency on drugs and fighting with depression. I know how hard this must be for her. She's the kind of mother who wants the very best for her family, wants to do it all for them, yet her health has made that impossible. I'm sure she tries to keep from us just how hard this has been for her.

And, I've also developed a greater compassion and respect—even honor—for my father. I can see the toll this has taken on him: the stress of trying to manage the household, be both mother and father, and maintain his job is a heavy load to bear. The medical bills have been huge. I know how much my parents love each other and their children, and I know he must work overtime picking up the slack to make sure we kids get the love and care we need. He's worked hard, and he hasn't complained. He's been a great husband and a wonderful dad.

Finally, being a part of all this has helped me deal with the roller coaster of first wanting to be anything but normal to then resenting that I didn't have a "normal, all-American family." But now, I question if "normal" really exists. The more I talk about my family with my friends, the more I learn how many other kids have special circumstances in their families, too. And when I look around at all the other teenagers everywhere, I wonder what kind of hardships or challenges their family has to face. And I wonder how they feel about it. I wonder if they feel left out of life, or accept their situation as "real life."

So if you're someone who has a challenge like mine that you're keeping a secret—maybe because you feel bad that your family is not normal—know that it's probably more normal than you think. If you talk about it with friends, you'll find that you're not alone, and other teens face challenges in their "normal, all-American" families, too. Who knows, maybe some day we will erase the idea of families as "perfect" and look at them in a whole new light—like a place where each member helps each other deal with life, real life. And then, like me, you'll realize that it is the nature of our families and the way each person in it loves and cares for each other (and makes concessions for each other, too) that sets each family apart from others. This is what makes each member special.

So, the next time you look at someone walking up to the front of the room or down the hallway at school, know that even if that person looks like your average sort of person, he or she probably isn't. Know that person has a place in a family and his or her relationship to his or her parents and brothers and sisters and the amount of love that person gets can make a big difference in just who he or she is—whether that person's family is supposedly "normal" or not.

Craig Buell, 16

Is Your Family "Normal"?
Family Hearts and Hurts

While your family may not have the trials that the Buell family has, most all families do have their own set of challenges. Likewise, each family develops its own "language," its own way to show love, affection and connection.

Because we see them every day, and know that we're going to see them again and again each day—because we count on their being there—it's easy to take our relationships with our family members for granted. But we shouldn't. Instead, we should shower as much love and support on each of our family members as we can.

Four Important Ways Family Members Lessen Your Stress—And Make a Big Difference in Your Game of Life

Here are some of the many ways having a good relationship with family lessens stress:

1. **With your family on "your side," the forces of stress seem less significant.** Being a success or failure at school or on the baseball field or with a friend is not the criteria for being welcomed home at the end of the day, for having family members admire you, or for getting (and giving) the love you each need on a daily basis. Even at those times when you've messed up, when you need to "fess up" to something you did that was inappropriate or wrong, you have others in your life who will listen, offer advice and counsel, and support you as you face up to it and come clean. You may be having a really terrible day, but you don't have to depend on that for your sole sense of satisfaction and gratification. You may have failed an important exam, but it's not the end of the world. Having others who love you and care about you and "vote" to have you on the "team" anyway is a great feeling.

   This love, support, advice and comfort during stressful times helps neutralize stress, making it seem less overwhelming.

2. **Parents are your *"fans, not foes,"* a lifeline you can always count on.** Your parents may be easy to get along with, or you may think they are difficult to get along with. You may think of them as fairly lenient in comparison to other parents, or you may think they are overly strict. You may feel it's easy for you to talk with them, or that it's tough to talk with them. For example, it can be scary to tell your parents that you feel in over your head on something—like experimenting with drugs or drinking or even getting bad grades—for fear that they will be upset with you. The truth is, they probably will be upset in the beginning because they may be as overwhelmed and frightened as you. But even if you think they will be upset, even if you feel you have let your parents down, you must tell them anyway. Once they work through their own fears and feelings, they will most always get to work to help you sort things out.

Your well-being is their number-one concern, so brave their reaction and know that in the end, your parents usually are the ones who know what's best for you and will do all they can to help you. Just knowing you are not alone and you have your problem out in the open reduces stress, and once your parents are on board, they will help you see it through to the end. Thousands of teens tell us it is their parents they admire most, it is their parents they turn to first in times of real stress and duress—and their parents don't let them down. What an incredible thing to know. In life, you have a lifeline that you can count on.

3. **Family members root for you—even when your team loses.** Your brothers and sisters may tease and scream at you, but just let outsiders try to do that! Even though at times you may think your siblings were put on the planet to stress you out, in reality they can be strong members of your stress-coping team. For example, you may constantly argue with your brother or sister over who gets to use the bathroom first. (Sometimes you may even wish you were the only child in the family so you could have it all to your-self!) Still, you know that your brothers and sisters would come to your rescue without a moment's hesitation when you really need it. Once again, you know you have a team: You aren't alone in thinking you are simply the best! Others think so, too.

4. **Family offers a place where you're not "on"—a place where you get to be just you.** Poet Robert Frost once said, *"Home is where you go and they have to take you in."* While there's always the exception to the rule, for the most part, family always "take you in." They "forgive and forget" more transgressions than most others are willing to do.

   With family, you get to be who you are—and you'll still belong. There's no struggle to fit in, you are simply a part of the family. You walk into your home after school and you know you don't have to impress anyone. It can really ease the stress of daily life to know there's a place where you will always be accepted as you are. Sometimes this same freedom to be you is also found in the unconditional love and acceptance of extended family members—with grandparents, aunts, uncles and cousins, for example. As part of their family, you are part of them, and so you're accepted as you are. What a comfort this can be when you may often feel pressured by so many expectations to perform in a certain way, to know there are those with whom acceptance is not based on performance. You, just you; with family, it's enough.

VIRTUAL PRACTICE: NAMING YOUR "HOME TEAM"

When our relationship with family is strong, it can be a potent source of good feelings and emotional security (a powerful coping tool in the face of stress). We asked teens to tell us ways in which the members of their family helped them to lessen the stress and strains they felt. Here's what teens Bob Mortola and Garret LaCross had to say.

Bob Mortola, 16, Los Angeles, California

Who: *My stepdad.*

An example of what he did to show me he's on my team: *Yesterday, when I forgot my history paper at home, my stepdad brought it to me at school, even though he had to take time to his leave his office, go home and then drive to my school.*

How that buffered stress for me: *He wasn't angry, and he didn't lecture me about being forgetful. He was concerned that I be able to turn in an assignment I'd worked so hard on in time to get a good grade on it.*

How having a good relationship with my stepdad makes me more resilient to stress: *It makes me feel like I'm not alone with whatever stress I have to face, and it gives me a safe place to go to when I'm feeling overwhelmed.*

Garret LaCross, 14, Denver, Colorado

Who: *My big brother, Ron.*

An example of what he did to show me he's on my team: *At lunch, one of the kids in my class teased me, and everyone who heard it laughed. Then no one asked me to sit with them, so Ron called me over to sit with him and his friends. It made me feel less alone, and because I'm with him, it makes me feel important.*

How that buffered stress for me: *Even though he teases me, when he hears other kids tease me—especially if he thinks they've gone too far with the teasing, and always when they're taunting me—he comes to my defense, my rescue.*

How being in a "good space" with my brother makes me more resilient to stress: *It's just great to know that I have*

someone who looks out for me, because I do get teased a lot.
And, I like the idea that he's a big brother. It's a good feeling.

How about for you? Using the form below, list a member of your family, and describe how you know that person is on "your team." Then, describe how having a good relationship with that person buffers stress for you.

Who: _____

An example of what he/she did to show me he/she is on my team: _____
_____
_____

How that buffered stress for me: _____
_____
_____

How having a good relationship with this person makes me more resilient to stress: _____
_____
_____

Cool Is Up to You!

It's much easier to get through times of stress with your family on your side. Do your part to keep these relationships strong and loving. Not only can they run interference against the blows of stress for life now as a teen, they'll also cheer you on for a long time to come.

When it comes to putting together a winning lineup against stress—and an all-star cheerleading team—besides family, few players rate higher than friends. The next chapter will show you how and why they join your team of taste berries.

22

Friends: On the Team—And the Pep Squad, Too!

While learning to be a part of "the team" begins in the family, it most definitely gets refined in "hanging out" with our friends. Good friends listen to us, hear us out, are there to pal around with and, in general, just enjoy being with us—which is what makes them friends in the first place! Friends who care about you and look out for you make for VIPs (Very Important Persons) when it comes to being members of your stress-management team.

The term *team* is particularly significant when we think of friends. We live in a world with others, and just about everything we do is done in concert with people. We live in families and within communities; we go to school and work with others. We communicate with people on a daily basis. Just as we experience the pleasure, fun and joy of being with others, should they be experiencing disappointment, upset or pain in their lives, we can feel it and be stressed by it, too. Certainly this was true for fifteen-year-old Gina Rivera (in the following story), whose best friend faced a life-threatening crisis—one that caused Gina to examine not only the friendship the two girls shared, but the extent to which she would go in order to help a friend choose victory over the challenge she faced, regardless of whether or not the friend approved.

A Secret Too Big to Keep

Morgan and I have been friends for three years, ever since the seventh grade. We were like sisters. We always called each other every night to decide what to wear the next day, and we always studied together whenever we could. We even chose the same elective classes so we could be together. We shared how we felt about everything from a new rock band to possible college majors. It was the best friendship that anyone could ever hope for. We looked for each other the moment we got to school. We were best friends in every way. Being friends with Morgan was awesome!

Even though we were both only average students, we never missed school. But then Morgan began to miss school, first for a day or two, and then for a couple of days together, and then once for a full week. It worried me, of course, and I really missed seeing her at school. During this time, sometimes she was even too sick to return my call at night, so I knew she was pretty sick. It was such a change from the way things used to be.

Every time Morgan would return to school from being sick, she was still tired and not feeling all that well. Then, she would become sick all over again from too much stress because of an overload of homework and makeup assignments. And she was getting so thin from being so sick. She sure didn't eat very much. At lunch time I was always starved and ate everything on my lunch tray. Morgan picked at her food and always complained she didn't like the food. (Who likes school food, anyway?) But in addition to not liking school food, she said she didn't want to eat it because she was afraid she'd get fat. I thought it was a strange comment given that she was already so thin, but kids are always saying things like that, so I still didn't think too much of it.

It wasn't too much longer when Morgan missed so much school that she dropped out and began a home tutoring program. Because she was so sick, and because we lived a long way away from each other, too long to walk, weeks at a time would go by before I'd see her. Then one Saturday, my parents told me I could have her over for the night so we could be together. We even made plans to go hang out at the mall together the next day, and do some shopping and, you know, the fun stuff of hanging out. I was really looking forward to that weekend; I even crossed off every day on my calendar until that weekend arrived.

When Morgan's parents dropped her off at my house, boy was I in for a surprise! Though she was happy to see me, she looked *soooo* different. There were dark circles around her eyes, and I could see her entire backbone right through her shirt. I never really thought that there was anything *threatening* about her situation until that moment. That's when I suspected that Morgan was anorexic. I was so shocked and so worried, but I didn't say anything that weekend, because I didn't really know for sure what was wrong with her. I didn't want her to be any more self-conscious than she already was, and I sure didn't want her to be mad at me or anything. So at the end of a nice weekend, I still hadn't mentioned her drastic weight loss. And I say a "nice" weekend because she had such low energy, it wasn't like she was her usual self, so we didn't do as much as I'd hoped we would. I mean, things weren't like they used to be. We used to laugh more and be more rambunctious.

I was already concerned for her, but when I saw a show on television about people who suffered from bulimia and anorexia, I got really concerned for my friend. It was at that moment, I realized that if Morgan had anorexia or bulimia, it could kill her. Talk about worry and stress! My friend might actually die.

I didn't know what to do about it. I began to think about all the stress that Morgan must be feeling, too. First of all, she had to be feeling a lot of stress about how she looked—about her weight—if she had taken it to such lengths as starving herself.

Then she had to feel stress about her health—she obviously felt terrible and tired all the time. She couldn't help but stress about that, since she couldn't do all the things she used to do with all her friends. And I knew Morgan, she had always cared so much about her grades—she had to be stressing about doing poorly in school. I mean, she had to be struggling with grades and keeping up in her classes, considering how much school she missed.

I called and called, but she hardly ever returned my phone calls. And when she did, I was too undecided about how to bring up the subject of her getting so skinny that she might be hurting herself. So finally, I decided to write her a letter. It ended up being three pages long, and in it I told her everything I thought she should know about anorexia and bulimia, everything I could remember from the television show. Then, I told her how much I cared about our friendship and let her know that I'd be willing to talk with her about what she was going through. I told her how concerned I was about her health and that I believed she needed to get help. And I told her that I was going to tell my parents and ask them what I could do for her—that even if she was mad at me for telling someone, she was special enough to me for me to do all I could to help get her help.

After reading my letter, Morgan called to tell me that she appreciated how much I care, and that she didn't mean to cause me so much grief. She said that her life was spinning out of control and she was stuck somewhere in the middle, feeling stressed and helpless and alone—until she received my letter.

Well, I'm happy to say that since then, Morgan is getting help for her eating disorder. And though it has been slow, she is getting better. In the last three months alone, she's gained six pounds. And, she's starting to be happy again. All this makes me feel good, or at least better.

I'll never forget how hard it was for me to write that letter, but it changed Morgan's life. I'm glad I was able to be there for her, but she needed more than just my help to deal with her problem.

In the end she needed the help of her parents, a psychologist and her doctor, too. I'm sure Morgan has less stress now; I know I do. It wasn't easy for me to do what it took to see Morgan got that help, but it was worth it. After all, Morgan is a friend—and I'm her friend. That's what friends are for: to be there for each other.

Gina Rivera, 15

Four Ways Friends Create—And Help You Make It Through—Stressful Times

Morgan's condition had to be a very scary and stressful time for her! (No doubt, Gina's friendship with Morgan created a great deal of stress for Gina as well.) You know firsthand that friends—while they're one of the first you turn to in times of stress—are a source of stress as well! Why? Because having friends is one of the most important mirrors we have. Here are four reasons that friends both create some of the stress we feel and can be the antidote to stress as well.

♥ **With friends, we "belong."** To be accepted by others, and to feel as if we belong, supports our natural instincts for self-acceptance—making us feel whole and complete. Having friends means that we are a part of something. This sense of belonging is a powerful contribution to how secure, happy and content we are. The happier we are, the better we weather the strains and pressures of life. And of course, when we feel left out or rejected by friends, well, that's a big source of stress. Losing a friend can be even more devastating. Losing a friend is simply a major loss: A friend offers understanding and acceptance during a time when we struggle to understand and accept ourselves. They like us in spite of our acne, braces, the D- on the quiz—and even that fib we told. How can we possibly navigate life without our friends? As teens, we feel we can't.

♥ **Having friends means we aren't alone.** A big part of the experience of being a teenager is exploring the world, a world spent away from your home and parents, even your own neighborhood. You're out there in school and in life—doing things for the first time and learning to do things your own way. It just wouldn't be fun to do those things all alone, so having someone to do them with is important. A good friend makes these experiences more than just fun; a good friend adds to them in just about every way. Perhaps, most important, in a world that can seem so big and over-whelming, friends offer us the comfort of connection—with friends, we're not in it alone! Walking down the hall in school alone—with all eyes on you—may be okay now and then, but it's an intimidating experience. But when you're walking down that same hall with your friend at your side, well, you just feel like you can take on—or fend off—the whole world.

♥ **Parents love you, but friends help you out; they *share in the experience*.** Friends have the same kinds of situations as you, so they serve as a comparison for you and your life. Friends help each other see if the world looks to others as it does to you—or not. It's confirmation, a baseline by which to gauge how you are doing.

While your parents try their best to help you with things, often it's your friends who best help you understand the situation at hand, and dissect the experience you are dealing with. They're going through the same problems, so each knows how the other feels inside.

While parents offer love, protection and direction, they sometimes can't relate to what a teen is going through as well as his or her friends can. Teenagers don't need or love their parents less than they do their friends, it's just a different kind of need and love. For example, take preparing for SATs: A teen's parents can provide encouragement, saying things like, "Let's get you some tutoring," or "You'll do just great," or "Don't worry, just do the best you can." But your friends will say, "Let's cram together Saturday, okay? You can help me with algebra; I'll help you with English." And your friends are apt to confess, "My stomach's been in knots for days just thinking about it!" or offer real words of camaraderie such as "I'm sure I bombed. How do you think you did?"

It's the "I know what you're going through," and the "I'm just as scared (or confident) as you are." The feedback of friends seems more real and authentic—because friends are right there with you. Times of stress are shared in this way, and the stress is lessened.

♥ **Through thick or thin, friends are "there for each other."** Friends listen to each other, are there for each other, comfort and console one another, and see each other through the rough times. Sometimes this means keeping each others' secrets, big and small, having someone who sees you at the top of your game and at your very lowest. No matter what, a good friend is willing to loan you his or her heart without judgment, without bias. So having a friend means you will receive this invaluable support and direction when you're faced with stress—or not.

VIRTUAL PRACTICE:
WHO AMONG YOUR FRIENDS "MAKES OR BREAKS" STRESS FOR YOU?

Wow! Having friends is pretty important! With so much at risk, no wonder friendships—making, keeping or losing—are stressful. Are your friends real "members of your team"? In

identifying those friends who are "on your team," it can be helpful to first think through questions such as:

- ♥ Who is always "there" for me?
- ♥ Who listens to me when I just need to talk?
- ♥ Who can I talk to, about anything and everything, and
  know for sure they won't share what I've told them with
  anyone else?
- ♥ Who really cares about me and wants what is best for me?
- ♥ Who makes me feel better when I'm feeling down?

This next exercise can help you assess which of your friends
you could turn to in times of stress. We asked Morgan (from the
story at the beginning of this chapter) to complete this exercise,
too, and we've provided it here as an example.

Friend: *Gina Rivera*

How do I know she/he is on my team? *Gina did all she could
to see I got the help and support I needed to get back on track
with my health. Not only did she tell me how worried she was
about me, she talked to her mother and the school nurse,
which I know couldn't have been easy for her.*

How my friend helps me cope with stress: *Gina listens, she
gives me good advice, she will always tell me the truth. Because
of her, I got the help I needed.*

Who among your friends would you name to your stress-management team? Using the form below, name one and tell how he or she helps you weather the stress and pressures in your life.

Friend: _____

How do I know he/she is on my team? _____

_____

_____

How my friend helps me cope with stress: _____

_____

_____

Cool Is Up to You!

There will always be times when your life feels bombarded by stress. Having friends who are there for you to help you work things through—even by just being a listening ear—is a real source of support when dealing with a tough issue or stressful time. It's easy to take friends for granted. Try not to. Friends, good friends, are a real asset; be sure to be considerate of their feelings. If you want to have friends, be one. Like the proverb says, "To have a friend, you have to be a friend."

So how big is your team anyway? Most teens probably don't think it's as extensive as it really is. In this next chapter, you'll discover that your support system may be larger than you think it is—which is always cool to know! Learn just who those players (taste berries) are, and what positions they play. And something else that's good to know: Your team can be as big as you want it to be!

23

Anchors, Mentors and Role Models: How Extensive Is Your Stress-Management Team?

The love and support of family and friends are a real help when it comes to coping with the stress and strains of life. An old adage, "1 + 1 = 3" implies that the synergy of two—which is the connection and combined power and strength of two genuinely caring hearts—can be a real plus. This heartfelt energy and knowing that others are willing to be there for us not just with the tough times, but also with helping move us forward towards positive goals and growth, is a solid feeling; we are not alone in the big playing field of life. Others care and are willing to go out of their way to do good for us. We are "connected."

Whether we call them teachers, coaches or mentors, they connect us to the world at large. This connection is one way we feel "powerful," cared about and worthy. This positive stroke of respect and attention is yet another way we learn that even when life dishes out curveballs, there are those willing and able to coach us on what we must do to not strike out. What a help.

Most all of us have "team members" who do this for us, whether mentors, promoters, anchors or role models. How fortunate: Their confidence and encouragement empowers us and can help make our "world" seem larger and more expansive—a feeling that makes some of the normal stress and strains in our lives seem small, mundane and trivial. Jennifer Newman, in the story below, tells us how much it meant to her to have a coach who felt her chances of doing poorly were "one in a million." Having team members who make you feel like you are "one in a million" is sure to be a win in your life, most especially as you go about the game of life.

One in a Million

I'd never been so eager to arrive home as I was that day two years ago when my family returned from our two-week vacation. It was a great vacation, but I was glad to be home. Everything familiar to me put a smile on my face, particularly the answering machine. It seemed as if just about all of my friends had called. I couldn't wait to tell my friends everything I had done on my vacation! Then came Krista's voice. She's one of my best friends on my gymnastics team. "Jen, I have something important to tell you, some bad news. Call me back soon!" She didn't say what the bad news was, but from the tone of her voice, I figured it had to be bad, really bad, more than being grounded for the next year, worse than breaking up with Tommy Smitts, worse than a fight with a best friend.

I called Krista right away. The minute she heard my voice, she began to cry. "Something terrible has happened," she sobbed. I thought that something had happened to our best friend, Ashley. "Please just tell me! What happened?" I pleaded. That was when Krista informed me that our coach, Mr. Ryan, had been killed in a motorcycle accident.

I was stunned. I could not believe what I was hearing. I could not imagine someone like Coach Ryan dead—he still had so much more to offer the world. Besides, he was too young to die.

The next few days were probably the toughest of my life. Even as I gathered details about the funeral, I couldn't make myself believe it. It just didn't seem right. And nothing could be more wrong than someone as good as my coach being killed in a senseless motorcycle accident.

Anyone who ever met Coach Ryan agreed he was the Coach of the Millennium. I mean, he was so awesome! He really, really cared about those he coached, and everyone knew it. It's one of the many reasons that he was so well liked by everyone in the community, and most especially, everyone in the gymnastics community. Co-owner of Le Club Gymnastics and a team coach, gymnastics was his life. Maybe that's why I admired him so much. It was always apparent that Coach Ryan enjoyed his life and what he did. He had a special coaching style that was unlike any other. Rather than being a strict dictator—as was the case with my first gymnastics coach—Coach Ryan acted as both a friend and second father to the entire team. Just being around him improved my life and my gymnastics so much. Whenever I would get discouraged and wail, "I'm not going to make it—I'm going to lose!" Coach Ryan would pump me up by saying, "Never! You're so good; why your chances of losing are one in a million." Something about his confidence in me completely turned my own doubts in myself around. I was sure one day I'd compete in the Olympics because of him.

Now, besides being filled with grief, I wondered how I would be able to complete my training for the regional finals, let alone actually compete or win without him. Never again would I hear his supportive voice, pushing me beyond what I thought I could do. Never again would I reach yet another new level with his help. Never again would he be there to cheer me up with his not-so-funny jokes that always made me laugh. It seemed unreal. Unfair. Impossible.

I couldn't make myself go to gymnastics practice for a full week after the funeral. But I knew I couldn't stay away forever. And I also knew that it was precisely because of him, and because of the way I honored him, that I had to go on. I had to make him proud. I had to show the world what he had taught me. I had to compete because of Coach Ryan. So in spite of my heavy heart, I returned to the gym. I knew that it wasn't going to be easy to go back to where most of my memories with him occurred, but I understood that I would have to deal with it sometime.

When I reached the gym, I took a deep breath, promising myself that I'd make him proud. Going back was hard, especially when I first walked in. Though everyone was stretching and warming up as usual, it was evident that something drastic and terrible had happened, because there was a completely different aura inside the gym. To begin with, no one wanted to look anyone directly in the eyes, because each of us was afraid that if we did we would end up crying. But it was hard not to cry for other reasons as well. There were so many reminders. The most glaring was the immensely empty space of Coach Ryan. For some reason, the wall filled with photos of the various teams—and champions—he'd coached over the years loomed especially large, as did the huge case of trophies and plaques that graced the walls. Coach Ryan kept a box to hold sweatbands, hair clips and other things needed by his "coachlings" as he would sometimes refer to us. Each of us would make a beeline to the box as we came in, hoping a missing barrette, headband or sweatband had found its way there. Today the box was empty of things—it seemed to mirror the emptiness that his absence left in my heart. Even though each of us gymnasts received a lot of comfort and hugs from his assistant coach, who had now taken over, it just wasn't the same in the gym without Coach Ryan. And I could tell that everyone else felt the same way. It wasn't the cheerful place I once loved and couldn't wait to get to. I spent the whole first practice teary-eyed, and so all did all the other gymnasts.

I knew that things would never be exactly the same at Le Club Gymnastics, nor would they ever be the same in my life. I also knew one other thing: I was not only going to continue with the sport of gymnastics, I was going to put my heart and soul into it as Coach Ryan would have wished. It was what he would have dreamed for me, and I was going to dedicate this season to winning—and my career in this field—in *his* honor. And it was my honor to do this, because as a coach and as a person, Coach Ryan was definitely one in a million.

Jennifer Newman, 16

The 1 + 1 = 3 Principle:
Are These 7 Players on Your Team?

Jennifer Newman's story makes it clear how important mentors can be in our lives. As she describes her relationship with Coach Ryan, it's easy to see how he helped Jennifer feel stronger, more capable and able to cope with the challenges and stress in her life—on and off the gymnastic bars.

It's important to take stock of those who clap and root for you. Knowing who is on your team can give you the added confidence you need to victoriously face the stress of your day—be it the stress of a crisis or of your day-to-day challenges.

Take a moment to think about:

♥ Who encourages me?
♥ Who helps me dream bigger than I might otherwise dream on my own?
♥ Who helps me stretch the expectations I hold for myself?
♥ Who nudges me to set worthy goals?

In answering these questions, most teens discover yet another group of players on their side. And, quite often, they find this "team" much greater, much larger, than they ever imagined. But, if we look closely, we will find this seven-member team: anchors, mentors, role models, challengers, recommenders, promoters and experts.

VIRTUAL PRACTICE:
WHO'S ROOTING FOR YOU?

We sometimes underestimate how large the base of people who support and clap, root and cheer for us really is. Who, besides your family and friends, is in your "camp" and on your side? Below are seven categories of those who provide support and a show of being on our side and in our camp. List the names of those who fit in each of the categories and describe ways they demonstrate support for you. (Don't be surprised if several names show up more than once; if they do, you know those people are *really, really* on your side!)

Anchors: These people make you feel centered, grounded, valued—you have a significant bond or "ties" with them. When your heart needs to turn to someone who you know loves you unconditionally—perhaps someone such as your grandmother—who would *you* turn to? Who is your number-one "anchor," and how does he or she demonstrate being on your side?

Who: _____

An example of what he/she did to show support: _____

_____

How I know he/she is rooting for me: _____

_____

Mentors: These people take an interest in you and offer you guidance. They provide you with opportunities and try to "teach you the ropes." Was there a particular someone you asked if you could "shadow" for your school's career day—and that person was happy to have you do that? Who is your number-one "mentor," and how does he or she demonstrate rooting for you?

Who: _____

An example of what he/she did to show support: _____

How I know he/she is rooting for me: _____

Role Models: These people have achieved what you hope to achieve yourself one day; they are your heroes. Because of them, you can look at how they achieved their goals and learn how to do the same for yourself. Maybe you'd like to work for NASA, and so you are fascinated by astronaut Steve Smith's career path. Or, maybe you'd like to be a professional athlete and Gabriela Reece is your idea of an all-around pro athlete. Who is your number-one "role model," and how does he or she demonstrate rooting for you?

Who: _____

An example of what he/she did to show support: _____

How I know he/she is rooting for me: _____

Challengers: These people cause you to look at the things you are doing, and the direction you are going in life. They encourage you to face some important questions about your own life. Has a teacher ever encouraged you to "believe in yourself," or a youth counselor witnessed the importance of actively living your faith? Who is your number-one "challenger," and how does he or she demonstrate rooting for you?

Who: _____

An example of what he/she did to show support: _____

_____

How I know he/she is rooting for me: _____

_____

Recommenders: These are the people who advise you of opportunities and encourage your visibility. Has anyone ever recommended you for a part-time job or some sort of responsibility that could be beneficial to you? Did you have an English teacher who said something like, "You're a good writer. You should enter the *Reader's Digest* Teen Writing Contest. I'm giving you a copy of the entry form"? Who is your number-one "recommender," and how does he or she demonstrate rooting for you?

Who: _____

An example of what he/she did to show support: _____

_____

How I know he/she is rooting for me: _____

_____

Promoters: These people think you're tops. They brag about you and promote you to others. Have you ever heard through the "grapevine" that a particular someone said you were a person who is "smart, dependable and an all-around good person"? Who is your number-one "promoter," and how does he or she demonstrate rooting for you?

Who: _____

An example of what he/she did to show support: _____

_____

How I know he/she is rooting for me: _____

_____

Experts: These people have expertise, information and "smarts" in key areas that are important or usable to you. Have you ever called upon a particular person to teach or advise you when you did a specialized project, such as your school's History Day or Science Fair competition? Who is your number-one "expert," and how does he or she demonstrate rooting for you?

Who: _____

An example of what he/she did to show support: _____

_____

How I know he/she is rooting for me: _____

_____

Cool Is Up to You!

Mentors, anchors, experts, promoters or role models and more—do you feel empowered just thinking about how many people are there to broaden your world and help you maneuver through the maze of it? Most teens do. Those who are in our lives and root for our well-being are real taste berries. How lucky we are to have them.

And yet, of all those who are there for you through thick and thin, the very most important person is *you*. In this next unit, you'll get an opportunity to see how managing life and its ups and downs begins with the fundamental basics: caring for yourself in ways that keep you healthy and fit. Up to now, maybe your health and wellness have been primarily the responsibility of your parents, but now it's up to you. Caring for your mind, body and soul is not only the most important thing you can do, but perhaps one of the biggest jobs you'll ever have. Not to worry, this next unit will give you a heads-up in self-care that is sure to help you ward off stress and is sure to give your self-esteem a real boost: What could be better for self-reputation than a thumbs-up that you are your number-one taste berry!

Part 7

Prevention and Intervention Skills: Great Ways to Take Care of Yourself

*It's better to look ahead and prepare
than to look back and regret.*

—Jackie Joyner-Kersee,
Olympic Track-and-Field Champion

24

A Message from the Authors

Dear Adam,

 We know that you are going through a lot of stress right now and hurting too much to know the right thing to do. But drinking and using drugs is really not helping, and is only making things worse. We're sorry that our trying to "talk some sense into you" the other day turned into a yelling match; we were only trying to get you to see how self-destructive drinking and drugs are to your coping with your life. We want you to know we are not down on you, and that we just want you to be okay. So many people care about you, even though it may seem like they've given up hope that you'll be the same person we once knew and liked so much. We want you to know we're here for you, and we hope you'll take better care of yourself. We want our Adam back.

Your good friends,
Tommy L., Candi M., Tara S.

Adam Harris is really fortunate to have friends like Tommy, Candi and Tara. Surely their friendship and support mean a lot to him, especially at a time when he's in such a frightening crisis. But in addition to the friendship and support of his friends— and their plea that he get some help—Adam will have to choose this, too. Just as you want others to be supportive of you, especially when going through stressful times, you've got to want to take care of yourself, as well. Up to now, your parents and teachers and other adults have looked out for you and your well-being. But you're a teenager now and growing wise enough to assume much of the responsibility for your well-being—especially as it relates to eating nutritiously, getting the rest and exercise you need, and doing those things that help you become a caring and competent person.

A large part of assuming responsibility means taking charge. It means that you can count on yourself to make the right and best choices for all the things that are a part of your life. For example, maybe you've been in the habit of doing things only when pressed to do them, such as starting on your homework or assigned family chores *only* when reminded (for the second time)! Taking care of yourself means that you no longer have to be told to get your homework done. After all, you know that if you don't, the next day you are not going to be prepared for your work (school) day. You see, taking care of yourself is a "bigger and better" idea than saying, "Gosh, if I don't get my homework done, my parents and teachers will be upset with me." Now that you're a teenager, you can take charge of your life in many ways. One of them is to take good care of yourself—and not always make it someone else's responsibility for overseeing that you do.

Taking care of yourself. What does that mean? We asked teens. Here are twelve things they listed as among the most important.

1. **Take good care of your body.** Don't take risks that could put your safety and your health in jeopardy (such as using drugs and alcohol).

2. **Take good care of your mental health.** Don't let the opinions and comments of others be more important than how you feel about yourself. Take care of your self-esteem; believe that the image (reputation) you hold of yourself is more important than what others think of you. No one else knows you as you know you, so believe in yourself. Treat yourself with respect, and as though you are your own best friend.

3. **Think about *your* life, and what you want out of it.** Don't think that your life just happens to you, and that you have no control over anything in it. Think about what you want, and make a plan and go for it. Why waste your life; why act like you are powerless to do anything for yourself?

4. **Don't be thrown off by life's daily ups and downs.** Accept that a certain amount of confusion and turmoil are common to everyone at all ages—even for those teens around whose lives appear to be "all roses." We all, at one time or another, feel unsure of ourselves, confused and even a little lost. These times pass. When times are tough, take extra good care of yourself. And don't forget to reach out for help if you need it.

5. **Make choices consistent with values you know to be good and right, those you can be proud to stand up for.**

6. **Find out who you are and what makes you tick.** Learn about yourself—your personality, your talents and what makes you happy.

7. **Set worthy goals and strive to achieve them.**

8. **Practice your faith.** Faith is about the timeless truths and provides leadership to your heart and soul—the core of your being.

9. **Learn all you can, about all that you can.** Read broadly and expose yourself to great minds. This allows you to examine your own assumptions, and to check your biases. Keep an open mind.

10. **Be respectful, considerate and friendly to others.** Accept differences. We are each making our way through life the best way we know how. We are all learning as we go. No one has the "only way." We are doing the best we can with what we have.

11. **When you screw up, admit it, apologize and then forgive yourself.** You will find others are willing to cut you some slack, especially if you are good-natured and courteous—so be sure to do this for yourself. It's only natural that sometimes you'll mess up. When this happens, admit it, talk about it, apologize for your shortcomings, and then vow to do better. Then let go and move on.

12. **Talk to others about how things are going for you.** Sharing things with others can not only lighten the load of the stress you're feeling, but help you see that everyone has tough times. When you talk about how you—and they—got through things, you'll feel better about yourself and be more confident in getting through the next "crisis"—and there will be others.

We think these twelve suggestions are insightful, and good advice. Certainly they are very important in your goal to minimize—even prevent—the normal stress and pressures of life. In this next unit, you'll learn other ways to take care of yourself so that you are at your best. All are important in your goal to be loving and caring to the number-one taste berry in your life—you.

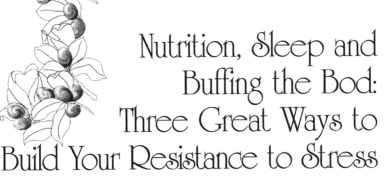

Nutrition, Sleep and Buffing the Bod: Three Great Ways to Build Your Resistance to Stress

As powerful and durable as the body is, it also a very sensitive and delicate machine. If you fuel it with all the nutrients it needs to keep running, it will hum right along with the schedule you keep. But if you fail to give it the nutrition it needs, it won't perform at peak efficiency. For example, if you give it an extra dose of pasta, its gears shift into slow, very slow; give it an extra dose of sugar, and its gears shift into high—as in, running out of control.

If you provide your body with the rest it needs, it will restore itself day after day, for years on end. If you fail to give it the sleep it needs, it will be sluggish, and may even go to sleep while on the job. It you give it more sleep than it needs, it may also be sluggish and unwilling to "get going." If you keep all its delicate and intricate parts in working order—via exercise—it will stay in top form and amaze you with its strength and energy. If you fail to give it the exercise it needs, it will be lazy and weak.

The body is an amazing machine—one that is also sensitive to stress, as seventeen-year-old Becca Chang—and her favorite uncle—discovered.

Shadow Day

My parents had a family gathering for my sixteenth birthday. My aunt and uncle—who live in the same town as we do—came, which made me really happy. I like them a lot. At the dinner table, my uncle made a comment about how busy and hectic—and stressful—things were in his office. "I've got so many projects going on," he commented, adding, "It's a very busy time. Very stressful."

"Sounds like my life!" I commented. "It's really stressful, too."

"*Your* life stressful," he commented while chuckling, and then asked, "What can possibly be stressful about your life?"

"Plenty!" I remarked.

"Oh, please!" he teased. "You don't have to go to work every day, and you don't have to deal with managing people, like I do."

"Yes, I do," I reminded him. "I go to work every day; it's called school. And, I deal with people every day, too. They're called teachers and classmates."

"Well, that's different," he said. "You don't have the pressures of real-world things, like you don't have to pay bills. You don't have to worry about taxes. You don't have to buy your own food, or cook it for that matter. I mean, what can possibly be stressful about going to school and hanging out with your friends? I'd love to have your life! I'd love being a carefree teenager again. I'd trade you positions any day."

I couldn't believe that my uncle thinks there's no stress in my life—because I'm a teen! Gosh, you'd think it were a thousand years since he's been a teenager, because all my friends feel as I do, that being a teenager is a very stressful time of life. From the minute the alarm clock goes off in the morning, I'm on the run. The buzzer sounds and in a matter of what feels like seconds, I rush to take a shower, get dressed and eat breakfast, and all the while, my head is overwhelmed with thoughts of organizing and managing the busy day ahead of me. There's almost always a paper that's due, or a test of some kind to face. Meeting deadlines is a way of life. Always there are a million things to do, every day, and everything is so urgent. And I do "manage people": I see six teachers (because I take six classes each day); there's my counselor, the school principal and vice-principal, classmates, friends. While I don't interact with the principal and vice-principal and counselor every day, on some days I do. But everyone else is in my life every hour, practically every minute.

When I get home from "work," all I want to do is watch television and relax—which I often do, but it's not like I get to be brain-dead when I do because I have some family chores I'm responsible for doing each day after school. Then, of course, I always have homework. After hours of studying for history tests, doing algebra problems and writing comparative essays—or whatever happens to be the night's homework—I finally fall into bed, only to wake up and do it all again the next day.

So when our school had a "Shadow a Teen for a Day" project, you can bet that I asked my uncle to be my guest to go with me on every little minute of that day. I was pretty excited when he said, "Sure," like it was going to be a great break for him to not have to be at his office for the day.

I'm not exactly sure what he envisioned the day would be like, but when he showed up school that day—with his cell phone in hand "to return a few calls between classes" and with a few business papers "to read when there's nothing else to do"—I knew he really didn't have any clue what a day in my life was like—or his on that day!

My uncle loved sitting next to me in homeroom. He just beamed. He looked pretty cute, too, sitting there in his blue jeans, "Go Navy" sweatshirt and old sneakers. He looked a bit nerdy, but I didn't tell him. I was happy he was there with me.

And, of course, I knew the day would change his mind about my having an easy, carefree life.

I could tell by the beam on his face that my uncle also enjoyed my first-hour class, history. While he listened to the teacher's lecture, he also thumbed through the book, really absorbed by some parts of what he saw there. But by the end of second hour, math, he was more somber. "Sure wished I'd paid a little more attention to math when I was in school," he commented as we walked to my third-hour class. I felt a little lost in that class today!"

By the end of third hour (Spanish II), well, let's just say my uncle looked pooped. It was only 11:30 A.M. when he announced, "I've got a throbbing headache." At 1:30 P.M. he said to me, "You know, sitting this long and listening so much is tiring. I need to get up and walk around a bit. Too bad that's not allowed in class." Then, while we were eating lunch in the cafeteria, my uncle asked, "Is the girl that's looking at me and laughing, laughing at me? How can you tell? I mean, I hope she doesn't think your uncle isn't with it, you know, on top of things."

"Relax, Uncle Bob," I said. "Well, she did giggle when in math I had to work out the answer to a question by figuring it out on paper rather than in my head." But if my uncle felt self-conscious then, he probably was embarrassed when in fifth-hour class the teacher called on him and asked him the name of the Secretary General of the United Nations, and he didn't know the answer. Looking horrified, my uncle looked at me and whispered, "I should have known that! I feel dumb, especially with everyone watching me!" By sixth hour I could tell he'd just about had enough. Looking at his watch, he asked, "How much more of this is there? I'm hungry, tired and whipped!"

At the end of the school day, my uncle admitted that maybe life as a teen isn't such a breeze at all. "This has been one of the longest and most stressful days I've had in a while," he commented and then pleaded, "Can I go now?"

"Sure," I told him. "I'm on my way to a job interview. I'm trying to get a part-time job at the video store."

"I honestly don't know how you manage," he said.

"Thanks for coming, Uncle Bob," I said to him. "And by the way, don't forget to do the homework you've been assigned."

"I'm leaving that to you!" he replied. "I've decided I'd rather have my job than yours!"

"Thought so!" I said, waving good-bye to him as he left.

So now my uncle knows that my life may resemble life in his office: intense and hurried—and a lot of work, not to mention that mine includes mounds of homework when I get home (and if I get the part-time job, there'll be some work hours, too). Thanks to the "Shadow a Teen for a Day," my uncle knows first-hand what real stress is like.

Becca Chang, 17

Do you, like Becca, wish you could convince someone that your life is as stressful as you find it to be? Or like her uncle experienced, so stressful that he succumbed to a headache? As Becca knows—and her uncle discovered—there is no such thing as a stress-free life. Going to school, dealing with friends and teachers, homework and part-time jobs—all are just a few ways that teen life makes for stressful times. But while you can't prevent stress, there are things you can do to be at your best so that you are as prepared as you can be. Eating nutritious foods, getting adequate exercise and rest head the list.

Food Is the Body's Fuel:
Three Ways "High Octane" Combats Stress

Eating nutritiously is your body's best and first line of defense in combating stress. What you eat affects your moods, energy level, how you feel, think and make decisions—all important to dealing with pressure-filled situations.

Nutrition can sometimes seem like a not-so-important, even a "ho-hum" issue. I mean, if you select the burger instead of the salad at lunch, you aren't going to collapse on the floor, right? And it can be difficult to connect eating healthy foods with whether or not that special someone is going to ask you to the dance, right? Still, there is a definite relationship between what you eat and how you handle the stress of when that special someone asks you out, or when he or she doesn't—to say nothing of how you handle all those stress-filled moments waiting to see which it will be.

The expression, "you are what you eat," has a lot of merit when it comes to coping with the demands of stress. Here are three ways nutrition is related to how you cope with stress.

1. **The way you fuel your body—the foods you eat—has a definite effect on how you feel (calm, energized, tired, irritable, sluggish, even hyper) and thus how you are able to cope with your day.** As an example, have you ever only eaten a couple of sugar-coated donuts for breakfast? You probably felt an initial burst of hyper-energy from all the sugar, but by lunchtime your energy was no doubt dragging. A stressful situation demands your attention and if you aren't up for it, you won't bring your best efforts to confrontation and resolution. Whether in the middle of a hyper-energy sugar rush or an energy-zapped droop, you won't be at your best in coping with the stress at hand.

   Let's say you're coping with the usual agenda of a million-and-one things to do, plus the excitement of being with friends, keeping up with the demands of school and the like, and then let's toss in an unexpected stressor—like an upset with a best friend, a flat tire or a pop quiz. If you're feeling good and up for the day, chances are, while being inconvenienced and throwing your day off schedule, you're not likely to go into a stressed-out frenzy or crash into tears. What's more, you'll be able to think clearly so you can better figure out solutions to the problem at hand. If you haven't adequately fueled your body—let's say you're on a sugar high or drooping, then you're not going to do too well with this added strain. You may even end up *creating* more problems with your stress-induced reactions.

2. **When you're under stress, you need your body to cope with the physical demands you make on it.** When the body is deprived of essential nutrients, it doesn't function as it should (such as having a good energy supply). This means you'll be less capable of withstanding the effects of stress—not to mention less capable of keeping up with your schedule. Health and nutrition experts say teen girls need about 2,500 to 2,700 calories a day, and that teen boys need about 2,800 to 3,000 calories daily—just to meet the demands of a growing body. But there is quite a distinction between a "good calorie" and an "empty calorie." If your 3,000 calories come from candy bars, this will not meet your body's need to run efficiently. Nor will it help you withstand the effects of stress.

In all, your body needs about forty-seven different nutritional substances to sustain itself. Vegetables, whole grain or enriched cereals and breads, a form of protein (such as beans and lean meat) and milk all help the body function properly. Medical experts and nutritionists agree that eating a balanced diet is the best way to get the proper mix of nutrients. (A diet that emphasizes one type of food—whether proteins, vegetables or carbohydrates—to the exclusion of other foods is harmful to the body because it deprives the body of the balance it needs to function efficiently.)

3. **Brain cells, like the rest of the body, require proper feeding in order to function correctly.** The brain is the body's most chemically sensitive organ. When deprived of proper nutrients, the brain cannot perform at peak efficiency. Too much sugar or vitamin deficiencies can seriously disrupt the brain's ability to function normally and effectively.

   Remember the goal: Use food to help your body be at its best. When you're facing a stressful time, such as a really big exam or semester finals, or you're trying out for the tennis team, or today is the day you really must break up (or make up) with someone, start your day with a high-energy breakfast and then feed it nutritious foods throughout the day. If your "stress attack" exam starts at 2:00 and you're not only tired but famished, eat a high-energy bar or a piece of fruit. If your energy is flagging, rather than grabbing a bag of cookies or chips from the dispenser, buy an energy bar or bag of nuts instead.

   The important thing is to eat foods that will feed your growing body, as well as provide energy to sustain your activities and help you manage the stress and pressures of life.

Five Stress-Busting Benefits of Exercise

The powerful machine that it is, the body needs exercise to stay strong and run efficiently. One obvious benefit of exercise is having buffed muscles, but exercise is also extremely important in helping you buffer the effects of stress. Here are five ways exercise can help you become more resilient to stress:

1. **Exercise relaxes nerves and balances emotions.** Have you ever gone for a jog or a bike ride when you're feeling really stressed-out and tense? If you have, chances are you noticed that you felt much more relaxed afterwards. That's because exercise burns off pent-up stress, and therefore, relaxes nerves, which in turn, balances emotions.

2. **Exercise increases your intake of oxygen, which improves your (physical and mental) alertness.** This in turn, helps you think more clearly—and, of course, the more clearly you can think, the better you are able to deal with stress. One way to get the type of workout that will increase your oxygen in this way also happens to be a great way to burn off the tension of stress—aerobic exercise. "Aerobic" means a level of activity that requires you to exert a good deal of effort, but doesn't consume oxygen faster than your heart and lungs can supply it. In keeping our bodies working efficiently and effectively on the inside, experts recommend three sessions of vigorous activity weekly, with each session lasting from twenty to thirty minutes. (You will be pleased to know that even a twenty- or thirty-minute impromptu game of basketball— or dancing—can provide the exercise you need to burn off stress and increase your oxygen levels.)

3. **Exercise heightens your energy level.** When you're feeling fatigued, it's more difficult to cope with stress. Exercise can help chase away fatigue because, while exercising burns energy, it also restores it. Have you ever been in a slump at school—just so tired you'd like to go home and forget your last-period class—when a friend comes along and starts a game of tag with you, and presto! After even a few minutes, you find your fatigue has evaporated and you're magically invigorated.

4. **Exercise improves your sense of well-being.** When you exercise, not only are you getting endorphins (our bodies' own mood lifters), but you're also doing something good for yourself: Between the increase in your body's endorphins and the added oxygen to your brain, you'll notice a sense of well-being. When you feel good about yourself and your life, those things that might otherwise stress you out seem less threatening, less looming, less "do or die."

5. **Exercise improves your quality of sleep.** You've gone hiking with friends and had a great workout; that night you crawl under your covers and get the best night of sleep you can imagine. Exercise actually helps you get a good night's sleep. When your body has had the rest it needs, you are more likely to find effective ways to cope with it—rather than to feel so overwhelmed by it that it simply debilitates you. Getting the sleep that you need helps set you up for your best coping possibilities; in short, you'll do better managing it effectively.

The good news is that there are all kinds of ways to get a good workout, and that can be interesting, even fun. From playing sports at school to working out at the fitness center; from running to in-line skating (or Rollerblading); from kick-boxing to dancing—all qualify as exercise and build your resilience to stress. It's nice to know you're not limited to jumping jacks; you can dance to your favorite CD while watching TV! Now that's not a hardship! Then, after spending all that energy, you'll have an even greater reason to chill and relax (which is also an important tool in keeping your cool when stressed).

Stressed-Out? Dream On:
Stress and Your Zzzzz's

Does the subject of getting all the sleep you need sound like information that would put you to sleep? It shouldn't. Sleep is so vital to your well-being that you can't function without it. Besides waking up fresh the next day and being able to handle things, like coping with the stress and pressures on a daily basis, here are three reasons that getting enough sleep is so important:

1. **A rested body is key to being alert and on top of things.** Have you ever found yourself to be too tired to be patient and sort things out? If so, did you make things worse by

ignoring the problem, or overreact, all because you were tired and not at your best? Health experts say that teens need between eight and twelve hours of sleep to maintain the intense stage of growth and development. Consider in addition to the demands of a growing body the toll of stress in coping with teen life!

2. **Sleep is your body's recovery period.** During sleep your muscles relax, your breathing and heart rates decrease, and your body temperature drops slightly. This recovery period primes your body to withstand stress. But not all sleep is the same.

   There are actually two different types of sleep: non-rapid eye movement (NREM) and rapid eye movement (REM). This sounds complicated, but it really isn't. In NREM, the "best sleep," your eyes move very little and your body reaches its state of deepest relaxation. NREM has four stages, each stage taking the body into a deeper and deeper phase of sleep, the last of these phases offering the body its best rest (primarily because the muscles in your entire body are most relaxed). Because it is during a state of deep relaxation that the body renews itself, the NREM stage of sleep is very important to the health of the body. Fitness experts tell us that people who exercise regularly and are in a relaxed state upon going to bed spend more time in the NREM state of sleep than those who don't exercise. In REM, which makes up about 25 percent of your sleeping time, the brain is still at a high level of brain activity. This is the stage of sleep in which you dream.

3. **Sleep is how the body renews itself.** Your body needs sleep. You've probably noticed a certain pattern to your body's ability to meet the demands of your life on a daily basis. For example, you probably wake up about the same time, get hungry around the same times each day, and get tired pretty much about the same time each evening. We

call this twenty-four-hour cycle of energy flow the *circadian rhythm.* Even your temperature, mood and alertness tend to rise and fall at roughly the same time every day. In other words, your body likes a predictable "routine"—such as going to bed at the same time each night, or even looking at your watch when it's lunch time. When your body experiences the comfort and renewal of this routine, it is less susceptible to both the physical and emotional effects of stress.

Are you getting all the sleep you need? Here are some things you can do to help ensure a restful night's sleep.

- ♥ Make sure you are getting adequate exercise. There is nothing like the rest that comes from the body being tired and wanting to rest itself.
- ♥ Go to bed at the same time every night. The body likes a routine, one it can count on.
- ♥ Don't play heavy metal or music with a fast tempo just prior to going to bed. This music will "rev" you up. Save it for the morning or after school when your goal is to re-energize. Instead, when getting ready for bed, put on soothing and relaxing sounds. This helps clear your mind of your schedule and hectic day.
- ♥ Fill your mind with uplifting, pleasant and reassuring thoughts, those that can help you wind down your day, and prepare to get the rest you need to have a great tomorrow. The goal is to relax so you can get to sleep.
- ♥ Don't eat right before bedtime. You don't want your body to have to work at digesting food when you are trying to shut down for the night.
- ♥ Avoid stimulants such as caffeine, sugar and nicotine. These will keep you awake.
- ♥ Create a soothing surrounding. Choose soothing colors for

your walls, decorate with your favorite pictures and snapshots of family and friends, and your favorite stuffed animals.

VIRTUAL PRACTICE:
FOOD, BOD AND ZZZZZ'S

1. "You are what you eat." How have you witnessed this expression in your daily life? _____

_____

_____

2. Describe a time when you were stressed, and exercise reduced the stress you were feeling. _____

_____

_____

3. What is the one most important thing you can do to improve the quality of sleep you get on a daily basis? _____

_____

_____

Cool Is Up to You!

Hmmm. Seems like nutrition, exercise and sleep are key to our ability to deal with stress. In the next chapter, you'll learn how breathing right can also help you rid yourself of stress, and prevent it as well. Bet you didn't know there was more than one way to breathe, right?

26

"Belly Breathing": Breathing Correctly Can Literally Blow Stress Away

"Breathing *correctly?*" Are you thinking, "Hey, breathing is breathing. You open your mouth, take air in, swallow it, and your body tells you when it's time to let it out. And besides, it's an automatic response. My body does it for me, as naturally as blinking."

Yes, it would seem that breathing the "right way" is an automatic response, but when stressed-out, your body changes its rhythm of breathing (it speeds up so that your body gets the oxygen it needs to make and act on its "flight or fight" decision). So getting your breathing back to normal is a little more complex than opening up your mouth and sucking in air—as sixteen-year-old Amber Mendoza (in the following story) found out when after she'd been waiting and waiting for the perfect guy to show up in her life—one who, according to her "list," had to have brown hair, green eyes and big feet—finds herself at a BBQ with a pretty serious question to address. Surprised, she finds herself momentarily unable to speak. So what can you do when brain freeze sets in? "Belly breathing" (a technique you'll learn in this chapter) is an effective way to rid your body of momentary brain freeze. When you take in air, your diaphragm expands and tenses. As you let the air out, or exhale, it relaxes. It's quick and convenient and can be used anytime, anywhere, such as before taking a test, making a presentation in class or trying to find the words to answer a surprise question by a special someone!

Brown Hair, Green Eyes, Big Feet

I've been waiting and waiting. Patiently waiting for the perfect guy to come into my life. I waited through sixth grade, and seventh grade and eighth grade and ninth grade. I've been extremely patient, too, and the reason is because I know that there is that one perfect person for each of us—even though we never know when that person will come along. But I was okay with waiting—because the guy for me had to be just perfect.

I was so sure what I wanted my perfect guy to look like and be like that I made a list of all the qualities he'd have to have. Things like brown hair, green eyes, big feet—and he'd have to pick me up to kiss me because he would be tall, much taller than me.

By the summer after my ninth-grade year, it seemed to me that every one of my friends had found that one perfect guy, while I was still waiting for mine. Mostly I'd pal around with Jenna, Chad, Brian, Kelsey and David, friends who also still had not met their perfect someone. The summer was nearly over, and still that perfect guy for me had not shown up. The fact that all my friends were doing fun things and going to fun events—like concerts, street fairs and state fairs—and each with their perfect someone (well, except for Jenna, Chad, Brian, Kelsey and David—who, along with me, all hung around together), made me very sure that I was more than ready for my perfect guy to show up.

If only he would.

It was one week before school was to begin, and everyone was talking about going back to school. And while I was looking forward to school beginning, it dawned on me that all my friends with their perfect someones would be going back to school, so now I'd really be left out. Then, as a "good-bye" to summer, my friends decided to have a BBQ. That sounded fun, and I was looking forward to it, even though I knew all my friends would be there with someone, while I'd be there alone.

Of course, I went to the BBQ. They were my friends, and this was a party of sorts. Just as I'd thought, all my friends came with their dates, and I was pretty much alone—at least that's the way it felt when everyone began to dance. The music was very loud and just great. And I really wanted to dance. So when my friend David, a really nice guy and someone I've known since elementary school, asked me to dance, I thought, *Well, why not? I love this music, and this is a party. And I'm supposed to have fun. David will do.*

David and I danced and danced. And when we took a break from dancing, we went to get food and sodas and sort of just hung out together. This went on for almost an hour, and then something totally unexpected happened. David started flirting with me—and I found myself flirting back. Then our friends teased us, and I felt okay with it. And then something completely out-of-the-blue happened, something that blew me away. When David and I were dancing to a slow song, he kissed me on the forehead. Speechless, I just kept dancing until the song was over, trying to get used to all the feelings going on inside of me. "Let's talk," he said when the music stopped, and steered me over to the corner of the dance area. Holding both of my hands in his he said, "I've liked you for a long time. And I'd like to ask you if you'd be my girl."

I didn't know what to say, except that my heart was fluttering and my whole being felt like dancing even though the music had stopped. Then David picked me up and kissed me again. Not one of those little weak kisses. This was an intensive kiss. And that's when I noticed: David has brown hair, green eyes and big feet. And he's so tall he had to pick me up to kiss me.

Amber Mendoza, 16

Four Reasons Breathing Correctly Reduces "Brain Freeze"

Amber Mendoza was feeling a great deal of stress—albeit euphoric—when she suddenly realized that after all her waiting and wishing for a perfect guy, in a moment's flash, he was standing right there in front of her! "It was an incredible heart-stopping moment, one that every time I even think about it, brings excitement," Amber told us. "I remember the very moment I suddenly realized that it was David who was my special someone. My heart fluttered and my brain sort of just shut down. When he told me he'd liked me for a long time and then asked me to be *his* girl—and especially when I realized that there in front of me stood the guy I'd described on my 'list,' well, I don't think I could even talk for a minute or two. It was total brain freeze."

Can you relate to the kinds of situations that bring on brain freeze? Many teens can. So many times there is the element of "first," or "on the spot"—such as when being called on in class or having to get up and give a speech or report—and when that moment arrives, you have to think fast! The momentary "brain freeze" we experience when in stressful or tense situations is caused by our change in breathing patterns, when we stop breathing in the amount of oxygen the body needs to function fully.

So how can you relax enough to stop "brain freeze" from happening or at least to keep it at a minimum? How do you relax when you're totally stressed out in the middle of the day? You breathe!

Here are four great reasons to breathe when you want to dissolve the stress that causes "brain freeze."

1. **Breathing correctly can help you control your emotions.** When your breathing is either frozen or rapid and out of

control, your emotions are also out of control. When you relax, you are also able to become aware of the relationship between your mind and body. When you relax your body, you relax your state of mind. When you control your breathing, you gain control of your emotions; you calm down.

2. **Breathing correctly gives you a sense of well-being.** Conscious relaxation produces changes in the electrical activity of the brain, which in turn produce more alpha waves, which are associated with feelings of well-being. These feelings of well-being will help you feel more confident in facing your stress head-on.

3. **Breathing correctly helps you slow down and regroup physically.** Along with the extra alpha waves, there is also a decrease in the rate of metabolism and oxygen consumption when you relax, even more than during sleep. These physical benefits help you feel less overwhelmed and more rested and equipped to deal with the stressors in your life.

4. **Breathing correctly helps you ease away tension.** Conscious relaxation is a simple but very effective method of eliminating tension. We've already seen how stress can cause tension in your muscles. When you avoid "brain freeze" and get the breath you need to perform at your best mentally and physically, those tense muscles also ease.

VIRTUAL PRACTICE: THAWING "BRAIN FREEZE"

Okay, you're convinced breathing the right way is important, but how? Here's how to check to see if you're doing it right: Stand in front of a mirror and watch yourself breathe as you normally do. Is it your body's natural desire to take deep slow breaths, or do you notice that you're breathing with your chest, in short shallow breaths? If you notice that you are taking short shallow breaths, you may be practicing what is called thoracic breathing. Shallow breathing (thoracic breathing) causes stale and unused air to be detained in the lungs—which is not good.

In diaphragmatic breathing, you use your full capacity for breathing, filling the lungs entirely with air, and then slowly exhaling (such as how a newborn baby breathes). In essence, it works like this: You stretch, filling the lungs and the diaphragm completely with air, and then sigh, letting all the air out slowly.

Here are the basic principles:

♥ INHALE deeply, first filling the diaphragm area with air (stomach goes out). Continue inhaling as the lower part of the chest expands. Finish inhaling as the upper ribs are expanded and the top of the lungs fill with air.

♥ EXHALE slowly. The air flows out smoothly from the top of the chest, down through the middle and completely out as the stomach draws in.

♥ REST. Allow yourself to experience the physical sensations that accompany breathing in this relaxing manner. Begin the process again by inhaling deeply.

Okay, time to try out this skill. To begin, concentrate on your breathing pattern. Focus on the air from the moment it enters your mouth until it enters the most distant reaches of your lungs. Picture the air making a return trip. Remember that the goal is to breathe in deeply through your nose, expanding your diaphragm, and then exhale through your mouth. If you concentrate on exhaling, inhaling should come naturally.

Follow these guidelines:

1. Close your eyes, or focus on a spot on the wall in front of you.

2. Place your hands very lightly on your abdomen just below the navel with your fingertips touching.

3. Take a deep breath in and count slowly: one . . . two . . . three . . . four. As you inhale through your nose, your abdomen should swell out. This may feel a bit awkward at first if you are used to more shallow chest breathing. You may have to make a conscious effort to push your stomach. An alternative method for checking to see whether you are using your diaphragm appropriately is to make a "bridge" by placing a notebook on your abdomen. When you inhale, you should see the lower end of the bridge tilting higher.

4. After inhaling deeply, begin to exhale through the nose. Let the air out very slowly, counting one . . . two . . . three . . . four. Draw in the stomach so that your fingertips come together again. If necessary, make a conscious effort to pull in the stomach slightly.

5. Breathe in deeply: one . . . two . . . three . . . four.

6. Let the air out slowly: one . . . two . . . three . . . four.

7. Repeat this five more times.

8. Open your eyes.

How do you feel? If you are like most teens, you'll find it's a great feeling, a peaceful, restful state of mind that makes you feel as if you've just had a nap! Now that's a good thing.

If you practice breathing this way as you lie in bed in the morning, and again just before you fall asleep, you will get into the habit of breathing correctly. And remember, when you breathe right it assists your mind in being alert and poised for action—which is always helpful in dealing with stress.

Cool Is Up to You!

Belly breathing is a very effective, easy and quick thing to do. It's sure to be one of your favorite stress-management skills. Isn't it nice to know that, with a little lung power, you can breathe yourself out of a stressful situation, and relax your mind as well as your body? The next chapter will show you how to achieve an even deeper level of relaxation.

27

Progressive Muscle Relaxation: A Cool Way to Chill Out (and Relax)

Being stressed can make you look like a Grinch. Think about it: When you're stressed to the max, do you look as though you have steam coming from your ears? Are your eyes pulled down? Are you wearing a scowl or a frown? Draw a caricature representative of what you look like when stressed-out.

So, do you look pretty frightening? Stress has a way of changing your cool to ghoul—from the way you look, to the way you act—as Gregory (in the following story) found out.

"Matilda the Hun"

My parents went away on a three-day weekend and hired a sitter to take care of me and my little sister. I told my parents that since I was in eighth grade, I didn't need a *baby*-sitter, that I was old enough to take care of the house and even my little sister, but they insisted that we have a *baby*-sitter. The woman they hired was old (she had to be at least thirty) and bossy. And she was a mite plump. So you can see, I had my reasons for not warming up to her.

She didn't think I was all that cool either. I'm not sure *what* it was about *me* that she didn't like, but it seemed to me that she always had a chore for me to do and was always telling me some rule I needed to follow. The minute I walked in the house after school on Friday (which was her first day there), her very first words to me were, "Take off your cleats before you walk on the wood floors." Like I don't know this. And it was only the beginning: "Hang up your jacket." "Take your books off the counter." "Start your homework." "Don't spill any of that popcorn on the couch." "Have you fed and watered your dog?" Geez, it was like she was going down some big checklist and felt she wasn't doing her job unless she had me doing something. I mean, I know what my responsibilities are. I don't need to be reminded of them again and again. What's more, she didn't seem to have so many orders and reminders for my little sister. I thought that was very unfair. So after the second day of her telling me to move my books and hang up my clothes and feed my dog—and right in the middle of my favorite television show—I was really ticked. "Why don't you just stop acting like Matilda the Hun!" I blurted.

At the time, telling her this felt good, but a minute after I said it, it didn't feel good at all. My parents are very strict about me having respect for others—especially my elders—so I knew I shouldn't have said it.

Matilda the Hun did not exactly like her new name—I could see this in the hurt look in her eyes. Then terror set in when she said, "That isn't very polite, and I intend to let your parents know about it. Now, go to your room."

Well, I was more than happy to go to my room, where I intended to stay the rest of the weekend. But then I remembered that my parents had promised me a host of goodies if I behaved myself for the sitter, like I could go to the senior all-star game on an upcoming Tuesday night with my friend, Hank, and stay out late for the school dance next weekend. Now, I saw these goodies as good-bye forever. My mouth had really gotten me into trouble. I'd be lucky if I wasn't grounded for a month!

I mean, I knew my father would be really mad. I also knew I had to be the one to tell him the sad news that his rebel son had defamed the sitter. I was so upset and so worried about things that I just couldn't get out of the terrible mood I was in. And my stomach was churning, my head hurt and I felt tense all over. I couldn't seem to think of anything but the trouble I was in— sleep was out of the question. I tossed and turned all night.

When my parents returned the next day, you can bet that I was waiting by the front door, all smiles, and more than happy to help them unload their luggage and bring things into the house. The second I got Mom alone, I told her about the incident. "Mom, promise me you won't be mad but I called the baby-sitter a name, and I'm really sorry and I promise to never to do it again," I said in one breath. "Please let me tell Dad about it myself. Please?"

My mom was pretty cool about it. She said simply, "I'm very disappointed in you. I know you know better than to call someone names. Let's go apologize to her. Then, I'll let you tell your father yourself at dinner. I'm sure he'll be very upset since we both want you to be a young man with good manners."

I was really grateful that my father seemed in an unusually good mood at dinner. Maybe it was because my room was cleaned, the dog was watered, fed and walked, and I had even mowed the lawn! And of course, I was on my very best and attentive behavior. Our family has a habit of taking turns telling about the events of the day, and sharing at least one really good or exciting thing that either happened or is coming up for them. My mother goes first, then my sister, and then me, then my dad. It's our ritual.

My mother had already talked about how much fun she'd had at the resort with my father, and my little sister had rambled about a good grade she got in school and about how she had gone bug-hunting in the backyard and captured a lightning bug, put it in a jar and was going to take it to her science class on Monday. Then, it was my turn. "Dad," I said, "I'm practicing having better manners. So, tonight *you* go first!"

"Okay," he smiled, seeming pleased, and he went on to tell us a little bit about what a good time he had on his long weekend with my mother. Then, he turned to me. "Well," I said, "I've been thinking about it and I see how it's really important to be kind to others, so I'm going to be more careful to be respectful. You can't just go around saying whatever pops into your head because you're mad at somebody. You have to think things out and treat people the way you want to be treated. I'm going to make sure that I never say anything that could be thought of as disrespect-ful to one of my elders—like say, a teacher, or a coach, or a baby-sitter. . . ." I could feel Mom's eyes drilling into me from across the table, letting me know it was time to level with my dad. I drew a deep breath and launched into the "downfall" of my weekend, "This isn't really a good thing, but it's something I need to tell you about. I called the baby-sitter Matilda the Hun."

As I expected, Dad was really upset. So furious, in fact, he looked like he could unleash a whole storm of reasons that this was grounds to lock me in my room until I turned eighteen. But surprisingly, he didn't say anything. He just glared into my soul for what seemed an eternity and seemed to punish me with-out even saying a word. Then he cleared his throat to speak. My punishment had come, and I just knew I was not going to make it to ninth grade. Just when I thought that the world was going to end right at my kitchen table, my dad said, "Calling your sitter Matilda the Hun is more than impolite, and maybe you need to think about just why it's so wrong. Besides rude and inconsiderate, what else is it?"

"Disrespectful?" I offered.

"Very disrespectful," he nodded, "And it's unkind. Do you know that?" he demanded. "Yes," I said as humbly as I could, waiting for the levy of my sentence.

"What you said was very wrong. Do you know why?"

"No," I answered, realizing that in this fragile moment "no" was the best response. The words he uttered will stay with me the rest of my life: "Well, the marauder was *Attila* the Hun, not *Matilda* the Hun." At that point, eight eyes looked around the table to decide how we should react to Dad's comment. Then, at the same time, everyone broke out in laughter at my mistake.

I was more relieved than I can express.

I know it's not nice to make fun of people, and I had mocked the baby-sitter. But aside from that, what I learned is what a gift it is to have someone "let you off the hook." My father made sure I knew I was in the wrong, but then created a door for me to escape from being forever condemned for doing wrong. It's a moment I will always cherish. Giving me a break and making it safe to be wrong without the world collapsing on my shoulders paved the way for a trust that let me know that I could talk with my father about anything—making our relationship a close one.

Of all the good "heart-to-heart" talks we've had, it was his laughing with me in that moment that makes him my best friend ever. It is a moment that will always stand out as a particularly "most excellent" moment between him and me.

Gregory Carl, 16

Like Gregory, have you ever been so stressed-out that you couldn't eat, sleep, relax—even think straight? Learning to relax can help you break the spell of stress.

Three Cool Reasons to Melt Stress via Relaxation

When the pressure you feel is overwhelming, it can be helpful to take a step back from the situation, and just let go of the stress—to really relax. Not only does this kind of relaxation help you renew your energy, it helps you ease up on the building aches of knotting muscles. Here are some other important reasons to learn the art of relaxation.

1. **Relaxation is an antidote to "overwhelm."** When you relax you are able to sort out your thoughts and feelings and come to a clearer, more manageable view of what's going on in your world and emotions. It helps you get a better perspective. Being able to sort things out this way helps you feel less overwhelmed and better able to deal with the task or stress at hand.

2. **Relaxation can "unstress" tense muscles.** Often when you are nervous, upset or afraid, your muscles get tense or tight. Sometimes they stay that way for a while—like a few hours or days, long after the stressful event. This tension can lead to headaches, muscle aches and cramps. Relaxing soothes muscles, helping you feel less tense, less irritable and you therefore feel better able to manage yourself.

3. **Relaxation keeps you from looking like a Grinch.** When you're under stress, do you look as though you have steam coming from your ears? Are the words "stressed out!" stamped on your forehead? Do your eyes pull down, looking sad? Stress can be seen in the face, the muscles and the posture. Try this. Think about a time when you were really

upset. Now stand in front of the mirror and think about that incident. Are your legs in a defensive stance? Is your jaw tight? Not a very attractive sight, is it? Learning to relax keeps you from looking like a close relative of the Grinch. Way cool!

Progressive Muscle Relaxation: Tension Meltdown

Okay, you say, "Count me in." You're convinced that relaxation is good thing—something you really want to be able to achieve. The question is how? One great answer is to relax away the tension and stress through progressive muscle relaxation.

Progressive muscle relaxation is a technique that uses physical exercise to achieve relaxation from tension. It's a systematic way to relax each muscle group by first tensing it and then releasing the tension and letting the muscles relax. The muscle groups around the head, face, neck and shoulders are particularly prone to stress, and when they are tense, you feel it. As you learn to relax the tension, the stress itself eases, too.

Once you see how progressive muscle relaxation works, the best and most convenient way to use it is to record the script provided below in your own voice so that it's available for you to use any time. When you're first learning this exercise, find a quiet location free of interruptions, like your room, or lay down on a sofa, or sit in a comfortable chair (preferably one that reclines). Your clothing should be comfortable and loose. It's best to remove shoes, eyeglasses or contact lenses. Dim the lights if you can.

If you don't have a tape recorder, you may want to ask your mother or father or a good friend to read the word-by-word script to you. You just lie back, close your eyes and concentrate on following along. If you don't have anyone to read this to you and you also don't have a tape recorder, just lie the script in your lap and do the exercise as best you can. Eventually, you can even memorize the script and exercise.

(You may also wish to play your favorite soothing music, but the key word is *soothing*. Most teens find it best to play just instrumental recordings, rather than those with words, because you really don't want to focus on the music at all, and for sure, you don't want to sing along to your favorite tune! Keep it just loud enough so that it is in the background but you are hardly aware of it at all. The goal is just to have it as a soothing sound in the background.)

VIRTUAL PRACTICE: TENSION MELTDOWN— HOW TO RELAX EVERY MUSCLE IN YOUR BODY

This virtual practice will take some time and dedication on your part, but you'll find if you stay with it you will most definitely feel the benefits. And, if you're like most teens, soon it will become one of your most important tools to reduce the tension of stress.

The Word-by-Word Progressive Muscle Relaxation Script

"[Head and Face.] Keeping the rest of your body relaxed, wrinkle up your forehead. Do you feel the tension? Hold it to a count of five: 1, 2, 3, 4, 5. Now relax and let go. Feel the tension draining away. Take another deep breath. Hold it to a count of five: 1, 2, 3, 4, 5. Breathe out and relax.

"Keeping the rest of your body relaxed, squint your eyes. Hold your squint to a count of five: 1, 2, 3, 4, 5. Now relax and let go. Feel the tension draining away. Take another deep breath. Hold it to a count of five: 1, 2, 3, 4, 5. Breathe out and relax.

"Open your mouth as wide as you can. Hold that position to a count of five: 1, 2, 3, 4, 5. Now relax and let go. Feel the tension draining away. Take another deep breath. Hold it to a count of five: 1, 2, 3, 4, 5. As you breathe out, relax and let go.

"Close your mouth. Push your tongue against the roof of your mouth. Hold it to a count of five: 1, 2, 3, 4, 5. Now relax and let go. Feel the tension draining away. Take another deep breath. Hold it to a count of five: 1, 2, 3, 4, 5. Breathe out and relax. When you breathe out, let your tongue rest comfortably in your mouth, and let your lips be slightly apart.

"Keep the rest of your body relaxed but clench your jaw tightly. Feel the tension in your jaw muscles. Briefly hold the tension to a count of five: 1, 2, 3, 4, 5. Now relax and let go. Feel the tension draining away. Take another deep breath. Hold it to a count of five: 1, 2, 3, 4, 5. Breathe out and relax.

"Think about the top of your head, your forehead, eyes, jaws and cheeks. Relax these muscles. Continue to let the tension slip away and feel the relaxation replace the tension. Feel your face becoming very smooth and soft as all the tension slips away. . . . Your eyes are relaxed. . . . Your tongue is relaxed. Your jaws are loose and limp. . . . All of your neck muscles are also very, very relaxed. All of the muscles of your face and head are relaxing more and more. . . . Your head feels as though it could roll from side to side.

"[Shoulder.] Now shrug your shoulders up and try to touch your ears with your shoulders. Feel the tension in the shoulders and neck. Hold the tension to a count of five: 1, 2, 3, 4, 5. Now relax and let go. Feel the tension draining away. Take another deep breath. Hold it to a count of five: 1, 2, 3, 4, 5. Breathe out and relax.

"Feel the tension giving way to relaxation. Shrug your right shoulder up and try to touch your right ear. Feel the tension in your right shoulder and along the right side of your neck. Hold the tension to a count of five: 1, 2, 3, 4, 5. Now relax and let go. Feel the tension draining away. Take another deep breath. Hold it to a count of five: 1, 2, 3, 4, 5. Breathe out and relax.

"Next, shrug your left shoulder up and try to touch your left ear. Feel the tension in your left shoulder and along the left side of your neck. Hold the tension to a count of five: 1, 2, 3, 4, 5. Now relax and let go. Feel the tension draining away. Take another deep breath. Hold it to a count of five: 1, 2, 3, 4, 5. Breathe out and relax. Feel the relaxation seeping into the shoulders. As you continue, you will become loose, limp and as relaxed as a sandbag.

"[Arms and Hands.] Stretch your arms out and make your hands into fists. Feel the tension in your hands and forearms. Hold the tension to a count of five: 1, 2, 3, 4, 5. Now relax and let go. Feel the tension draining away. Take another deep breath. Hold it to a count of five: 1, 2, 3, 4, 5. Breathe out and relax.

"Push your right hand down into the surface it is resting on. Feel the tension in your arm and shoulder. Hold the tension to a count of five: 1, 2, 3, 4, 5. Now relax and let go. Feel the tension draining away. Take another deep breath. Breathe out and relax.

"Next, push your left hand down into whatever it is resting on. Feel the tension in your arm and shoulder. Hold the tension to a count of five: 1, 2, 3, 4, 5. Now relax and let go. Feel the tension draining away. Take another deep breath. Breathe out and relax.

"Bend your arms toward your shoulders and double them up as you would do to show off your muscles. Feel the tension. Hold the tension to a count of five: 1, 2, 3, 4, 5. Now relax and let go. Feel the tension draining away. Take another deep breath. Breathe out and relax.

"[Chest and Lungs.] Move on to the relaxation of your chest. Begin by taking a deep breath that totally fills your lungs. Hold the tension to a count of five: 1, 2, 3, 4, 5. Now relax and let go. Feel the tension draining away. Take another deep breath. Hold it to a count of five: 1, 2, 3, 4, 5. Breathe out and relax.

"Take in another deep breath. Hold it and again feel the contrast between tension and relaxation. As you do, tighten your chest muscles. Hold the tension to a count of five: 1, 2, 3, 4, 5. Now relax and let go. Feel the tension draining away. Take another deep breath. Hold it to a count of five: 1, 2, 3, 4, 5.

Breathe as smoothly as you can. You will become more and more relaxed with every breath.

"[Back.] Keep your face, neck, arms and chest as relaxed as possible. Arch your back up (or forward, if you are sitting). Arch it as though you had a pillow under the middle and lower parts of your back. Hold the tension to a count of five: 1, 2, 3, 4, 5. Now relax and let go. Feel the tension draining away. Take another deep breath. Hold it to a count of five: 1, 2, 3, 4, 5. Breathe out and relax. Let that relaxation spread deep into your shoulders and down into your back muscles.

"Feel the slow relaxation developing and spreading all over. Feel it going deeper and deeper. Allow your entire body to relax. Face and head relaxed . . . neck relaxed . . . shoulders relaxed . . . arms relaxed . . . chest relaxed . . . back relaxed. . . . All these areas are relaxing more and more, becoming more deeply relaxed.

"[Stomach.] Now begin the relaxation of the stomach area. Tighten up this area. Briefly hold the tension . . . Relax and let go. Feel the relaxation pour into your stomach area. All the tension is being replaced with relaxation. Take a deep breath. Hold it. Relax and let go as you slowly breathe out.

"Now experience a different type of tension in the stomach area. Push your stomach out as far as you can. Briefly hold the tension . . . Now, relax and let go. Take a deep breath. Hold it. Relax and let go as you slowly breathe out. Now pull your stomach in. Try to pull your stomach in so far that it touches your backbone. Hold it . . . Now relax and let go. Take a deep breath. Hold it. Relax and let go as you breathe out. You are becoming more and more relaxed. Each time you breathe out, feel the gentle relaxation in your lungs and in your body.

"[Hips, Legs, and Feet.] Begin the relaxation of your hips and legs. Tighten your hips and legs by pressing down the heels of your feet into the surface they are resting on. Tighten these muscles. Keep the rest of your body as relaxed as you can and press your heels down . . . Hold the tension to a count of five: 1,

2, 3, 4, 5. Now relax and let go. Feel the tension draining away. Take another deep breath. Hold it to a count of five: 1, 2, 3, 4, 5. Breathe out and relax. Your legs feel as if they could float up. Take a deep breath. Relax and let go as you slowly breathe out. Feel the relaxation pouring in.

"Next, tighten your lower leg muscles. Feel the tension. Hold the tension to a count of five: 1, 2, 3, 4, 5. Now relax and let go. Feel the tension draining away. Take another deep breath. Hold it to a count of five: 1, 2, 3, 4, 5. Breathe out and relax.

"Now, curl your toes downward. Curl them down and try to touch the bottom of your feet with your toes. Hold the tension to a count of five: 1, 2, 3, 4, 5. Now relax and let go. Wiggle your toes gently as you let go of the tension. Take another deep breath. Hold it to a count of five: 1, 2, 3, 4, 5. Breathe out and relax. Take a deep breath. Hold it. Relax and let go as you breathe out.

"Bend your toes back the other way. Bend your toes right up toward your knees. Feel the tension. Try to touch your knees with your toes. Hold the tension to a count of five: 1, 2, 3, 4, 5. Now relax and let go. Feel the tension draining away. Take another deep breath. Hold it to a count of five: 1, 2, 3, 4, 5. Breathe out and relax. Feel the relaxation seeping in.

"Continue to feel yourself becoming more and more relaxed each time you breathe out."

"It's A Wrap!" Closing Down Your Relaxation Time

It's important to end the relaxation exercise gently by saying something like, "Now flex your arms. Take a deep breath and release it slowly. I'm now going to count from four to one. When I reach one, your eyes will open and you will be awake, feeling calm and comfortable. Four . . . three . . . two . . . one. Open your eyes, feeling calm and comfortable."

Doing this slowly allows this time of relaxation to end gently. This helps you adjust gradually to the higher state of arousal needed for getting up and walking around.

This really is a very simple exercise, and a very effective one to use whenever you begin to feel your muscles beginning to get tense. But of course, you needn't wait until your stress has set in to the extent it is now affecting your muscles getting tense. When you find yourself getting anxious or worried about something during the day, try using even some portions of this, such as relaxing your hands, face and neck.

You can use it while sitting at your desk in school, and no one will even notice. For example, you are about ready to take a test, so you take a deep breath, hold it and slowly breathe out silently.

And of course, this exercise is also a great way to calm down before going to bed on an evening when you are feeling particularly excited or keyed up.

Cool Is Up to You!

When your body has experienced the tension meltdown of progressive muscle relaxation, you'll find yourself more relaxed and mellow, and better able to manage the stress at hand. And, of course, your body won't be screaming "I ache!" and your face won't be shrieking, "Grinchville!"—which is always a cool thing.

And here's something else that's good to know: Just as you can relax your body, you can relax your mind—especially at those times when it's racing wildly, fueled by the stress of living—where else than in the "land of overwhelm."

28

Mental Imagery: Reducing "Brain Strain"

Do you ever find yourself in a daydream, even while a flurry of activities are going on around you? You probably thought not being able to concentrate on the task at hand—especially when something important is going on around you, like the teacher giving a lecture on algorithms, or your parents laying out the new rules for curfew—meant you had a poor attention span. Au contraire! Hold on to that skill! Yes, skill.

If you are successful at taking short trips in your mind, you already know a great way to reduce the (brain) strain of stress. Certainly this skill served thirteen-year-old Stephanie Anderson when she was all set to be a popular girl at school, but was upstaged by a group of other girls. What did they know that she didn't? It seemed to Stephanie this particular group could get away with just about anything. Until . . .

The "Supergirls"

What bugged me the most during my seventh-grade year was this thing about the "popular" girls. At first, it didn't bother me—though I did notice I felt a definite "attitude" about "them." It just seemed so unfair that for no known reasons, one small group of girls were considered so in, so with it, that everything they did set the standard for what was cool. They did things no one else would have dreamed of doing, such as putting glitter on their arms and face, and applying makeup and combing their hair in class! They passed notes during class time and seemed to never get caught, whereas the moment one of us "just ordinary" kids did, you can bet the teacher would snatch it up in a moment. It seemed to me that these popular girls had immunity from the teacher's gaze and wrath, but who knew why? We'd heard of supermodels; well, here were "Supergirls." But for the rest of us, it meant that this handful of popular supergirls was obviously even more special than we could understand—or be. The Supergirls thought they were the stars of our school—and they were.

And, of course, the Supergirls expected "model" treatment. And wouldn't you know, everyone seemed to be at their every little beck and call. If one of them should ask someone to "loan" them their homework "for a few minutes" (so as to copy it, of course), hardly anyone said no. And nearly everyone else in the school was at their mercy for running errands, such as returning a book, going up and requesting a second piece of pizza from the cafeteria cooks (which took a lot of begging because if the cook gave a second piece, everyone would want seconds, and thirds, and fourths!) and the Supergirls were simply too cool to ever be turned down, so if a second piece of pizza wasn't forthcoming, well, it only made the "beggar" look unsuccessful, or worse, like a pig, and the Supergirl was allowed to save face. Stuff like that.

Since the Supergirls seemed to have it all together—and the rest of us were their trained flock of followers—we felt not as much helpful as stupid for not having the courage to have a life of our own. And of course, we were just dying to be like them, even if we had no idea how to do that, so we were willing to accept membership by association.

I didn't feel so much like a groupie as I felt left out. I have to admit that in the early months, the moment I got home I'd head to my room, put on my favorite CD and just think of the injustice of it all, and sometimes, I'd rehearse all the things I intended to say to one or all of the Supergirls the next time one of them asked me to be her errand girl. But mostly, I just lay on my bed and imagined I was one of the Supergirls—really popular, with glitter on my arms and all the other kids thinking I was so cool, too.

But then one day, the Supergirls started a pretty terrible rumor about Ben Tappan and Jennifer Olds. We all knew that both Ben and Jennifer liked each other ever since the sixth grade. And, when the two started walking each other to their lockers—and then began to hold hands—well, it looked like they were lucky to us. I mean, we were all hoping to find someone of our own to do that with. But the rumor that the Supergirls started was really bad, and of course, not at all true. They had Ben and Jennifer doing more than holding hands, and in the seventh grade, a rumor of that nature can quickly ruin your reputation as being a nice girl. Of course, the other kids at school all believed the rumor, mostly because of the simple fact that it was told by the Supergirls, who could do no wrong. Everyone wanted to believe what the Supergirls said. And did. And you could tell it affected how Ben and Jennifer felt about us all, because when they'd see their friends coming, they quickly dropped hands. I thought that was sad.

Of course, when the Supergirls started dating, they thought holding hands and walking to lockers together was innocent and didn't mean anything else was going on—and of course, it was the perfectly cool thing to do! And all on their own, they spread the rumor that they'd all been kissed. Well, we never did see them with any of the boys in our class, so I asked one who it was she was "kissing," and she flat-out told me that the three of them were seeing upperclass boys from Wilson High across town.

Well, this sort of one-upsmanship went on all semester, and finally, I got so frustrated with not being able to be anybody without their approval, that I told one of these girls exactly how I felt. I said that I did not like most of the "popular" girls because of how they acted. She told all her friends what I said, and pretty soon, no one in the whole entire school was talking to me! Talk about feeling like I had the plague or something. I just don't get it how a group of girls can have so much influence, but they sure seemed to! So, after that little—well, actually, huge—ordeal, I decided to keep my thoughts to myself. But at night, I'd still lay awake sometimes and visualize myself as one of the Supergirls.

But you know what? Pretty soon, the "popular" group of girls got in trouble for putting on glitter and combing their hair in class. I guess the teachers just got tired of how they acted as if they could do anything they wanted in class, especially since they went from putting on glitter and combing their hair to coming in late and talking all the time. Finally the teacher just said, "That's it! Absolutely, positively no more tubes and containers of glitter in this classroom, or I'll confiscate it!" Then some of the Supergirls started rumors about each other and wound up being enemies. Two even got in a fight: It was pretty awful to watch two supergirls—our heroines—in a regular knock-down drag-out fight. I mean, everybody was shocked. That fight sure seemed to change how a lot of kids felt about the popularity of the Supergirls. And, from that time on, there wasn't any major thing that was "Super" or special about the Supergirls.

It just goes to show that if you're stressing out about something someone else is doing, like trying to act like they're better than everyone else, it's really a waste of energy and stress. I know I sure could've saved myself all the worry. What another person does eventually catches up with that person, so why stress out over it? I know that it caught up with these girls! All the hurt they had caused others came back to hurt them in the end. It's just one more reason I know that it's always best to be nice to everyone. And ever since all this happened, when I listen to CDs and imagine myself with glitter and being really "popular," I also see myself being really nice to everybody at the same time—and making that the "cool" thing to do.

Stephanie Anderson, 13

Four Ways Mental Imagery
Floats Stress Right Out of Your Life

Stephanie obviously had a rough time throughout the semester not having the sense of belonging she desired and deserved. But when Stephanie listened to music and imagined herself with glitter and acceptance, she had actually come upon a very effective tool for not only visualizing as one of the supergirls, but for dealing with stress as well. Here are four ways that using mental imagery reduces your stress:

1. **Mental imagery directs your thoughts to a more positive perspective.** When you are able to visualize a beautiful place and outcome, it helps you open to a more positive perspective. Being able to hold a vision of calm helps you move towards solutions and away from the problem and the stress of thinking about it.

2. **Mental imagery calms your emotions.** When your thoughts are directed towards a more positive perspective, you feel more calm and hopeful. Your stress is lowered as your confidence in your ability to cope and succeed is raised.

3. **Mental imagery helps you relax mind and body in tense situations.** We already know how the mind and the body are connected when it comes to stress: well, when you visualize paradise and good with the mind, the body comes along for the ride. The calm images, outcomes and scenarios your mind creates seep into the body, easing away tension.

4. **Mental imagery improves your ability to find creative ways out of a jam.** Have you ever been in a spot (like Mom or Dad give you a lecture, and your mind took a little time out) and thought of a very creative way to get out of the jam? Very useful, right? Maybe the time you were "taking a mental break" you actually did come up with a creative

solution. As you visualize, you are better able to come to creative solutions for coping with stress.

VIRTUAL PRACTICE: HOW TO TRAIN YOUR MIND TO TAKE A MINI-VACATION WHEN IT NEEDS RELIEF FROM STRESS

To begin using visualization to help you stay "cool" in the heat of stress, simply think of the most beautiful, serene setting you can imagine and place yourself right there in the middle of that setting. Try to experience the scene in every way you can, including the use of images from your senses—such as smell (for example, the scent of flowers), touch (the feel of the grass beneath your feet), sound (the sound of birds singing in the trees), and taste (the salt air at the beach). And by the way, you can also use soothing music along with this exercise to create a calm state. Be patient with yourself as you begin to learn mental relaxation. Don't get too concerned if at first your mind wanders off to other places. Simply redirect your thoughts. Following are some helpful step-by-step tips:

Step 1: Find a quiet place without distractions.

Step 2: Sit or lie down and get comfortable and loosen any tight-fitting clothing.

Step 3: Close your eyes.

Step 4: Take a deep breath. Imagine breathing in the clean air. As you breathe out, feel the relaxation spread over your body. As you take another breath, feel yourself floating down.

Step 5: Tense and relax your muscles.

Step 6: Imagine or picture yourself doing something relaxing (such as soothing your pet, picking flowers, floating peacefully in a swimming pool, relaxing by the fireplace).

Step 7: When you are finished, stretch your arms, take a deep breath and open your eyes.

Mental maps for your imaginary journey to a place that is stress free: What a great (and inexpensive) journey.

Cool Is Up to You!

When you find yourself feeling stressed-out over a problem, see yourself dealing with it successfully. When you do this, you have a much better chance of being in charge of your emotions, which makes you much more likely to be in control of your behavior. Being in charge of your emotions and being able to control your behavior is sure to lower your stress.

You've learned how what you *see* (even in your mind's eye) can help lower your stress. Well, guess what? What you *hear* can turn down the volume on your stress level, too. In the next chapter, you'll learn how music can be used to help you relax away your stress and tension.

29

The Magical Power of Music: How to Sing and Dance Your Way Through Stress

Have you ever put on one of your favorite CDs and then found yourself dancing around the room, filled with an exuberant feeling that gave you an extra burst of energy—the kind of energy that's free of all tension—sort of a vibrant, but calm and joyful feeling? In the same sort of way, have you ever listened to a tune that made you feel sad and depressed? Almost everyone has—because sounds exert a powerful influence over the way a person feels.

Music has a very powerful effect in influencing our moods and attitudes. Music can make us melancholy, cheerful, even sad. It can give us energy, and it can put us in a great mood. It can also relieve our stress by helping us to relax.

But what if you lost your ability to hear and feel music? That almost happened to Amanda Martinez's favorite niece Ciara—until a benevolent group made sure she received a very, very special music box. As both Ciara and Amanda find out, the real importance of music is to not only give us pleasure, but to soothe us as well.

Ciara's "Music Box"

Life as a teenager is extremely stressful; there all the worries about grades, friends and the future. But I discovered that if you're really close to someone, and they're having a hard time with life, that can also cause you stress. This was true for me with my little cousin Ciara. She and her mother lived with us from the time she was born, so I was really close with her anyway. But what made us even closer was that I really love what a happy little girl she is. She always has a huge grin on her little round face, and her big brown eyes are always filled with one of her many expressions. Have you ever known someone who is simply gleeful? Well, Ciara is. She's a happy-go-lucky little person. She's just darling.

I've always adored her, but even more now.

Ciara especially loves music. We all thought that maybe music would be her talent, because whenever the radio was on—especially if I had it on full blast—she'd hum or sing along, always in full motion, swinging and swaying away. And she had a little ritual that I thought was especially cute. I took piano lessons (which I wasn't all that thrilled about) and whenever I would practice, Ciara would come running over. Sometimes she would sit on the bench with me, but mostly she would rest her head against the piano as if to *feel* the melody. She'd listen for a minute or so, and then, once she'd hear it, Ciara would break out in an ear-to-ear grin. Should I momentarily stop, Ciara would motion for me to keep playing. It was so cute. If there was any fun to my having to practice the piano, it was because of Ciara's enjoyment of hearing me play.

She was only three and a half years old. So you can only imagine how shocked I was (as was my entire family) to learn that Ciara was slowly losing her hearing. Doctors said she would be deaf in one to two years. When I first heard the news, I couldn't believe it; I didn't want to believe it. How could such a terrible thing happen to her, and to someone so young? But it was true. When only an infant, Ciara had come down with a terrible inner-ear infection, one that over time would eventually destroy her hearing. I wondered how as a family we didn't know this earlier, and that's when I realized that the reason for her resting her little head on the piano was because it was the only way she could hear it. Is that sad or what?

When Ciara was four years old, her hearing had deteriorated to the point that she could hardly hear at all. It was a stressful time for the family, and I could only imagine how stressful it must have been for her. And then, something wonderful happened. We learned that a new surgery—called a *cochlear implant*—had just been invented and that Ciara, because she was so young, was considered a "good candidate" for this surgical procedure. The specialists told us that the cochlear implant is named after the cochlea, a seashell-shaped organ in the inner ear. I know that sounds technical, but when something so terrible as losing your hearing happens to someone you love, it's amazing how interested you get in learning how to "fix" the problem. We were told by doctors that the cochlear implant could restore nearly 85 percent of Ciara's hearing. Well, you can imagine how excited we were. And then came the bad news. The operation would cost nearly fifty thousand dollars! There was no way our family could afford that. Knowing there was a procedure to help Ciara, and then not being able to afford it in order to help her, was a stress all its own.

And then a miracle happened. Some organizations in our town got together and raised the money to help us help Ciara. It was so wonderful. But then a new set of worries began for me: "What if something goes wrong with the operation? . . . What if it isn't successful and she has to go through this again? . . . How much pain will she feel afterwards with an implant in her ear? . . . And what if it simply doesn't work for Ciara? We were told that in the operation, if the damage to her ear was worse than they had thought, it might be possible that the device wouldn't give her hearing. So, even though the chances were pretty good that wouldn't be the case, it was a possibility. And that would be devastating to Ciara. This little girl was absolutely convinced that from the moment she woke up from the operation, Presto! She'd be able to hear. But what if that didn't happen? I had grown so close to her that I didn't want her to be hurt or sad, and I didn't want her to have to feel any pain. I worried about her constantly days before the operation, and throughout it.

Well, if you feel all the ups and downs of this by now, you know sort of how I felt up to this point. Every step of the way, through every twist and turn, we all had our lives changed by this situation. Even when she came home there was still all the drama. Ciara was in the hospital for one day, and then we got to bring her home. Then, for the next couple of days, she was pretty drowsy from the medication she was taking to keep her from having too much pain. I sat beside her bed, and just watched as she lay sleeping. On the third day, they removed the bandages. True to her nature, the first words she blurted were, "I have a new *music box*!" She was obviously delighted. "Do you want to see it?" she asked and, without waiting for my response, put her head on my lap so I could check it out. Her ear was pretty swollen and, while I couldn't see a thing, I said simply, "Wow, too cool!" That made her happy.

I am so happy for her. And I know her life is changed, and will be in the years to come. "C'mon," I coaxed her. "I'd like to play the new songs I've learned just for you!"

Amanda Martinez, 15

From Stress-Out to Chill-Out:
The Colorful Cool of Music

Amanda learned an important lesson about courage as she watched her little niece weather the experience of losing hearing. And she had the satisfaction of watching the little girl be helped by a benevolent organization who made the operation for the little girl and her family possible. In the process, Amanda discovered a newfound respect for our ability to hear, namely the importance of music to our lives.

Not only does music have the power to change both your energy level and your mood, it can also change your stress level. The work of numerous researchers has proven that whether you hear a sound consciously or unconsciously, your body hears the vibration and responds to it at the cellular level. While some sounds can keep you well and "in tune" with yourself, others create stress and can literally make you sick. For example, the research of Dr. Sheldon Deal, a nationally known chiropractor and author, shows that loud and harsh sounds have a definite weakening effect on muscle strength. Over 90 percent of the people tested on an instrument designed to measure the effect of noise on muscle strength (called the electronic strain gauge) register an instant loss of two thirds of their normal muscle strength while listening to loud and harsh sounds.

Knowing that sound has such a powerful effect on us, the goal is to use music in a way that works for you, and not against you. Just as you can use soothing music to lull yourself to sleep, you can also put on music that will put you in a positive and upbeat mood in the morning when you begin getting ready for the day. This will help you feel jazzed and ready to "tackle" your day. Listening to upbeat sounds in the morning helps give you energy for your day, and put you in a better temperament to deal with everyday life and the problems that come along with it.

Five Ways to Use Music to De-Stress

If your mood needs changing, your stress needs easing and your cool needs refuel, turn to your CD collection!

Here are five different ways you can use music to de-stress:

1. **To change your mood:** After school, you run into your ex-girlfriend holding hands with her new boyfriend. You are completely upset because you are still hurt from the breakup. You practically run to your car, dump all your books in the backseat, slide in and put on your favorite CD—all the songs are so upbeat. Soon you're tapping along with the sound of the drums on your steering wheel. Just listening to that music brings up your mood as you hum along.

2. **To focus:** You're on your school's basketball team, and you're about to play in the biggest game of the season for the state championship. Everyone's going to be there watching you, and you're totally nervous. You slip on your headphones, and you immediately feel more focused and ready for the game as your "game music," your favorite song of triumph and victory, gives you the confidence you need.

3. **To energize:** It's sixth hour and you're sagging—which is not good timing since you're about to take a very big algebra test. You figure that it's probably a good idea to swing by the student center, where you know you can count on music that rocks to give you a boost. Arriving at the student center, you're not disappointed: You perk up and are soon revitalized by the fast-paced melodies filling the air.

4. **To relax and unwind:** Your day has been one high-stress thing after another—the big test, the argument with your best friend, finding out you need to ace your next biology exam or you won't be getting the grade you need to stay on the honor roll. Now it's time for dinner and with your

nerves on edge and stress level soaring, sitting down to polite dinner conversation with your family is the last thing you feel like you can pull off. You tell your mom you've had a rough day and ask if you can put on some music. She agrees as long as it isn't heavy metal. Great decision on your mom's part—you put on a CD of your most mellow music, and soon you find your stress has mellowed, too.

5. **To go to sleep:** You are so stoked! Today you asked that super-sweet, super-cute special someone out for tomorrow night. Lying in bed, you just can't get to sleep. Your mind is racing: What are you going to wear tomorrow night? What are you going to say? What if that person doesn't have a good time? Should you try to hold hands on the first date? You know that you should get some sleep tonight so you can be your charming self tomorrow, so you decide to put on some music. You're flipping through the radio stations when you come across a station playing "elevator music." What a brilliant choice: After about two minutes of listening, you are fast asleep.

VIRTUAL PRACTICE: USING MUSIC TO DE-STRESS

The following exercise will help you chart how you can use music to manage stress.

1. **To start your day right.** For the next seven mornings, try listening to upbeat music first thing when you "rev up" for the day. This could mean turning your radio on to your favorite station when you get out of bed, or putting your favorite CD on while you're picking out what to wear to school. Each day for the next week, jot down how listening to that music "got you going."

Monday: _____

Tuesday: _____

Wednesday: _____

Thursday: _____

Friday: _____

Saturday: _____

Sunday: _____

2. **To get a restful night's sleep.** Try listening to soothing, calm music at night while you are preparing for bed or when you're trying to fall asleep. Do this for seven nights. Using the form below, in the morning, record if you noticed it helped you to relax and forget about all the activities going on in your life, and, to wake up feeling well-rested.

Day _____: How listening to music helped me feel relaxed and "close down" the many thoughts and activities going on in my mind, and wake up feeling well-rested:

_____

_____

3. **To pick up your spirits.** Over the next week, notice those times you use music to pick up your spirits. For each of those times when you were feeling stressed, describe how the music helped you. And here's a great tip from some of the teens we worked with: *Record the songs that lifted your mood and eased your stress* (so that you have tried and true back-up for the next time you're stressed)!

Date: _____ Time: _____

What I was stressing over: _____

_____

How music helped me get beyond my stress: _____

_____

The name of the song(s) that lifted my spirits: _____

_____

4. **To focus.** Over the next week, notice those times you use music to focus. Describe why you needed to focus and how the music helped you. Don't forget to record the songs that helped you focus, so you'll have a reminder the next time you could use the help.

Date: _____ Time: _____

How I used music to help me focus: _____

_____

The name of the song(s) that helped me focus: _____

_____

5. **To energize.** Over the next week, notice those times you use music to energize. Jot down why you were feeling drained, and how the music helped you get energized.

Date: _____ Time: _____

How I used music to help me energize: _____

_____

The name of the song(s) that helped me energize: _____

_____

Cool Is Up to You!

Music! What could be more fun in managing stress? And just think of all the ways you can use this information to your advantage! For example, the next time your mom or dad shouts "Turn down that music!" you can cheerfully say something like, "But I'm trying to de-stress—and you know what a good mood I'm in when I get rid of my pent-up stress from the day!" How could your parents possibly object to that, right?

Epilogue

Using Your Newly Acquired Skills: It's Up to You!

That's it for this book, but as you can imagine, there are more ways to cope with the stress and pressures of life than those we've included here. To find the humor in a situation, for example, to laugh at ourselves and not take ourselves too seriously, can be one of life's great coping skills—as so many teens know. When seventeen-year-old Tony Johnson *finally* got a date with his dream girl, Rosalee Whitamore, he wanted everything to be perfect. He practiced his smile and suave compliments, borrowed and buffed his brother's car, and took great pains to look his very best. You can imagine his horror when he climbed in the driver's seat after seating Rosalee and promptly sat on and crushed her delicate beaded purse. Tony needed a dose of humor—and quick. Luckily, he found it, and it saved the day— well, night that is.

Some people think that humor is a genetic trait, that to be funny, you have to be born with a funny bone. This is not necessarily so. While some people—like comedian Robin Williams, for example—seem to be innately funny, you can learn to use humor as a way to give levity to a tense situation, too. And that's an important point: The skills presented in this book are ones we can all learn. We invite you to read each one over and practice using them. As with most things, they'll get easier (and more automatic) with practice.

Just as laughter is another way we get to choose our attitude and perspective, managing stress and pressures is, too. Doing so is a real sign that you're learning from your experiences and growing wiser as a result. In short, you're growing up. Which brings us to another important point: Now that you're on your way to becoming an adult, you're going to have more and more say in the things you do and in the choices you make. Having more control of your life means more than just lifestyle choices—staying up later or spending even more time with your friends, for example. It means that almost everything is up to you: *You* are responsible for your health and well-being, for planning the events of your days and seeing things through to fruition, to planning your future and doing those things that will bring about your goals and desires. In short, *growing up is about taking responsibility for yourself.* Taking responsibility means you think about your life, who you are, and how you would like to shape your life—to become the person you'd truly like to be. As you go about doing that, as you get even more busy and involved with your life, you're going to experience stress. But you can be cool to cope.

Throughout this book, you've been reading about a number of skills and techniques that you can use to reduce the stress, strains and pressures of life, and learning how you can change undesired behaviors and adapt new ones. As with anything, these skills must be incorporated into your *lifestyle;* you have to practice daily.

You can do it! You can deal with stress in healthy, esteeming ways. As always, we'd like to hear from you. Tell us how this book made a difference to you, and which of these stress-management skills worked best for you and why, as well as how you've adapted these skills to draw strength, courage and vitality from the stress and pressures you face. Wishing you happiness, achievement and fulfillment and, most of all, a taste-berry experience in Teenville! You can write to us at:

Youngs, Youngs & Associates
3060 Racetrack View Drive #101–103
Del Mar, CA 92014

Suggested Resources

When going through tough stuff, sometimes you need to turn to someone for help—but don't know exactly where to turn. Remember, you don't have to go it alone! Following is a list of hotlines of organizations that are there to help you. Hotlines are a great resource when you need to talk about something confidential, or need a referral for a particular problem. Listed according to the problems they deal with, you will find both the names of organizations that are there to help you and how you can reach those organizations.

Most of these hotlines have 800 numbers, so that you can call them free of charge from anywhere in the United States. For those that don't have 800 numbers, we've included addresses, so you can write to them. This list is just a sample of what's out there—there are any number of local and national hotlines available to help you through almost any crisis or the tough issues you may be facing. You can find other hotlines in your yellow page directory.

Abuse (domestic violence and sexual abuse)
Childhelp USA
24-hour hotline: 800-4-A-CHILD
(English/Spanish)
or
Rape
Rape Crisis Center
800-352-7273

Adoption Services
National Council for Adoption
419 17th Street N.W.
Washington, DC 20009
800-704-4841
800-289-9111

AIDS
AIDS Hotline for Teens
800-234-8336
or
Teens AIDS Hotline
800-440-8336

Cancer
American Cancer Society
(can refer you to local support groups)
800-ACS-2345
or
National Cancer Institute/National Childhood Cancer Foundation
800-4-CANCER

Depression
National Depressive and Manic-Depressive Association
800-82-NDMDA
Provides information about teenage depression and referrals for
local physicians who can help.

Disabilities
National Information Center for Youth with Disabilities
800-695-0295

Drug and Alcohol Abuse
Focus on Recovery:
Alcohol/Drug Abuse Hotline
24-hour hotline: 800-222-0828

or
Youth Crisis Hotline for Teens
800-448-4663
or
National Council on Alcoholism and Drug Dependence Hope Line
24-hour hotline: 800-622-2255
Family Recovery:
AL-ANON and ALATEEN Family Headquarters
800-356-9996
or
National Association for Children of Alcoholics
301-468-0985

Eating Disorders
American Anorexia and Bulimia Association
293 Central Park West, Suite 1R
New York, NY 10024
212-501-8351
or
Anorexia Nervosa and Related Eating Disorders
P.O. Box 102
Eugene, OR 97405
503-344-1144

Pregnancy (and Prevention)
(Consult the yellow pages for your local offices.)
Planned Parenthood provides reproductive health services: birth control, pregnancy tests, STD testing and treatment, abortion services and counseling.
or
The Reproductive Health Technologies Project
800-584-9911
Information about emergency contraception and referrals to local services.

or
Birthright USA National Office
Information about abstinence, safe sex and caring for infants,
including getting your baby adopted.
P.O. Box 98363
Atlanta, GA 30359
800-550-4900
or
National Office of Post-Abortion
Post-Abortion Counseling, Reconciliation and Healing
P.O. Box 07477
Milwaukee, WI 53207
414-483-4141

Runaway and Homeless Teenagers
National Runaway Hotline
24-hour hotline: 800-621-4000
Counseling and referrals for runaways and homeless teens.
or
Runaway Hotline
800-231-6945

Suicide
National Commission on Youth Suicide Prevention
67 Irving Place South
New York, NY 10003
212-532-2400

Sexuality
Sexuality Information and Education Council of the United States
(SIECUS)
30 West 42nd Street, Suite 350
New York, NY 10036
212-819-9770

Suggested Readings

Benson, Herbert, M.D., with M. Z. Klipper. *The Relaxation Response.* New York: Avon, 1990.

Cobain, Bev. *When Nothing Matters Anymore: A Survival Guide for Depressed Teens.* Minneapolis, MN: Free Spirit Publishing, 1998.

Combs, H. S. *Teenage Survival Manual: How to Reach 20 in One Piece (and Enjoy Every Step of the Journey).* Laugunitas, CA: Discovery Books, 1993.

Covey, Sean. *The 7 Habits of Highly Effective Teens: The Ultimate Teenage Success Guide.* New York: Simon & Schuster, 1998.

Davis, Martha, E.R. Eshelman, and M. McKay. *Relaxation and Stress Reduction.* Oakland, CA: New Harbinger Publishers, 1998.

Edelson, E. *Sleep.* New York: Chelsea House, 1992.

Feller, R. M. *Everything You Need to Know About Peer Pressure.* New York: Rosen Publishing Group, 1995.

Glassman, B. *Coping with Stepfamilies.* New York: Rosen Publishing Group, 1994.

Hipp, Earl, P. Espeland, and M. Fleishman. *Fighting Invisible Tigers: A Stress Management Guide for Teens.* Minneapolis, MN: Free Spirit Publishing, 1995.

Honor Books Staff. *God's Little Instruction Book for Teens.* Tulsa, OK: Honor Books, 1998.

Hurwitz, S. *Staying Healthy.* New York: Rosen Publishing Group, 1992.

Ignoffo, M. *Everything You Need to Know About Self-Confidence.* New York: Rosen Publishing Group, 1995.

Johnson, Greg P. *If I Could Ask God One Question: Answers to Teens' Most Asked Questions.* Minneapolis, MN: Bethany House, 1998.

Koyler, D. *Everything You Need to Know About Dating.* New York: Rosen Publishing Group, 1994.

Lang, Susan S., with Beth H. Marks. *Teens and Tobacco: A Fatal Attraction.* New York: Twenty First Century Books, 1996.

Licata, R. *Everything You Need to Know About Anger.* New York: Rosen Publishing Group, 1994.

McClauslin, M. *Sexually Transmitted Diseases.* New York: Macmillan, 1992.

McFarland, R. *Coping Through Assertiveness.* New York: Rosen Publishing Group, 1992.

Meier, Paul D., and Jan Meier. *Happiness Is a Choice for Teens.* Nashville, TN: Thomas Nelson, 1997.

Moe, B. *Everything You Need to Know About PMS.* New York: Rosen Publishing Group, 1995.

Ojeda, Linda. *Safe Dieting for Teens: Design Your Own Diet, Lose Weight Effectively, Feel Good About Yourself.* Alameda, CA: Hunter House, 1992.

Peterson, Lorraine. *How to Get a Life. . . No Strings Attached: The Power of Grace in a Teen's Life.* Minneapolis, MN: Bethany House, 1997.

Pruitt, B.E., Ed.D., CHES, Kathy Teer Crumpler, M.P.H., and Deborah Prothrow-Stith, M.D. *Health Skills for Wellness.* Needham, MA: Prentice Hall, 1997.

Reybold, L. *Everything You Need to Know About the Dangers of Tattooing and Body Piercing.* New York: Rosen Publishing Group, 1995.

Roehlkepartain, J. L. *Surviving School Stress.* Loveland, CO: Group Publishing, 1991.

Saltzer, C. A. *The Nutrition-Fitness Link: How Diet Can Help Your Body and Mind.* Brookfield, CT: Millbrook Press, 1993.

Sonder, B. *Eating Disorders: When Food Turns Against You.* New York: Franklin Watts, 1993.

Stewart, William. *Building Self-Esteem: How to Replace Self-Doubt with Confidence and Well-Being.* Philadelphia, PA: How To Books, Ltd., 1998.

Versace, Gianni. *The Art of Being You.* New York: Abbeville Press, Inc., 1998.

Wagonseller, B. R., L. C. Ruegamer, and M. C. Harrington. *Coping in a Single-Parent Home.* New York: Rosen Publishing Group, 1995.

Walker, Rebecca. *Adios Barbie: Young Women Write About Body Image and Identity.* Seattle, WA: Seal Press Feminist Pub., 1999.

Youngs, Bettie B., and Jennifer Leigh Youngs. *Taste Berries for Teens: Short Stories and Encouragement on Life, Love, Friendship and Tough Issues.* Deerfield Beach, FL: Health Communications, Inc., 1999.

———. *Taste Berries for Teens Journal: My Thoughts on Life, Love and Making a Difference.* Deerfield Beach, FL: Health Communications, Inc., 2000.

———. *More Taste Berries for Teens: A Second Collection of Inspirational Short Stories and Encouragement on Life, Love, Friendship and Tough Issues.* Deerfield Beach, FL: Health Communications, Inc., 2000.

Youngs, Bettie B. *You & Self-Esteem: A Book for Young People* (Grades 5-12). Rolling Hills Estates, CA: Jalmar Press, 1996.

———. *Friendship Is Forever, Isn't It?* Rolling Hills Estates, CA: Jalmar Press, 1992.

Youngs, Jennifer Leigh. *Feeling Great, Looking Hot & Loving Yourself: Health, Fitness and Beauty for Teens.* Deerfield Beach, FL: Health Communications, Inc., 2000.

———. *Getting What You Want Out of Life: Goal-Setting Skills for Young Adults.* Del Mar, CA: Learning Tools Press, 2001.

About the Authors

Bettie B. Youngs, Ph.D., Ed.D., is a professional speaker and the internationally renowned author of eighteen books translated into twenty-nine languages. She is a former Teacher-of-the-Year, university professor and executive director of the Phoenix Foundation and president of Professional Development, Inc. She is a long-acknowledged expert on teens and has frequently appeared on NBC *Nightly News,* CNN, *Oprah* and *Geraldo. USA Today,* the *Washington Post, Redbook, McCall's, Working Woman, Family Circle, Parents Magazine, Better Homes & Gardens, Woman's Day* and the National Association for Secondary School Principals (NASSP) have all recognized her work. Her acclaimed books include: *Taste Berries for Teens: Inspirational Short Stories and Encouragement on Life, Love, Friendship and Tough Issues; Taste Berries for Teens Journal: My Thoughts on Life, Love and Making a Difference; More Taste Berries for Teens: A Second Collection of Inspirational Short Stories and Encouragement on Life, Love, Friendship and Tough Issues; Safeguarding Your Teenager from the Dragons of Life; How to Develop Self-Esteem in Your Child; You and Self-Esteem: A Book for Young People; Taste-Berry Tales;* the Pulitzer Prize–nominated *Gifts of the Heart;* and the award-winning *Values from the Heartland.* Dr. Youngs is the author of a number of videocassette programs for Sybervision and Nightingale/Conant, and is the coauthor of the nationally acclaimed *Parents on Board,* a video-based training program to help schools and parents work together to increase student achievement.

Jennifer Leigh Youngs, twenty-six, is a speaker and workshop presenter for teens and parents nationwide. She is the coauthor of *Taste Berries for Teens: Inspirational Short Stories and Encouragement on Life, Love, Friendship and Tough Issues; Taste Berries for Teens Journal: My Thoughts on Life, Love and Making a Difference; More Taste Berries for Teens: A Second Collection of Inspirational Short Stories and Encouragement on Life, Love, Friendship and Tough Issues;* and author of *Feeling Great, Looking Hot and Loving Yourself: Health, Fitness and Beauty for Teens.* Jennifer is a former Miss Teen California finalist and Rotary International Goodwill Ambassador and Exchange Scholar. She serves on a number of advisory boards for teens and is the International Youth Coordinator for Airline Ambassadors, an international organization affiliated with the United Nations that involves youth in programs to build cross-cultural friend-ships; escorts orphans to new homes and children to hospitals for medical care; and delivers humanitarian aid to those in need worldwide.

To contact Bettie B. Youngs or Jennifer Leigh Youngs, write to:

Youngs, Youngs & Associates
3060 Racetrack View Drive, #101–103
Del Mar, CA 92014

More Taste Berries
for Teens!

Taste Berries™ for Teens

Inspirational short stories and encouragement on life, love, friendship and tough issues

With contributions from teens for teens

Bettie B. Youngs, Ph.D.
One of the best-loved contributors to *Chicken Soup for the Teenage Soul*
Jennifer Leigh Youngs

Code #6692 • $12.95

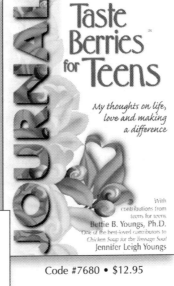

Taste Berries™ for Teens JOURNAL

My thoughts on life, love and making a difference

With contributions from teens for teens
Bettie B. Youngs, Ph.D.
One of the best-loved contributors to *Chicken Soup for the Teenage Soul*
Jennifer Leigh Youngs

Code #7680 • $12.95

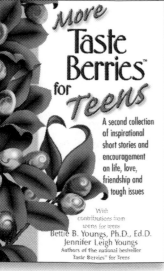

More Taste Berries™ for Teens

A second collection of inspirational short stories and encouragement on life, love, friendship and tough issues

With contributions from teens for teens
Bettie B. Youngs, Ph.D., Ed.D.
Jennifer Leigh Youngs
Authors of the national bestseller
Taste Berries™ for Teens

Code #813X • $12.95

Code #7672 • Paperback • $14.95

Beautiful–
Inside and Out!

Jennifer Leigh Youngs, coauthor of the bestseller, *Taste Berries for Teens,* created this complete guidebook for every girl's teen years. Ranging the gamut from healthy eating, fitness and stress reduction, to skin and hair care, fashion, makeup and more, this book offers you all you'll need to feel beautiful, inside and out.